T0128129

FATHERLESS DAUGHTERS

*Turning the Pain of Loss
into the Power of Forgiveness*

PAMELA THOMAS

Simon & Schuster
NEW YORK LONDON TORONTO SYDNEY

SIMON & SCHUSTER
1230 Avenue of the Americas
New York, NY 10020

First Simon & Schuster hardcover edition August 2009.

SIMON & SCHUSTER and colophon are registered trademarks
of Simon & Schuster, Inc.

Some names and details have been changed.

For information about special discounts for bulk purchases,
please contact Simon & Schuster Special Sales at
1-866-506-1949 or business@simonandschuster.com.

The Simon & Schuster Speakers Bureau can bring authors
to your live event. For more information or to book an event
contact the Simon & Schuster Speakers Bureau at
1-866-248-3049 or visit our website at www.simonspeakers.com.

Designed by Paul Dippolito

Manufactured in the United States of America

1   3   5   7   9   10   8   6   4   2

Library of Congress Cataloging-in-Publication Data
Thomas, Pamela, date.
Fatherless daughters: turning the pain of loss into the power of
forgiveness / Pamela Thomas.
p.   cm.
1. Loss (Psychology) 2. Fathers and daughters.
3. Thomas, Pamela, date. I. Title.
BF575.D35T46   2009
155.9'3—dc22   2009008518
ISBN 978-1-9821-0104-6

For my dad
Roy Vernon Thomas
March 13, 1908 – February 24, 1957
With love

CONTENTS

INTRODUCTION

"My mother died when I was nineteen. For a long time, it was all you needed to know about me . . . a kind of vest-pocket description of my emotional complexion: 'Meet you in the lobby in ten minutes—I have long brown hair, am on the short side, have on a red coat, and my mother died when I was nineteen.'"

This is how writer Anna Quindlen described herself, and the impact of her mother's death, a few years back in her "Life in the Thirties" column in the *New York Times*. Her description is imbued with irony, but her bittersweet humor brings a lump to my throat. Clearly Anna, or anyone who has endured the untimely death of a parent, knows that the loss is not so much an abridged edition of an emotional life story as it is a line of existential poetry. In one phrase, you've said it all.

My father died when I was ten. My situation was a bit different from Anna Quindlen's. I lost my father, not my mother. I was a child about to embark on puberty, not an adolescent emerging into adulthood. But the end result was the same: my dad's early death and the fact that I was brought up without his influence shaped my life in every way, and forever.

Nothing traumatizes a child more than the death of a parent. Hope Edelman, in her thoughtful book *Motherless Daughters,* speaks movingly about the death of her mother when she was seventeen. Edelman believes that the death of the mother is the worst death any girl can, and probably ever will, endure, and I agree. For boys and girls alike, our mother is our first love, our primordial source of sustenance and care. If we are lucky, Mother is the one—and perhaps the only—person in our lives who will love us unconditionally. Her loss, especially if it occurs at an early age, is absolutely devastating.

But I believe firmly that the death of a father, especially if you're still a child, is almost as dreadful. Although the effects of the loss of your father are perhaps initially less obvious, the pain runs just as deep. The loss of a father on a daughter is particularly and exquisitely affecting. (I hasten to add that the loss of a father on boys is equally traumatic; however, the impact is psychologically different and deserves a study of its own. Although I grew up with three brothers who were as affected by our dad's death as I was, and I talk about them frequently here, I don't address issues of father loss on sons to a great extent in this book.)

For most of my life (I am now in my early sixties), describing the consequences of my dad's death was rather like trying to define the perimeter of a void, or opening a file in my computer labeled "Influence of My Father" and finding it empty. I simply could not find the words to articulate the nothingness I felt.

In recent years, however, I began to see that my dad's death produced not so much a void but a cluster of deep, rigid emotions that have profoundly influenced my life. Without quite knowing it, I was absolutely terrified of these feelings; as a result, I denied them, bringing the whole emotional morass full circle, hardening those emotions into a place I called nothingness or a void. I began to think that perhaps my father's loss was even more crushing than I had initially imagined.

Which brings me to this book.

I began writing down my memories of my dad more than twenty years ago. Around the same time, I also began reading books about fathers, fathering, and father loss. In retrospect, I realize that I approached the topic in a rather intellectual, almost clinical way. Again, I suspect those scary feelings were at work, preventing me from really experiencing what all this abstract research had to do with me.

Coincidentally, as I was delving into father research for my own private reasons, the subject of fathering began to receive a tremendous amount of public attention. Indeed, by the early 1990s, the issue of fatherlessness and the importance of a father's influence on a child had become central to any discussion of American family values.

In 1993, Barbara Dafoe Whitehead, a sociologist from the Institute for American Values, published a controversial article in the *Atlantic Monthly* entitled "Dan Quayle Was Right." Vice President Dan

Quayle had publicly criticized the popular television program *Murphy Brown* (and its star, Candice Bergen) for glamorizing the lifestyle of the single mother. Dan Quayle had, in turn, been blasted by the liberal press for being too conservative and out of touch.

In her article, Whitehead argued that Quayle was right and the writers of *Murphy Brown,* as well as many members of the liberal establishment, were wrong. According to Whitehead, choosing unwed motherhood was neither noble nor desirable, especially from the child's perspective, since the absence of a father fueled everything from delinquency to drug abuse.

This skirmish marked the beginning of a new wave of battles over American family values, especially on issues involving marriage and parenting. Since then, the subject of fatherlessness has come up repeatedly as a primary contributor to many of our society's ills. In recent years, countless magazine and newspaper articles and several important books, particularly *Fatherhood in America: A History* by Robert L. Griswold, *Fatherless America* by David Blankenhorn, *Strong Fathers, Strong Daughters* by Meg Meeker, *For Better or For Worse: Divorce Reconsidered* by C. Mavis Hetherington, and several books by esteemed sociologist Judith Wallerstein have been published on the subject. Virtually all of the experts agree with Whitehead: a father's influence is essential for bringing up healthy children, and his absence can be devastating.

Still, although I found this material informative, in the end, none of the books I read really spoke to my yearning to know precisely how my own father's loss had affected me personally. Ultimately, the books seemed rather academic and abstract, so I decided to try to research and write the book I wanted to read. I wanted my book to serve two purposes.

First, I hoped that the act of researching and writing a book on father loss would be a personal journey for me, a pilgrimage to better understand myself in relation to losing my father. I hoped writing this book would allow me to answer particular questions: Did the fact that Daddy died when I was still a child affect my relationships with men? Did it help that I was raised with three brothers? How did my mother's behavior, and the fact that she was a relatively young, single woman throughout my adolescence, influence my life? Would things have been different if Daddy had lived? Would life have been better?

Second, I wanted to write a book that would serve as a guide for other women seeking answers to their own issues with father loss. I am not a professional sociologist or a psychologist; I am a longtime book editor and a writer, so I approached this book as an investigative journalist tracking down a complex story. Toward that end, I rather arbitrarily decided I would interview 100 fatherless daughters—a goal that seemed substantial but not overwhelming. Ultimately, I interviewed 106 fatherless daughters: 66 women who had lost their fathers through death and 40 who had lost their fathers through divorce. (In addition, I interviewed nine men, all fathers of daughters, and have incorporated many of their insights into this text. I also consulted with five psychotherapists for professional viewpoints.)

I debated with myself about including women whose dads disappeared from their lives as a result of divorce or conscious desertion. In the end, I chose to include them because so many women, especially those born after 1960, were fatherless as a result of divorce, and I was curious as to how their experiences with loss differed from my own.

I defined a fatherless daughter as a woman who lost her father between birth and age eighteen, though many women who lose their fathers after age eighteen consider themselves to be fatherless daughters. In her book *Fatherless Women: How We Change After We Lose Our Dads,* Clea Simon addresses issues of father loss among adult women, explaining that a father's death for a woman in her twenties, thirties, or even forties is, indeed, often life altering. However, I was interested in exploring the effects of father loss on women who were raised from childhood without the influence of their dads and how this absence affected their development.

The women I interviewed ranged in age from nineteen to ninety-four. Not surprisingly, because of the broad range in their ages, these women experienced father loss in decidedly different ways, in part because of the nature of the society in which they were raised. Mores, particularly attitudes toward death, divorce, and the rights of women, changed dramatically during the twentieth century, and this strongly colored each woman's experience of father loss. Most of the women were American, although I also talked to women from Canada, Mexico, England, and Japan. They ranged across the board geographically, ethnically, socially, and economically.

To my surprise, I had no trouble finding women who would agree to be interviewed. Early on, I considered putting ads in newspapers, magazines, and online to find potential subjects, but I found more than enough appropriate women simply by word of mouth, and most of the fatherless daughters I met were as interested in exploring their experiences with father loss as I was.

I found all of these women's stories utterly fascinating and came to feel that it was important that I share as many of these biographies as I possibly could. Therefore, in addition to my research and observations, I have included vignettes of women whose experiences cast a special light on a particular issue. (To insure privacy, some of their names and details of their lives have been changed.)

Finally, I was deeply moved by the intensity of the emotion virtually all of the daughters expressed about their dads. Only rarely did I encounter a woman who expressed hateful feelings about her father— indeed, I can think of only two or three who felt mostly negative attitudes toward their dads. The rest all loved their fathers passionately, even if these men had died when their daughters were infants; even if they had been absent from their children's lives for years; even if these fathers didn't deserve it!

People who lose their parents early in life are like fellow war veterans. As soon as they discover that they are talking to someone else who has lost a parent, they know they are speaking the same language without uttering a word. In a certain sense, although each fatherless daughter's story is unique, each woman's experience with regard to losing her dad is the same. What follows is my journey and what I discovered about those ineffable similarities.

PART I

FATHERING

———◆———

1. SNAPSHOTS OF MY FATHER

Losing a father in childhood forever changes the shape of a daughter's identity—how she views the world and herself. Not only is her connection to the first and most important man in her life sharply curtailed or extinguished, but all her perceptions, all her decisions, all her future relationships are filtered through that early, unimaginable, ineffable loss.

—Victoria Secunda, *Women and Their Fathers*

There's a photo of a man kneeling on a manicured lawn in front of a prosperous-looking house—a house I've never seen and can't identify. A little girl is perched on his lap. She is smiling, clearly happy to be perched on this particular knee. She has a sweet face, one surrounded by soft, dark curls. Her eyes are wide-apart and curious, her mouth delicate and upturned in that way only a child can manage without appearing supercilious.

The man is my father. I know him by his wide-open smile, as warm as bath water, and his distinctively thick, dark, wavy hair, parted just left of center. He is a much thinner Daddy than the one I finally remember, but the gesture fits. It's him. The little girl, unfortunately, is not me. It's my cousin Frances, the daughter of my mother's older sister.

Frannie adored my father, a man who would become her uncle shortly after this photo was taken, and he delighted in her. He once traveled from Cleveland to Philadelphia, or so

I've been told, just to be by her side when she convalesced after a double-mastoid operation. He took her a red velvet muff.

I have no picture of myself sitting on my father's knee, although I must have done so; every small girl does. He once brought me a red velvet muff, too, and I hadn't even been sick. Still, this photo has always troubled me. Perhaps it ignited my first feelings of female rage that erupts with Vesuvian heat in the midst of any love triangle. To put it another way, I wish that happy percher were me.

I wrote this little vignette (and a variation on the story that follows) about my dad almost twenty years ago. I don't believe it had yet occurred to me to write this book, so I guess I was acting on a desire to collect my memories of my dad and put them into words. In any case, since then, I've shown this little memoir—or various incarnations of it—to several friends and family members. With the exception of my brother Steve, who perhaps understands better than most people the subconscious emotions that led me to write this snippet, everyone found it sort of confusing. Why start out a chapter about my dad and me with an anecdote that not only does not include me but instead shows him adoring somebody else?

I listened to my critics. I knew they were caring and honest. I also could tell they were couching their comments in the most tactful language. (As an editor, I can spot that sort of literary diplomacy pretty easily.) Yet I couldn't seem to cut it. This little snapshot touched something deep inside me, and I realized that I needed to get at that something, to explore it, to understand it.

I come to this chapter—indeed, to this book—as a searcher. I am on a quest to find my father, who I feel in the deepest sense of the word is lost to me. In actual fact, my dad died when I was ten, so in the literal life-and-death sense, of course, he was and is lost. Over the sixty-plus years of my life, many other people I have loved have also died: my grandfather, my grandmother, my stepfather, two beloved aunts, several close friends, my cousin Frances, but I don't have that same sense that they are lost to me, that I am cut off from them. I know with certainty that I loved them; I know that they loved me. I have my memories of them, which will stay with me as long as I live, and those memories are warm and comforting.

Yet, with regard to my dad, I feel quite removed from him. I have the facts of his life, and I know that he was a good man. I also have memories of him—lots of them—and except for the last few months of his life, they are happy ones. Yet somehow I don't have that confident feeling that he loved me. And worse, I don't have a real sense of knowing that I loved *him*.

When I think of my dad and try to describe what his effect on me was, I feel as though I am in a dark, damp, chilly place without any form or anything to grab onto. It feels empty, yet I sense fear in myself, which leads me to believe that there probably is something there, but I'm afraid to look at it. It's hard for me to write these words, but I feel that I must. I sense that by saying them, by attempting to articulate these emotions, I'll bring warmth and light into that dark void. Perhaps I'll be able to grapple with the fear, to look at it, maybe even make it disappear. Perhaps then I'll find my dad. And I'll be able to let him go.

My father's name was Roy Vernon Thomas, and he was born on March 13, 1908, in Youngstown, Ohio, the youngest of seven children. His father, Mose Thomas, was an immigrant from Pontyprydd, Wales, who had settled in Youngstown sometime in the mid-1880s when he was in his late teens, undoubtedly to work in the coal mines or steel mills along the Ohio River. His mother, Mary Porter Thomas, a native of England, had also come to America as a young girl.

Shortly after Daddy was born, his family moved to Cleveland, where my dad grew up in a tidy working-class neighborhood on the south side. In the photographs we have of him and his brothers and sisters, they always appear impeccably dressed, although posed in a decidedly modest place, which I can only assume was their backyard. Still, according to my mother, they were a fun-loving family, and they all loved to laugh.

Daddy was definitely a man's man sort of guy. He adored sports of any kind—football, baseball, basketball, golf, wrestling, bowling, horse racing, boating, bicycling—and he loved the male camaraderie that went along with them. When he was in high school, he served as the captain of his football team, which went on to win an Ohio state championship during his senior year. During the 1920s, the big Cleveland newspapers played up these events, and Daddy's team was covered regularly in the *Cleveland Plain Dealer* and the *Cleveland Press*. We have many pictures and news clippings of my dad with his team: very skinny, very handsome, and, to me, very glamorous.

Daddy graduated from high school in 1926 and spent the next eight years working his way through Baldwin-Wallace College, a small school in nearby Berea, Ohio. To meet expenses, he alternated one year in college with the next in the steel mills in Cleveland's flats. My mother believes that my dad's final illness—cancer of the esophagus—was the result of damage to his body due to the years he spent working in mills. He graduated with a B.A. in psychology (of all things!) in 1934.

He met my mother, Roberta Frances Bosworth, sometime that spring of his senior year. He had started dating her younger sister, Ruthie, and according to my aunt, they would go out dancing until they dropped (literally), or else take in a movie at the local theater, where they were sometimes asked to leave because they were making too much noise laughing. This was not a particularly serious relationship; what's more, according to Ruthie, she and my dad, despite the fun times, occasionally fought, apparently rather vociferously. It was an upshot of one of these tiffs that my dad met my mother.

My mother came from a different background than my father. While Daddy's family was working-class, my mother's parents were firmly middle class. Not only were they old-school Yankees from Boston (to the point of claiming *Mayflower* ancestry), but my grandfather, Herbert Holt Bosworth, had done well in business, ending up by the mid-1930s as an executive for the General Electric Company in Cleveland.

My mom was one of three sisters: Beatrice (mother of cousin Frances), Roberta (my mother), and the aforementioned Ruthie. As often happens in families, the girls were typecast: Beatrice was the smart one; Ruthie was the cute, funny one; and my mother was the pretty one. And, as often happens with typecasting, there was some truth to the labels. My mother was exceptionally beautiful, but somehow, despite compliments about her beauty, she deduced that she was not terribly intelligent or cute! This lack of self-confidence would haunt her throughout her life and would ultimately have its effects on me.

Because of my grandfather's career trajectory at GE, my mom's family moved frequently when she was very young, but they ended up living in Lakewood, Ohio, a suburb to the west of Cleveland with tree-lined streets and comfortable houses with big front porches. It was the sort of town that encouraged a kind of neighborliness that rarely exists today.

It was on the front porch of that Lakewood house that my parents met in the spring of 1934. By that time, both Aunt Ruthie and my mother were also attending Baldwin-Wallace College. Although the two sisters were only a year apart in age, they had separate friends and social lives. So while Ruthie had known my dad for quite some time, my mother had never met him.

On the fateful day, Daddy pulled up in front of the house. As Ruthie got out of his car and slammed the door, my mom, who was sitting on the porch, heard Daddy say: "If I never see you again, it'll be too soon." No one remembers what their fight was about or how the hostility got diffused, but somehow Daddy and Mother were introduced, and the joke was that Ruthie remained part of his life until the day he died.

For the next five years, my mother and dad dated, but apparently it was something of an on-again/off-again relationship. Daddy graduated from college within weeks of meeting my mother, while Mother wouldn't graduate for another two years.

Daddy labored at several jobs over the next few years, eventually specializing in personnel management and labor relations. After Mother finished college, she worked for a while as a demonstrator for GE and ultimately landed a teaching position at a high school in a small mining town in southern Ohio. Still, they kept their relationship going and finally married in 1939.

The early years of their marriage were warm, happy times for them, I believe. Occasionally, we children witnessed wisps of those moments, like glimpses of my mother washing Daddy's hair, or hearing him tell her a joke at dinner and her laughing until tears rolled down her face. I once asked her why she had married my dad. She thought for a minute, then said, "Because he could make me laugh."

They rented half of a double house in Lakewood, just a few blocks from where my mother had grown up. A son, Stephan Bosworth, arrived three years later, in August 1942. World War II disrupted many people's lives, but because Daddy was by then working for a company that supplied materials for the war effort, he did not enlist. I was born immediately after the war, nine months almost to the day after the bombing of Hiroshima, on May 7, 1946. Two more boys arrived within five years of me: Herbert Roy, in 1947; and Robert James, known from birth as Bo, in late 1950.

Shortly before I was born, my Grampa Bosworth married a widow named Sarah Porter Thorne, who happened to live down the street from him. (My mother's mother had died in the late 1930s.) Grampa's marriage to Sarah (which is what we always called her) caused a shift in our family dynamic. First, my parents bought the house with the big front porch that my mother had grown up in from my grandfather, and this was the house in which I would live until I left home for college. In addition, Grampa and Sarah now lived less than a ten-minute walk away and would become very important people in the lives of my brothers and me—even more so after the death of our father.

Photographs of my parents taken during the years when we children were young attest to their continued happiness together. Mother still looked very beautiful, and even with two, three, and finally four children to care for, she took the time to mound her hair up in one of those 1940s Betty Grable rolls and pin grosgrain bows to the neck of her blouses.

Daddy didn't change much, either. There is a picture of him taken in the early 1940s at what looks as if it were a class for expectant fathers. He's changing a diaper on a baby doll, laughing, with a cigarette hanging out of his mouth. In most other family photos, he's usually posed holding one child in his arms with one or two others hanging by his side.

Still, for Daddy, after his wife and children, sports remained his abiding love. As we children got bigger, he introduced us to softball games, ice skating, and horseback riding. He even occasionally gave us "professional" rubdowns, which we loved. As a younger man, he had played a lot of baseball and coached various company teams, but by the time I can remember, he was catching baseball games from an armchair, over a car radio, or even through a window. Warm summer evenings and the sounds of a ball game always make me think of him. I can see him now mowing our back lawn, a glass of beer on the fence, and our old ivory-colored Bakelite radio somehow rigged up in the kitchen window tuned into the clearest game he could get. He'd cut the back part of the lawn very quickly, since it was far away from the radio. But the front part, the part near the radio, boy, he clipped that to perfection.

When I was a little girl, I always liked to dress up for special events. Once, when I was seven or eight, my dad invited me to take a drive with him to his country club to pick up his golf clubs. For me, this was a particular treat, since he usually took my older brother, Steve, on such outings. I decked myself out in a favorite little red-and-white sundress and wore my black patent leather shoes with air vents. Daddy escorted me around the club, introducing me to all his buddies and bragging about my naturally curly hair and my straight-A report card, of which he was very proud. His friends treated me with a courtliness I'm sure was not wasted on my brother. I guess they thought I was cute; I was pretty sure he thought so.

Daddy was very good about teaching us children the pleasures of treats. From him, I learned how to drink a chocolate ice-cream soda without breaking the straw, that clowns were not dangerous, and that little girls were as entitled to "real leather" two-gun holsters as their older brothers. He introduced me to cherry pie à la mode, the scariest roller coasters, and elaborate jump ropes designed for prize fighters. Early on, before I had clearly separated (or put together) Daddy and Santa Claus, I knew I could request the most expensive doll for Christmas and could count on getting it. At the age of eight, I asked for a sterling silver identification bracelet, the latest rage among third graders. A friend assured me: "No way you'll get it. It's not even your birthday." Daddy brought it home nestled in his pocket. For my brothers, there were airplanes, cowboy suits, electric trains, horseback rides, and very fancy bicycles. The usual, plus.

Daddy was the prince of games, the king of good times. He was a vacation man, a party guy, a lover of the spontaneous. My brother Steve once brought eighteen teenagers home for lunch after a morning of ice skating. My mother retired in frustration to their bedroom with a magazine, but Daddy fixed hamburgers for the kids, then organized a Ping-Pong tournament in our basement. If the PTA needed men to dress up like ballerinas to raise money for the school, Daddy was there. If I wanted to drive two hundred miles on a Sunday afternoon to see an obscure Indian site, Daddy would take me.

Discipline, however—that tough-love province of the responsible parent—was anathema to him. To my memory, he never reprimanded or corrected any of us children, and I know for sure he never spanked us. Occasionally he would "blow his stack," as my mother would put it, but he would rail at the situation, not at the child.

Nor was he particularly disciplined about himself. By the end of his life, at the age of forty-eight, he was quite overweight, deeply in debt, and unable to balance his work life and his home life. Despite all the special occasions I remember, he was a workaholic, leaving for the plant before dawn and often arriving home long after we children had gone to bed. My mother was not so great at discipline herself, so the fabric of their lives—of our lives—began to fray. Minor outbursts over trivial matters became major explosions because, perhaps, they had too many children, too little money, too many treats, and not enough sense.

It became obvious that Daddy was sick during the summer of 1956. We took a family vacation to an inn at Clear Lake, Indiana. I don't believe anyone knew how desperate Daddy's health situation had become, but he was showing alarming signs of discomfort. He had very little energy (which was unlike him), and when he tried to eat, he couldn't keep anything down. Almost nightly, he would leave the dinner table, undoubtedly to be sick and lie down.

I had just turned ten and was still very much a child. I played with dolls, sulked when my mother wanted me to wash the dishes or practice the piano, and played kick the can with my brothers and the kids in the neighborhood after supper. Nevertheless, I did seem to be tiptoeing up to adolescence. Although I was emotionally still a ten-year-old, I looked like a teenager. I was very tall for my age, about five-five or more, but not charmingly fawnlike. I had rounded arms and legs, hips, and more than just the beginning of breasts. Mostly, at this age, I was oblivious to how I looked, but I was beginning to sense things were changing. One day, as I walked down our street, some older boys, age sixteen or so, drove by in a convertible and began cat-calling and whistling. I was absolutely floored, and more than a little frightened, when I figured out that they were whistling at me!

I insert this here because it is background for one of the dearest memories I have of my dad. While we were vacationing in Indiana and he was often so sick, he decided to take us skating at a nearby roller rink. As he helped my younger brothers with their skates, he left my older brother and me to our own devices. Steve was fourteen and hardly interested in his younger sister, so he just skated off.

I stood there alone, wondering what to do. Then around the circle came a boy about Steve's age who asked me to skate. This was, in effect, like being asked out on a first date, and it scared me. You have got to be kidding! I thought, although I somehow summoned the good grace to politely say, "No, thank you." But Daddy, not feeling so good and busy with the little boys' skates, quickly jumped in.

"Go ahead, skate!" he said, half laughing. "It's okay. I'm here."

Many years later, I learned that Daddy did precisely what a "good" daddy is supposed to do: He let his little girl know that of course other men were going to want to skate with her and it was okay. And if she got into any trouble, she shouldn't worry because he would be there.

Daddy went into the hospital for two operations in the fall of 1956. The first was an exploratory one and was nothing too serious, or so everyone said. All he had to do was quit smoking—which, of course, he didn't do. However, within weeks he was back in the hospital for a second operation. Later my mother would tell me that before the procedure the doctor had said that if Daddy was in the operating room for three hours, she could hope; if he was gone for less than an hour, she should know that the situation was extremely serious. He was back in his room in thirty minutes.

By December, my father could barely get out of bed without help. He would walk behind my mother to the bathroom, supporting himself with his hands on her shoulders. Between August and December, he had lost more than seventy pounds and was skinnier than he had been in his glamorous high school football pictures. The last time he came downstairs was on Christmas Eve, when he convinced my mother to take him shopping. He bought me a pale blue blouse with a scalloped collar and tiny pearl buttons, a grown-up lady's blouse, not a little girl's garment. I think he got my brothers fishing rods, but I don't believe they ever took up the sport. He never got out of bed again.

A few weeks later, I threw a fit when my mother asked me to clean up my bedroom. Actually, I remember having several temper tantrums during these months that Daddy was so sick. Once he asked me to get him a pillow, and I recall throwing it at him as he lay in bed, then running into my bedroom and slamming the door. On this particular day, as I was storming around, jamming my clothes into drawers and throwing hangers across the room, my mother came into the room and quietly closed the door.

"You have to calm down and let your father sleep," she said. Then she added: "He's not going to get well."

She said this without tears, and the front of my mind thought: What a drag; he'll be sick like this forever. But the back of my mind—the part that had yet to experience the death of even a pet—knew she was saying something more. For a moment, I considered asking

Mother to explain exactly what she meant, but I guess I figured she might tell me the truth.

Early in the evening of the night he died, I was organizing my doll clothes on the floor of our living room, and I overheard my mother talking to my dad's doctor on the telephone in the kitchen. "My husband is dying," she said, this time without shading her words. "When will it be?" I continued fussing with my dolls and pretended that I had not heard her. An hour or so later, the doctor arrived, smiling, genial, and gave Daddy a shot.

I've always been self-conscious about praying. Nevertheless, on the night he died, as I lay in bed, I went over the Lord's Prayer and the Twenty-Third Psalm, prayers I'd been taught either by my mother or at Sunday school. I didn't yet know words like *futile* or *despair,* yet somehow, even as I was saying my prayers, I recognized utter hopelessness when I saw it. So I got out of bed, pulled a length of Lustre Lace from the top drawer of my dresser, and braided myself a whistle chain by the light in the hall.

In the morning, he was gone.

My childhood ended that night, February 24, 1957. Although I was only in the fifth grade and still wore little-girl dresses with bows in the back, my life no longer focused on childhood pursuits. More, I immediately began running up against the grown-up behavior that often surrounds a civilized death, and I found it utterly bewildering.

Early in the morning after Daddy died, my mother came into my bedroom before I'd gotten out of bed and said with feeling but, again, without tears: "Your dad died last night." I cried for a few minutes while she rubbed my back, and then she said: "Don't cry; everything will be all right." As young as I was, I knew she didn't mean "Don't cry"—literally. But then, what did she mean? Don't cry *now?* Don't cry *ever?* Don't *worry?* I didn't understand. But I didn't cry anymore.

Later that day, I was playing catch in the street with my brother Herb. As we listlessly tossed the ball back and forth, a distant relative pulled into our driveway, and in a perky voice she asked us if we had the day off from school. Herb and I solemnly told her that our dad had died, but we both knew that she knew that already. So why had she asked us such a ridiculous question?

I did not go to my dad's funeral. Steve went, but Mother decided that my younger brothers and I were too little, although to this day, she wonders if it was the right decision. I, for one, have never been sorry that she made that choice. I don't think I could have handled seeing Daddy—or the shell of my dad—in a casket.

Instead, on the day of his funeral I went to school. In retrospect, I suspect my teacher had been told that my father had died; after all, the death of a parent would be a significant event in any family, especially in a town like ours. But she said nothing to me about it and behaved as if nothing was wrong. When I got home that afternoon at about 3:30 or 4:00, our house was filled with friends and relations, including some cousins from Boston. I knew that Daddy's funeral had taken place earlier in the day, but I didn't know that funerals were followed by what looked an awful lot like a party. No one was weeping and wailing. In fact, they were talking loud and fast; laughing even. I didn't get it, but I took my cues from the grown-ups and, again, I didn't cry.

Within days of Daddy's death, Grampa Bosworth sat me down in a big wing chair in his living room and told me in no uncertain terms that my life was now going to change. For starters, I had to accept responsibility for helping my mother. In fact, the words *responsibility* and *helpfulness* became hallmarks in our home, not only for me, but also for my brothers, particularly my older brother, Steve.

From that moment until I left home for college almost eight years later, I often cooked dinner, washed the dishes most nights, helped clean the house on Saturdays, and did a fair amount of the family ironing. By the time I was in seventh grade, just eighteen months after my dad's death, my mother had taught me how to sew, and from then on, I made many of my own clothes. By the eighth grade and throughout high school, I held a full-time job in the summer and often had part-time jobs during the school year, usually working in a local department store. Being a typical adolescent, I did my share of complaining about these responsibilities, but, frankly, I didn't feel unusually abused. My brothers carried a similar load, as did several of my friends who lived in conventional two-parent homes.

My life progressed in ways that were at once ordinary and perhaps not so ordinary for a middle-class girl from the Midwest. I made my way through high school, went on to college (a private college, Ohio Wesleyan, partially paid for with two scholarships), spent a year studying in Europe, and then, after college, came directly to New York City. When I was in my early twenties, I married my college boyfriend, but our marriage never quite solidified and we amicably divorced before we were thirty. Although I thought I would marry again, I have not; although I thought about (and wanted) children, I did not have them.

Instead I established a career as a book editor and later as a writer in New York City. I have loved my work and I have loved New York. I have had a very full life, rich with friends and activities, but it is not the life I thought I would have; nor is it the life I suspect my father expected me to have or perhaps even would have wanted me to have.

It would be easy to sum up my story by saying that any problems or disappointments in my life are the result of the trauma from my father's death and my upbringing in a fatherless home. This, of course, is not only too simple; it's not entirely true. Another personality dealt the same hand may well have played her cards differently. Each of my three brothers, products of the same parents and the same home situation, has faced his life and its choices in an entirely different way. Temperament and character play a role in how your life turns out. Still, my dad's loss shaped me profoundly, and I've struggled with its consequences all my life.

There's a photo of my dad that sits in a glass frame over my desk and has been with me since I started writing this book. It's a black-and-white shot, catching him from the waist up. He's standing in front of a picnic table. On the table in front of him, I can see an open bag of potato chips and a couple of bottles of Vernor's Ginger Ale, an old-fashioned Midwestern soft drink that has disappeared, although I can recall its distinctively sweet/spicy scent and flavor, both of which I associate with my childhood and with my dad.

I suspect the photo was taken in 1955 when I was nine, because Daddy looks pretty much as he did at the end of his life, except that in this picture he still looks happy and strong, which would not be true by the summer of 1956. His face is in shadow, but I can see that he's relaxed and smiling. Someone may have said something funny or told a joke. There's a lit cigarette in his fingers, and he appears to be toying with something, but I can't make out what it is.

I recognize the park in the background. Cleveland is ringed with beautiful parks, and this one, Clague Park, had a duck pond at one end; a play area with swings, slides, a merry-go-round, and a jungle gym at the other; and a cluster of picnic tables and grills conveniently scattered in between.

I have a distinct memory of my dad in that park, but it's a troubling one. We were at a picnic with many other families with children; I think it may have been a company picnic, because I don't remember knowing the other children. Dad was leading games with the kids—three-legged races, water balloon tosses, relay races, and the like.

I participated in one of these events. We kids took off our shoes and scattered them in a row about twenty yards away. Then we lined up; Daddy said go; and the first one to find his or her shoes, put them on, and run back to the starting point was the winner, which turned out to be me. What was disturbing was that I sensed that Daddy was disappointed in me.

I remember I was wearing sandals with buckles that day, and during the race, I just loosely buckled my shoes—sort of cheating, or, at least I thought so. To complicate the matter, I received a bag of peanuts as a prize—a pretty dopey prize, I thought, and may have even complained about it. More than fifty years later, the thought of my behavior that day shames me.

I can't remember what my dad said or did to make me feel that he was unhappy with me. Did he think I had cheated at the race? Was he embarrassed that his own kid had won and not someone else's child—

perhaps his boss's? Had I shamed him by behaving like a brat about the bag of peanuts? I don't know.

Why do I dredge up this rather insignificant event now? And why is it tinged with such sadness, shame, and regret? I think it is because it serves as a hook on which to hang all my unresolved and unarticulated feelings about my father. If he had died when I was five, I would have fewer memories of him, but I suspect they all would be of an adoring daddy, unconditionally proud of his bright, curly-headed little girl. If he had died when I was twenty-five or thirty, I would have collected many more memories, probably some good and others not so good, but I would remember him as a real man, and he would have known me as a real young woman. I would have learned what his boundaries were; what he liked, what he didn't like. Perhaps I would have learned how to please him, and perhaps I would know that he loved me even when I did things that did not please him.

But he died when I was ten. My memories of him, while numerous, are colored by my perceptions of him, which remain, to this day, immature and childlike. Still, at that age, I was old enough to perceive something new in him and in our relationship as father and daughter, but I was not mature enough to make sense of it. It is this confusion of emotions that I want to explore, explain, and hopefully put to rest.

2. SO, WHAT'S A FATHER?

It is a father's task to help raise his children so that they can be constructive members of society, and to transmit to his children those cultural values they must have to succeed in life.

—David Popenoe, *Life Without Father*

It would be almost impossible to write about growing up fatherless without first defining what it means to be a father, or, perhaps more to the point, what it means to *have* a father. What is it that fathers do? And, more particularly for this book, what is it that fathers do for their daughters?

Of course, the first father image that comes to my mind is that of my own dad. Except for the vivid images I have of him lying in bed during his last illness, most of my memories involve him either coming home from the outside world (usually his job) or going out into the world (also usually his job)—that is, most of my recollections of him are not of him at home, intimately involved with the goings on of our family.

Oddly enough, my dad's seeming lack of involvement is not at all disturbing to me. On the contrary, it was through my dad that my brothers and I were introduced to the pleasures of the outside world. Whether we were visiting relatives on the other side of town, going to a circus or an amusement park, leaving for a vacation, or just picking up jelly donuts from the local bakery on a Saturday morning, these were fun-filled adventures for us, and they were almost always instigated by my dad.

To my amusement (and, in some ways, my horror), many of the other strong father images that lurk in my brain are figures I came to know through television. Being an American girl whose childhood spanned the 1950s, television dads like Ozzie Nelson, and actors Robert Young and Fred MacMurray (who played the fathers in the popular shows *Father Knows Best* and *My Three Sons,* respectively), were part of my life for years.

In a rather powerful way, these television shows shaped my views of what a father was, or, at least what a dad ought to be. These television dads were almost always portrayed in situations (and, in the 1950s, these were almost always comic circumstances) involving the home and family. Although it was implied that these men held jobs, I can't for the life of me remember what it was that they did for a living; nor did I ever see them doing it. In retrospect, this strikes me as odd, since my personal sense of a father is of a man who was inextricably tied to his work. What's more, my memories of my own father doing things with us children usually involved leaving home, not staying home.

Also, with these 1950s TV dads, a benign but ever-present patriarchal force was very much in effect. If a child got into trouble (which meant a son failed his geometry test, or a daughter spilled soda on her prom dress), the mother would invariably announce that Dad would deal with the problem when he got home. Indeed, the premise of the popular show *My Three Sons* was that the father, Fred Mac-Murray, was running a house full of boys virtually all by himself. The mother of these children had apparently died—a huge tragedy for most people, but an issue that went unmentioned and unaddressed in this family. Also, the father managed to handle everything with ease, including coping with the household, with the help of the boys' grandfather, making the patriarchy absolute.

Actually, the mothers in these TV shows (and most of them did feature mother figures) were as unreal as the fathers. They were always perfectly groomed and usually wore high-heeled shoes and a spanking clean dress, sometimes protected by a little apron presumably to indicate that they were involved in housework. Somehow, too, the house was always spotless, yet you never saw Harriet Nelson, June

Cleaver, or Donna Reed, or any of the other 1950s TV moms, running a vacuum cleaner or washing a dish. Like the fathers' careers, the women's work was sort of a mystery.

The mothers on these programs were sweet, kind, occasionally witty, seemingly competent, but never forceful. The fathers, even dads as goofy as Ozzie Nelson, made all the tough decisions. What's more, these men did so in a calm, rational manner, never losing their temper, often adding a light touch of humor, and certainly never harshly disciplining the children.

Needless to say, this is not at all how I remember the dynamics of my own household. By the time I was five years old, our family consisted of four children under the age of nine, and our house looked it. Being the only girl, I had a bedroom of my own, but our house was not particularly large and my brothers shared a room. Toys were strewn throughout, dust and magazines collected on the tables, and an ironing board was often set up in the living room so that my mother could iron as we played or watched television. We always had meals as a family, although my father was frequently absent from the dinner table because he was at work.

Although my dad never yelled at us or spanked us, my parents fought a lot between themselves. My dad was away much of the time—according to my mother, this was the reason for many of their disagreements—and my mother made virtually all of the decisions pertaining to the house and the children. And, of course, she continued to do so after my father died.

Because my father died when I was ten, I might be inclined to suspect that my memories are a little faulty; that my dad was home more than I remember and that he was much more involved in the family decision making. But I know that's not true. My brothers and my mother confirm my memories. What's more, most of my friends experienced their fathers in much the same way.

The image of the father has a very strong impact on children. Even when he is romanticized, as he was on television in the 1950s (and often is today!), children acknowledge these images and attempt to integrate them into their own truth. So what is that truth, and how did it develop?

THE EVOLUTION OF THE FATHER

In the great sweep of history, the concept of fathering as we know it is a relatively modern one. In his book *The Father: Historical, Psychological, and Cultural Perspectives,* Luigi Zoja talks about the history of fathering in a fascinating way. Using the symbol of a year-long calendar to describe evolution, Zoja shows that mammals did not appear on the face of the earth, symbolically speaking, until mid-December; the human species did not develop until about 9:00 P.M. on December 31; and the contemporary idea of fathering evolved in the last five minutes.

Not only did the concept of fathering come late, but, according to Zoja and others, the notions of masculinity and fathering have traditionally been at odds with one another and continue to be so to this day. Throughout the animal kingdom, survival of the fittest was always the ultimate life issue. The strongest, or the most "masculine" male survived, and, as a result, was the one who would provide the seed for the next generation.

As mammals and ultimately humans developed, their offspring often required the care and training of their parents for a relatively long period of time before they were able to survive on their own. Hardwired by biology to care for her babies, the female stayed with them while the male went off, sometimes to hunt, sometimes to create more progeny, sometimes simply abandoning mother and baby because his job to spread as much of his genetic material around as possible was completed. Eventually males learned that they needed to protect their females and babies if their own genes were going to survive.

To put it another way, females cared for their offspring because they were biologically and instinctually created to do so; males cared for them because it was in their best interest to do so, even though the learned behavior of fathering was at odds with fundamental "masculine" instincts.

Fathers in Classical Myth

Greek and Roman myths are rife with father images, from Zeus, the supreme symbol of the patriarch, to Ulysses, the ultimate absentee dad. It is in classical myth that the concept of the father begins to evolve into a more sophisticated cultural form. As Zoja points out, Hector is the only Trojan hero who is both a warrior and a family man with a private life that includes a wife and a child. Zoja says, "Hector is both patriot and father, patriot and *pater,* two words that ring with a similar sound, and with nearly the same meaning."

In Homer's *Iliad,* the scenes between Hector and his child reflect the conflict between the macho, warring male and the warm, empathic father. When Hector tries to embrace his child before going to war, the child pulls away in fear. Only when Hector removes his armor will the child permit his father to hold him. Still, although Hector is considered to be one of the greatest warriors in Greek mythology, he ultimately is slain by Achilles. The message: the macho warrior prevails, not the more "feminized" family man. This conflict between the masculine and the fatherly remained deeply imbued in Western culture for centuries.

From the Ancients to the Victorians

From the fall of Greece and Rome through the Dark Ages, the concept of patriarchy endured, exemplified most powerfully through the rise of the Christian Church and the worship of the Heavenly Father and his son, Jesus Christ. In the sixteenth and seventeenth centuries in Western Europe and especially in Colonial America, families and the community at large were closely linked, but fathers were supreme, serving as the moral and authoritarian center of the home.

Beginning in the late seventeenth century with the Enlightenment (and the rise of radical notions such as that formally educating women might benefit the family and society as a whole), the strong patriarchal base of Western culture began to soften a bit. By the mid-nineteenth century, when industrialization took the father out of the home and into the factory, dramatic shifts began to occur that would alter the role of the father in the family, although these changes would take close to one hundred fifty years to come to fruition.

Victorian Fathers and the Nuclear Family

The concept of the nuclear family, the small, private entity made up of two parents and a few children, emerged in Western Europe and the United States in the early- to mid-nineteenth century during the so-called Victorian era. Unlike families of earlier generations, which consisted of vast webs of relatives, neighbors, and social equals linked together often merely by the need to survive, the nuclear family was characterized (at least in theory) by warmth and affection. The marriage between the parents was not arranged or based on economic or social necessity; instead it was the result of romantic love. The family or nuclear unit was meant to serve as a refuge, as opposed to a cog in the wheel of society as a whole.

Also, for the first time in history, the father worked outside of the home instead of on the farm or in the shop, which previously was almost always attached to the living quarters. Socially, at least among the middle classes, it reflected badly on the adequacy of the male if his wife needed to work in order to support the family. As a result, the parenting roles began to shift.

Since the father was gone from dawn to dusk throughout the week, most of the parenting responsibilities fell to the mother. Not only was she expected to run an efficient household, she was required to deal with the day-to-day problems of raising the children. Although the father remained the moral authority (the image of the severe patriarch remained strong), he, in fact, gradually became only a part-time presence.

Robert Griswold, author of *Fatherhood in America,* explains that industrialization also gave rise to stronger female bonding, which in turn played a role in reducing the importance of the father:

> The simultaneous emergence of industrialization and domesticity in the nineteenth century gave rise to a distinctive world of "female love and ritual." . . . These developments created social and psychological spaces in which women established lasting bonds with one another. Brought together by frequent pregnancies and childbirth, nurturing lifelong friendships with impassioned letters and frequent visits, bonding together in reform and church associations, women created a world in which men, fathers included, made but a shadowy appearance.

Fathering and the American Melting Pot

In the United States in the late nineteenth century, the huge influx of immigrants, especially from Europe, also altered the notion of fathering. Irish, German, Scandinavian, Italian, and Jewish peoples flooded into America between 1850 and 1920, each nationality bringing a somewhat different notion of the father role, but often, especially in German, Jewish, and Italian families, a strongly patriarchal one.

For example, in the majority of Italian homes the father was usually the dominating force, demanding obedience and deference, which was often given out of fear rather than love. According to Griswold, "In the formal, patriarchal [Italian] home, life was especially difficult for daughters. Many found their mothers more flexible than their fathers, less suspicious of American ways, more tolerant of their social lives, and far less demanding of elaborate displays of deference." By the late 1920s, when the first generation of the children of immigrants was coming of age, the authority of the father had broken down considerably.

The Impact of the Depression and World War II

By the mid-twentieth century, although the strong patriarchal legacy and the deeply entrenched concept of the nuclear family were beginning to break down in the United States, two events occurred that stalled the decline of the nuclear family for at least another generation: the Depression of the 1930s and World War II in the 1940s.

Because of the fragile economy during the Depression years, families tended to stick together in order to survive. During World War II, the idea of a man going off to war was heralded as a heroic gesture, even if he had children. Also, family life was romanticized, in part to keep people in a positive frame of mind in order to promote the war effort.

However, beneath the surface, aspects of family life were continuing to change. During both the Depression and World War II, it became not only necessary but acceptable for women to work outside the home. What's more, women often ended up enjoying escaping from the confinement of housework and child care and took great pride in their pursuits. It also became clear to both men and women that the role of breadwinner could be assumed by women, and, as a result, one of the primary roles of the traditional father was threatened.

In addition, other sociological trends were chipping away at American beliefs about marriage and the nuclear family. One was the American concept of masculinity. Beliefs about fatherhood versus the macho ideal of manhood were often at odds. On one hand, fathers were considered to be highly respectable; often a man's sense of himself was measured by his success as a husband, father, and family man. On the other hand, the ultimate masculine archetype, especially in America, was the strong silent male, the loner, the cowboy, the tough warrior, the man who didn't need anybody—all models antithetical to being a good husband, father, or family man.

So, on the surface, although the nuclear family seemed to remain intact, changes surrounding the concept of family began to appear as early as the first quarter of the twentieth century. The divorce rate jumped nearly 100 percent between 1900 and 1920, although it then slowed during the 1930s and 1940s as a result of the economy and the war. Men who went off to war in the 1940s returned with a strong sense of male pride, a sense that they had prevailed as men and with men. Women worked outside the home and sustained the family by themselves, emerging from the war years equally proud of their accomplishments. These strong feelings would eventually explode, but not before the men and women of this generation would make one more stab at raising their children according to the tenets of the happy nuclear family and the American dream. In the end, of course, it didn't really work.

The Myth of the 1950s

The years between 1946 and 1960 were among the most affluent in the history of the world. Not only were people of the middle class secure, but many members of the working class were finally able to enjoy some of the benefits of relative financial security, including a house of their own, a new car, and a college education for their children. It was the Eisenhower era, and Conservatism was the prevailing philosophy. Women who had joined the work force during World War

II returned to their lives as "perfect" wives and loving mothers. Men stored their dress uniforms, their combat helmets, and their medals in the attic and started anew as commuting businessmen, contented husbands, and suburban dads. In theory, everyone was comfortably well off and life had returned to normal.

But, of course, this supposed normalcy was a myth, and nowhere was that myth more idealized than on American television. According to sociologist Elaine Tyler May, in the 1950s—at least on television—"fatherhood became the center of a man's identity"; these men "forged their screen identities as fathers, not workers. Secure in their suburban homes, untouched by financial problems, marital discord, or political passions of any kind, these men's 'work' was the resolution of minor crises that beset their children. Only men like Ed Norton, the feckless and childless sewer worker in the *Honeymooners,* made much mention of their occupations." According to the television culture—which by then was a reflection of the notions of the culture at large—the ideal American man was an easygoing Ozzie Nelson–like dad who in his sort of goofy way solved the problems of the world. (Curiously, that same sort of lovingly silly dad is seen again in a more recent television dad, Raymond Barone, in the popular sitcom *Everybody Loves Raymond.*)

However, the reality was more in line with what I and others of the baby boom generation experienced with our own 1950s fathers. Despite the message presented on television concerning the ideal dad, most post–World War II fathers identified strongly with the notion of breadwinning as the primary responsibility of the father. By the 1950s, breadwinning assumed not only the defining element of a successful father but the ultimate macho ideal. The more prestigious your job or position, the more money you earned, the bigger your house, the more cars you owned, the more successful you were considered to be, not only in the world at large but as a father and as a man.

As men became more successful (that is, earned more and more money), the macho ideal often superseded any wish to be an involved father. In addition, it also began to color how men viewed their wives and their wives' roles in the family. In a study conducted at Stanford

University in the late 1950s, the researchers found it "striking how clearly the men saw breadwinning as a male obligation and how casually they accepted the responsibilities of fatherhood in general."

The 1950s code for success was that men went out into the world and earned a living while women kept the house and took care of the children. Griswold states, "Quite clearly fatherly responsibilities had little to do with the day-to-day care of the children or upkeep of the home. Men's belief in the sanctity of the division of labor and the ideology of male breadwinning precluded sustained involvement in daily housework and the less appealing aspects of child care."

Still, most men continued to believe that they were necessary advisors to the intellectual and social success of their children. It was still the father, most people felt, who shaped the character of their children. According to Ruth Tasch, in her study "The Role of the Father in the Family," "Fathers emphasized . . . their efforts to mold their offsprings' characters."

But inevitably, the happy 1950s, the nirvana of the nuclear family turned out to be a myth. According to Popenoe, by the late 1950s, "Expectations for love, happiness and the good life within the family had reached new heights . . . With such high expectations, many adults were bound to end up disenchanted, disappointed, and discontented . . ." And this included the job of parenting. Women began to perceive that motherhood was not the all-consuming joy they had been led to believe it would be. Men, often enthralled with their work, became distant both as husbands and as fathers. And children were caught in the middle.

The 1960s and Later

By the mid-1960s, thanks in large part to Betty Friedan's landmark book *The Feminine Mystique* and the influence of the 1960s feminist movement, women were demanding change. (In my research for this book, I was struck by the number of feminists who grew up fatherless. Although Friedan was reared in a conventional two-parent home, Gloria Steinem, Susan Sontag, Bella Abzug, Geraldine Ferraro, and many other well-known feminists were fatherless daughters either through death or divorce.) At the same time, men began rethinking their roles as husbands and fathers, and their sons, the males of the postwar baby boom generation, to a great extent, decided to postpone fatherhood or to alter its meaning to suit their own ideals and lifestyles.

Social historian and writer Marty Jezer is a perfect example of such a father. Born in the late 1930s, Marty was brought up in New York City and was active in radical politics long before the label "hippie" entered the lexicon. Although Marty had had several committed relationships, he didn't father his one and only child until he was in his early forties in 1982.

When Marty and Mimi, his partner, learned that their baby was to be a girl, Marty was especially pleased. He had lost his beloved older sister, Ruth, to cancer ten years before, and to him this baby was a gift. Also, Marty considered himself to be a feminist, and having a daughter fit nicely into his view of himself and his politics.

"I never thought I'd be a father," Marty says. "Until I held Kathryn, I had never even wanted to hold a baby. Then I got into it, liked the image, and was very proud and conscientious. Because of the influence of my sister, my own politics, and the radical pacifist circle I worked in, I was very aware of feminist issues and very supportive of them.

"The decisive moment for me was when I was in the birthing room where Kathryn was born. The doctor delivered the baby, showed her to Mimi, and handed her to me, and I bonded instantly. From that moment on, I knew I could do it. It was like holding one of my cats, which I was comfortable doing and very cavalier about.

"When we got home, Mimi became slightly ill and had to go back to the hospital, leaving me with Kathryn (and some bottles). I lay on the bed and she lay on my stomach. When she cried, I held her and gave her a bottle. It seemed a very natural and easy thing to do. Throughout her babyhood, I was the one who woke up at night to give her a bottle and also did most of the diapering. I liked the image of myself as a feminist man, but I also enjoyed doing it."

Screenwriter and novelist Jonathan Day, born in 1946, reports an almost identical experience with regard to relating to both his daughters, Julia and Sophia, immediately after their births. Jon and his wife, Nina, had been married for twelve years before they decided it was time to have a child. Even after Nina became pregnant, Jon was rather neutral about the notion of fatherhood. However, from the moment his first child was in his arms, Jon's feelings changed radically.

"During Julia's birth, Nina went into toxic shock. They kicked me out of the room, and the procedure became totally medical. I was sitting outside when they brought Julia to me. I can remember how she looked at me, which was totally Julia—just straight up at me with wide eyes—sort of saying, 'So, you're my dad. Well, okay.' "

Holding her at that moment, says Jon, "just opened a door into a world that I'd never imagined. I'd never known that depth of feeling could overwhelm you in a moment, like love at first sight. It opened up a door to a well of emotion within me that I hadn't anticipated. I am very much in love with [my wife] Nina, but I don't think I was ever overwhelmed with emotion like that, partly because I think guys have to protect themselves a little bit."

Bob Stein, a New York City attorney, also reported a unique connection with his eldest daughter at the moment of her birth. "When my first was born, bonding was instant. I fell asleep that first night in an armchair [at the hospital] with her on my shoulder. We just slept there like that for a couple of hours. It was the most wonderful moment in my entire life."

Like Marty and Jon, Bob had not given much thought to being a father before his children were born. However, to "the extent to which I thought through my relationship [with my kids], I was going to be an involved parent, unlike my father, and unlike the whole generation of the fifties that I, as a [sixties] hippie, had rejected. I was not going to go off to the office every day and never see my kids." So, for the first few months of Bob's daughter's life, he came home at six o'clock every evening and took his baby daughter, Miriam, out in a backpack for long walks in the park. "Those were treasured moments for me," Bob says. "I was determined to be as important in my children's life as their mother was."

The sad fact is that despite this powerful desire among many of the fathers of the post–World War II generation to participate more fully in the lives of their children, an equally strong—if not stronger—tendency among many men to avoid or relinquish their fatherly responsibilities came into play in the 1970s and continues to this day. In addition, over the last two decades, many women have chosen to give birth to or adopt babies without being married or partnered. As a result, today more than 30 percent of children under age eighteen are being raised in single-parent homes, primarily by women. And many of today's dads are not just distant; they have disappeared altogether.

The Age of the Disappearing Dads

In 1992, Vice President Dan Quayle ignited a firestorm of controversy when he criticized the television character Murphy Brown, a powerful, intelligent journalist in an eponymous sitcom, for having a child out of wedlock without any father in the picture whatsoever. (Once again, a television sitcom reflected the prevailing values.) Specifically, Quayle said: "It doesn't help matters when prime-time TV has Murphy Brown, a character who supposedly epitomizes today's intelligent, highly paid professional woman, mocking the importance of fathers by bearing a child alone and calling it just another lifestyle choice."

Articles and editorials flared up for weeks in every journal imaginable from the *New York Times* and the *Washington Post* to *Time* magazine and the *National Review,* most raging over Quayle's seeming criticism of single mothers. A few months later, however, the (liberal) sociologist Barbara Dafoe Whitehead published a long article in the *Atlantic Monthly* entitled "Dan Quayle Was Right," in which she took issue with the press and explained that the controversy was not over single motherhood; it was about the absence of fathers.

A decade later, in early 2003, Quayle again commented on the Murphy Brown controversy on a national news show: "As you recall, in that famous sound bite that ran over and over again, I talk about mocking the importance of fathers, and that's what I really didn't like about the show. There was no father. The message was that fathers need not be involved; fathers can go ahead and have children, but they don't have to raise the children."

Whitehead's thoughtful *Atlantic Monthly* piece explored in detail the social trends that had led to the Murphy Brown explosion. She pointed out the fact that as a result of a series of shifts in social values over the preceding twenty-five years, fathering had almost disappeared. Specifically, she cited the lifting of taboos against divorce, couples openly living together without being married, and having children out of wedlock as the reasons for the high rate of absentee dads. Whitehead says, "At some point in the 1970s, Americans changed their minds about the meaning of these disruptive behaviors. What had once been regarded as hostile to children's best interests was now considered essential to adults' happiness."

For an entire generation, starting in the early 1970s in an almost natural progression from the swinging sixties, couples got together (either in marriage or simply through living together or even just casually dating), had children (in or out of wedlock), and then split up with apparent ease if the going got rough or they fell in love with another person or they just got bored. The upshot of the quest for happiness was, of course, an inordinate percentage of broken families. More often than not, it was the fathers who became detached from their children. The fact that many fathers virtually disappeared from the lives of their children was not necessarily intentional, but it had become the reality.

Fatherhood Today

Paradoxically, although fatherlessness continues to rise, the problem of disappearing dads may be beginning to correct itself to some extent. Fatherhood organizations like the National Fatherhood Initiative have sprung up and are supported by politicians of every stripe. Even the world of television reflects a more complex response to social mores. Rachel, a character on the once extremely popular program *Friends,* had a baby. Like Murphy Brown a decade before, Rachel was a single woman living in New York City. But in this situation, she had a baby with Ross, a former lover and one of her best friends, and a man who you sensed would be an important and present part of the child's life. Indeed, when the series ended in 2004, the finale implied that Rachel and Ross would end up together in a conventional upper-middle-class marriage. The seemingly risqué television program *Sex in the City* carried this issue to its obvious ending. The character of Miranda, who accidentally gets pregnant after a casual one-night stand with an old-shoe boyfriend, decides to keep her baby and allows the baby's father to participate fully. After a year, the couple realize that they love each other and marry!

SO, WHAT DO FATHERS DO?

The role a father plays in the life of his children has changed over the centuries and will, no doubt, continue to evolve. Many tomes have been written on the topic of what men bring to the task of parenting. Also, much has been said about what fathers can provide that mothers cannot, although in this age of the supermom and the single mom perhaps some of these roles have become superfluous— or have they?

Some of the traditional responsibilities of the father developed simply because of the relative physical size and strength of men versus women. In addition, some of the fatherly roles have been imbued with macho values in order to appeal to male pride, and perhaps to ensure that men would stay around to protect the young. Still, at a basic level, these are the primary responsibilities that fathers have traditionally assumed, although some of them may have diminished in importance or changed in quality:

- Protector
- Guide to the world at large
- Breadwinner
- Alternative parent
- Second opinion
- Male role model

Protector

The role of protector is probably the most primitive of the fatherly functions. In earlier times, it was the larger, stronger, more aggressive male who protected the female and the children against predators and enemies. Traditionally, men fought the wars; indeed, some still argue whether women should participate in combat. In our current age, the notion of father as protector has lost some of its value, simply because it is not required. Most mothers are as able to protect their children from modern-day dangers as fathers.

Guide to the World at Large

A guide to the outside world is another traditional fatherly role that has changed with the general melding of men's and women's roles, especially in the workplace. As a person born in the mid-twentieth century, my generation may be the last that perceived the father as the door to the outside world and the mother as the symbol of home. In 2003, less than 20 percent of families operated as a conventional (perhaps now old-fashioned) nuclear family, with the father as the primary breadwinner and the mother as the homemaker. Today, mothers as easily as fathers can introduce children to the world at large in any number of ways. It is interesting to contemplate who symbolizes home, and does it matter?

Breadwinner

Like the protector and the guide, the role of the breadwinner has traditionally been perceived to be a function of the father. Nevertheless, throughout history, men have typically shared this task with women. Among early primates, man was the hunter, woman the gatherer; in agricultural societies, men and women typically worked the farm together; in the urban, industrial world, the mom-and-pop business is a convention. Men—and fathers—as the exclusive breadwinners have been a part of Western culture for only the last one hundred fifty years, and then only within the middle and upper-middle classes. Even then, during times of distress, such as the Depression and World War II, women were required to earn some of the income.

Still, in American society, even to this day, men are often valued for their earning power. What's more, men still take pride in their money-making capability and women usually look for it when seeking a husband.

Despite the inroads of the feminist movement, women still earn less than seventy-five cents on the dollar as compared to men. Also, although some couples have chosen to reverse roles, with the father caring for the children and the mother bringing home the bacon, these families are in the minority. Nevertheless, because so many women are in the workforce and expect to be treated and paid equally, these values are changing, albeit slowly.

In short, mothers can be the sole breadwinner, if necessary. In today's world, most mothers are required to do so just to make ends meet. But the role of the father as breadwinner remains part of our culture, if not so much literally, then certainly emotionally.

Alternative Parent

Men and women parent differently. Women tend to be calm, thoughtful, protective, and fair, whereas men lean toward being less emotional and more results oriented, disciplined, and demanding. In *Life Without Father,* David Popenoe points out that the differences in parenting styles between men and women come out especially dramatically when it comes to play and discipline:

> Fathers' play tends to be both physically stimulating and exciting, consisting of what has been called a "rough-and-tumble approach." In play, too, fathers tend to stress competition, challenge, initiative, risk-taking, and independence. Mothers, in their roles as caretakers, stress emotional security and personal safety.

Fathers often encourage team sports as a way for children to learn how to relate to the world. "I loved to play sports with my kids," reported Jon Day, who coached a number of his daughters' sports teams. Jon and his two daughters "wound up doing a lot of team sports together. With team sports, you have to learn not only how to deal with a coach but how to negotiate with other kids. You have to find out who is good and who isn't good; how you deal with the good kids and how you deal with the kids who aren't so good."

According to Jon, "It was important, too, that my girls were physically strong and have the confidence that strength builds. Along with that, I wanted them to have a certain toughness. If they got whacked down, I wanted them to get back up and not come crying to me and say, 'Somebody pushed me down.' This is life. I wanted them to have a certain toughness so that they could face the world. Not meanness, by any means, but a certain ability, a resilience."

Second Opinion

Many sociologists and child development experts believe that an important aspect of the father's role is simply that of a second opinion. This comment sounds a bit flip, as though all a father might be is one of Mom's friends offering an alternative way of viewing a particular issue. However, a second opinion is not only often welcome, it is essential. Children who lose their fathers often put inordinate value in their mothers' opinions, when these opinions may well be in error, or at least worthy of examination. Especially during the teen years, two parents working (and agreeing) in tandem can be helpful to both parents and children alike.

Male Role Model

What it means to be male is the one role that women cannot provide for their children. Mothers are women; fathers are men. From their fathers, sons learn how to be men and daughters learn how to relate to them.

As sociologist David Popenoe succinctly and beautifully confirms,

> Daughters learn from their fathers, as they cannot from their mothers, how to relate to men. They learn from their fathers about heterosexual trust and intimacy. They learn to appreciate their own femininity from the one male who is most special in their lives, assuming that they love and respect their fathers. Most importantly, through loving and being loved by their fathers, they learn that they are love-worthy.

If a father dies or departs, his daughters and sons lose their strongest source of male love, trust, and understanding. It cannot be replaced or compensated for by the mother, and it is a loss that will affect them in every facet of their lives.

WHY FATHERS MATTER

The more that fathers are involved in the day-to-day activities of their children—assuming the fathers are loving and sensitive to their children's needs—the better off those children will be. Not only do children who have had good fathering tend to feel safe and secure, they usually excel intellectually and academically; they are happier, exhibiting less psychological distress; and they seem to be more compassionate and better able to relate to the needs of others. Most children who have been raised by great fathers exhibit self-confidence—intellectually, emotionally, psychologically, and sexually.

These are the qualities and values that a good father provides for his children. So, what happens if he dies or abandons them? What happens if and when, for whatever reason, he simply isn't there?

PART II

SHOCK

◆

When a Girl Loses Her Father

3. DEATH, DIVORCE, OR SIMPLY FADING AWAY

Today the principal cause of fatherlessness is paternal choice. Over the course of [the twentieth] century, the declining rate of paternal death has been matched, and rapidly surpassed, by the rising rate of paternal abandonment.

—David Blankenhorn, *Fatherless America*

Many factors enter into how a woman experiences the loss of her father. It can depend on how old she is when he dies or leaves, whether she has siblings and where she fits in the birth order, how well her mother copes with the family changes, and whether her mother remarries. However, the initial most compelling factor that affects how a woman experiences her father's loss is whether her father dies or whether he abandons the family by choice.

My family, being of conservative New England stock, accepted my father's death with great stoicism. No one, most particularly my mother, broke down. It seemed to me that we were expected to pick up and go on, almost as if nothing had happened. This attitude, which was not uncommon in that time and place, ultimately took a terrible toll on my brothers and me.

Not long ago, I went to my fortieth high school reunion. Since I had lived in Lakewood, Ohio, a suburb of Cleveland, throughout my entire childhood, I had gone to public schools with the same kids since kindergarten, and many of them came to our reunion. At one point, I was chatting with two men I had known since I was five, Barry and Parker. They asked me what I did for a living. I said that I was a writer and was working on a book about girls who are raised without fathers. Since both Barry and Parker were in my class the year my dad died, I said, "I don't know if you remember, but my dad died when we were in fifth grade." The men looked at each other, sort of meaningfully, and then Barry said, "Pam, your father's death was one of the most formative events of my childhood."

I was shocked. I had truly thought that except for my closest friends, perhaps no one knew that my dad had died, or if they had known at the time, they would not remember forty years later. That my dad's death had affected both of these men so deeply absolutely astonished me!

Barry then went on to explain that the children in our class were told that my dad had died, but they were instructed not to say anything to me about it. And, perhaps not amazingly, none of them ever did! I vividly remember returning to school two days after my dad's death, as if I'd simply been absent due to a slight cold. Life just went on as usual.

Still, I recall that two other childhood friends also behaved in especially compassionate ways during the days immediately following my dad's death. One of them, Peggy, asked me to come to her house for lunch on the day of my dad's funeral, an event undoubtedly arranged by our mothers. (In my hometown, children went home for lunch, then returned to school in the afternoon.) Only years later did I learn that Peggy's younger brother had been killed in an automobile accident a year or two before. Clearly Peggy's mother knew much about the importance of extending kindnesses during a time of mourning.

Another friend, Margaret, came over to my house during the days immediately following my dad's death, brought me a box of chocolates, and asked me to come over for a sleepover at her aunt's home. Years later, I learned that Margaret's parents had divorced around the same time that my dad died. She and I certainly never discussed her parents' divorce, which in the late fifties in middle-class America was still considered quite shocking.

Both these girls (and their parents) reached out to me with concern and kindness, and yet neither one of them said anything to me at any time about my dad's death or about their own losses. For me, initially, my dad's death was a bewildering, private, almost shameful event. Literally for decades, except for a few awkward instances, I discussed his death and my feelings about it with no one—not my mother, not my brothers, not my grandparents, not my friends.

CHANGING STATISTICS: A SOCIOLOGICAL FLIP-FLOP

My experience was not unusual. During my childhood in the 1950s and in my middle-class Midwestern social milieu, death was dealt with privately with stoicism and frequently with a sense of embarrassment. Divorce in the family was even more hidden and shameful. However, starting in the 1960s, the outward reaction to death or divorce in the family began to change, and by the 1970s the overt response was decidedly more open and less tinged with shame.

The notion of the nuclear family truly solidified when society became industrialized, allowing middle-class mothers to stay at home to raise their children and fathers to go out into the workforce. Still, until well into the twentieth century, it was not uncommon for the breadwinning father to die at an early age, often due to various diseases that only became curable in the mid-twentieth century.

At the end of the nineteenth century, more than 20 percent of American children endured the loss of a parent before the age of fifteen, and more than half the time, the loss was the father. Divorce or abandonment as a reason for father loss was not unheard of, but it was rare. In 1900, only about 5 percent of children who lived in single-parent homes lived with a parent who was divorced or had never been married. Most of the time, that parent was the mother.

By the early 1960s, the death rate for young and middle-aged men had slowed while divorce in the early years of the twentieth century still appeared to be unusual. In fact, the incidence of divorce was slowly increasing but had not risen enough for anyone to notice, and the death rate was falling faster than the divorce rate was rising. As a result, by 1960 about 80 percent of children in the United States were living in two-parent homes, which is the highest percentage in history.

Suddenly a sociological earthquake shook the institution of marriage, rattling the concept of the nuclear family to its foundation. By the mid-1960s, the so-called sexual revolution had arrived and the post–World War II baby boomers were out to change the world. By the mid-1970s, open marriage was considered by many to be an acceptable lifestyle. Journalist Tom Wolfe dubbed this time frame the "Me Decade," in which significantly more marriages ended as a result of divorce rather than due to the death of a partner, and the statistics concerning the reasons for father loss flip-flopped. Whereas in 1900 only 5 percent of fatherless children were fatherless because of divorce or abandonment, by 1980 (and continuing to today) only 5 percent of fatherless children were fatherless because their dads had died; the remaining 95 percent were fatherless because their fathers had abandoned the family through divorce or were never married to the mothers in the first place.

For children born between 1970 and 1990 (interestingly, a "baby bust" period in American social history), only about 50 percent of children made it through their childhoods living simultaneously with both their natural parents. This was a staggering drop from 1960. (Other variables such as race and, to some extent, class, affect these statistics.) It is also important to note that most of these children were fatherless, since in over 85 percent of single-parent families the custodial parent is the mother.

Today, as we come to the end of the first decade of the twenty-first century, the main reason for fatherlessness within American families is paternal choice. While divorce remains the principal reason for father loss in our time, nonmarital births and adoptions are emerging as significant causes for the absence of fathers. While the effects of the lack of traditional fathering among these children have yet to be felt, we should be prepared for some potentially serious repercussions.

WHEN A FATHER DIES, WHEN A FATHER LEAVES

In his landmark book, *Fatherless America,* David Blankenhorn, founder of the Institute for American Values, virtually sums up the differences in tone and quality between losing a father through death and losing him through desertion:

> When a father dies, a child grieves. (I have lost someone I love.) When a father leaves, a child feels anxiety and self-blame. (What did I do wrong? Why doesn't my father love me?) Death is final. (He won't come back.) Abandonment is indeterminate. (What would make him come back?)
>
> When a father dies, his fatherhood lives on, inside the head and heart of his child. In this sense the child is still fathered. When a father leaves, his fatherhood leaves with him to wither away. The child is unfathered.
>
> When a father dies, the mother typically sustains his fatherhood by keeping his memory alive. When a father leaves, the mother typically diminishes his fatherhood by either forgetting him or keeping her resentments alive.
>
> Death kills men but sustains fatherhood. Abandonment sustains men but kills fatherhood. Death is more personally final, but departure is more culturally lethal. From a societal perspective, the former is an individual tragedy. The latter is a cultural tragedy.

When I began working on this book, some people (including editors and interviewees) urged me to focus solely on father loss through death because they believed father loss through divorce was a very different animal. However, I found through my interviews that the effects of father loss on women, whether through death or through divorce, were fundamentally more alike than different, and it was the relative weight of the effects and when they were experienced that accounted for their seeming differences.

Many sociologists believe that losing a father to death results in fewer negative effects on children than losing him through divorce and desertion. That is, the death of one's father is less traumatic emotionally because the father did not *choose* to leave.

At first glance, this statement seems true. When a child's father dies, if she is over the age of four or five, although she may be shocked and saddened, she understands that he did not choose to leave her. Nevertheless, almost everyone I interviewed whose father had died, myself included, experienced the loss, at some level, as *abandonment.* Granted, these abandonment feelings were not as sharp and cruel as those feelings of rejection experienced by children whose fathers had overtly deserted them. They were not as close to the surface, but they are present nonetheless.

Conversely, a fair number of the women I interviewed whose parents had divorced, especially girls born after 1960, did not feel a profound sense of abandonment or rejection by their fathers because of their parents' divorce. For example, one young woman, Libby, whose parents divorced when she was nine, found that she developed a deeper relationship with her dad after her parents' divorce, since the turmoil in their home due to hostility had ceased. Even after her father remarried, Libby found that she and her father enjoyed far happier, more meaningful times together than when he had actually been living in their home. It would seem that once the problematic marriage was resolved, the father could focus more clearly on his relationship with his daughter.

In addition to choice, many sociologists cite other variables that may make the effects of father loss due to death less damaging to children. These include:

- Absence of family acrimony and trauma that usually accompany divorce
- Fewer immediate life changes, such as moving to a new home or the emergence of a stepparent
- Fewer serious economic problems
- Maintenance of a positive, even idealized, image of the father
- A sense of finality as opposed to feelings of chaos

Again, superficially, these observations appear true. However, with closer scrutiny, it becomes clear that families experiencing father loss through death may be facing the same problems but at different times and perhaps in slightly different forms. In any case, ultimately the emotional effect is essentially the same.

Family Trauma

Marital discord and family trauma may well have been present before a father's death to the same degree as it may be before and during a divorce. One woman I interviewed was haunted by the fact that her father, who died suddenly in an automobile accident, had just had a terrible argument with her mother before storming out the door to his death. My own parents' marriage was in a rocky state at the time my father became ill, and I don't believe it was ever repaired or even discussed. Even if the parents' marriage is a happy one, the shock of watching a beloved father die of a long (or even a short) illness, an automobile accident, or even an event as outrageous and unforeseen as the September 11 terrorist attack is every bit as traumatic for a child as enduring the tribulations of an unhappy marriage surrounding a divorce; perhaps, in some ways, even more so.

Life Changes

Many sociologists believe that children experience fewer life changes after a father's death than those whose parents divorce. Frankly, I disagree based on my own experience and the life stories of the women I interviewed. With regard to divorce, it is true that a man often leaves his family for another woman, forcing the children to come to terms not only with his immediate absence but also the presence of an unwanted stepmother. However, among the women I interviewed, a number of widowed mothers, especially younger ones, remarried quickly, often precipitously, causing chaos for their families.

Life changes following divorce often result from a shortage of money, and statistics show that divorce puts a strain on a family's relative wealth. In *Life Without Father,* David Popenoe states that "widowed mothers tend to be financially better off than divorced mothers, and relatives and friends are more likely to provide assistance." But I found that many widows often were seriously strapped for money, while many divorcées, although sometimes left financially high and dry, often did receive child support if not alimony. Most women stated that friends were attentive immediately after the death of their father, but that attention quickly evaporated.

The Idealized Dad

Women who lose their fathers through death, especially those whose fathers were killed in war, maintain a heroic picture of their dads. With rare exception, the women I interviewed spoke of their late fathers in loving terms and with unconditional praise. Conversely, most of the women I interviewed whose fathers had deserted the family referred to their dads in harsh terms, some in almost hateful ways. Neither of these responses is surprising.

When a father dies, he is usually remembered favorably, gently, with longing and love. Within the family, he remains a positive force. However, when a father abandons his family, his influence diminishes drastically and often completely disappears. Even a very young child recognizes that Mom is now not only in charge but is very possibly both very unhappy and very angry. And, of course, so is the child.

Nevertheless, this picture is not as absolute as it may appear initially. Many of the women I talked to whose fathers had left the home sustained positive feelings about their dads, sometimes even despite strong evidence that their love was not warranted, appreciated, or even reciprocated. Even women who spoke disparagingly about their fathers' desertion eventually revealed that often they had gone to great lengths to secure the attention and affection of these same fathers. After all was said and done, they loved him and wanted him to love them in return.

In contrast, women whose fathers died when they were children must occasionally come to terms with harsh realities concerning their beloved and much idealized fathers. One woman whose father had died a hero in France during World War II was appalled and angry to learn from an officer who had served with her dad that her father had had a serious drinking problem. She insisted on denying this revelation, although she had long since come to terms with her mother's debilitating alcoholism. Novelist Mary Gordon wrote a heart-wrenching memoir called *The Shadow Man* about her father, who died when she was seven, having spent his life lying about his background and accomplishments. Still, Gordon closes her book with the wonderful thought that love is stronger than death. And, indeed, for the fatherless daughter, it is.

Is Death Really Final?

Finally, some sociologists believe that a father's death, because it is so utterly final, is less problematic than desertion. In other words, desertion is more damaging to a fatherless daughter than experiencing her father's death because a daughter isn't left hanging, yearning for her "lost" father, wondering if someday he will return.

It is true that women whose fathers abandoned the family almost always spend years—if not their whole lives—wondering if Daddy will return, and later, when they are adults, if he will finally seek a relationship with them. It is also true that fathers who desert their families rarely return; indeed, among the women I interviewed, none of the fathers who had abandoned their families came back. (Bear in mind that I'm talking about complete desertion; usually in divorce situations, fathers do maintain contact with their children, even if the situation is not ideal.) Nevertheless, because he is alive, the hope that he might return to her remains burning inside a fatherless daughter, and indeed this can be very problematic.

However, among women whose fathers have died, even though they clearly understand the concept of death and know full well that their father can never return to them, a sense of unfinished business with regard to their dads remains strong—and alive!—throughout their lives. This seems to be true if a girl's father died when she was an infant and she never knew him, or if he died when she was a rebellious teenager, already working through classic adolescent emotions with her dad. The fact that he has died does not resolve her feelings about him. In this sense, a father's death is no more final—and no less problematic—than if he had walked out the door of his own volition.

↭ PATRICIA ↝

Patricia lives in one of the world's most enviable apartments. It is positioned a block from the Promenade that runs along the western edge of fashionable Brooklyn Heights in New York City. Apartments with windows facing the Promenade enjoy a world-class view of southern Manhattan, a vista that most people would pay a fortune to possess, and most who live there do.

Unless, of course, you bought your apartment in the 1970s when co-ops were affordable, which is Patricia's fortunate situation.

When Patricia opened the door to her apartment, she made me feel instantly welcome, not an easy task for someone who is greeting a stranger who is about to ask incredibly intimate questions. Her natural warmth seemed at one with her Southern background, although all traces of her Virginia accent have been eradicated, thanks, I suspect, to her training as an actress.

Patricia is on the tall side. Her honey-colored hair is shoulder length, long for a woman in her early fifties, but very appealing on her and adds to her Bohemian aura. She is wearing soft blue jeans that look as if they have been washed a hundred times and a pretty blouse that hangs loosely over them.

Patricia grew up in a little town in southern Virginia. Her mother, Anne, was the daughter of a prominent local judge. Her dad, Henry Ames, known as Hank, had grown up on an Iowa farm and had entered the University of Virginia on a football scholarship. Her parents met at the university during World War II. Two years later, Hank went off to fight in Europe, shortly after Anne and Hank were married. He returned a lieutenant, only to be sent to Korea in 1947. Patricia was born in April 1947, in Fort Lewis, Washington, where her mother was staying while her dad was serving in Korea.

"Honestly, I have no physical memory of him," Patricia explained. "He survived World War II, survived Korea, and was finishing up his military duties in Washington when he was killed in a freak accident. He was driving a Jeep with other military men near the base and a drunk driver ran into them."

Shortly after her husband's death, Patricia's mother returned to her hometown with her toddler daughter and infant son. Actually, Patricia's mother was no stranger to tragedy. Her own mother had died when she was a child. It would seem that she gained strength from her family because she remained near them for the rest of her life. At the same time, she made sure her children maintained a connection with their own father's family in Iowa.

But maintaining ties with her husband's family was not enough. "My mother felt strongly that we needed a father," Patricia explains, "and she remarried about four years after my father died." Her new husband, Jim Harris, had lost his wife to cancer and had two children, a boy and a girl, who were several years older than Patricia. Together they had one more child, Jamie, who was born when Patricia was twelve. Patricia's stepfather was a successful electrical engineer, and the family settled into a comfortable small-town life.

"I liked my stepfather," Patricia says. "He was a very nice man and a good father. I grew up calling him Daddy."

Like many of the fatherless daughters, Patricia grew up a bit shy and reserved, and seemed to have a fairly fertile fantasy life, particularly with regard to boys but also with respect to her own future.

"Growing up, I was this goody-two-shoes," Patricia says openly. "I didn't date a lot as a teenager. I had a big crush on [one older boy], and I know he had one on me, but my mother didn't like me having anything to do with him because he was a 'bad' boy. He rode a motorcycle. I liked that—a little walk on the wild side."

Despite her "wild" fantasies, Patricia couldn't imagine herself with someone who wasn't considering higher education. She started college in 1965 at Northwestern University in Evanston, Illinois, primarily because she was interested in their theater program but also to satisfy some of those yearnings for something a bit "wilder."

"I went to Northwestern, thinking: Oh this is going to be a wonderful, liberal place. It's near Chicago, you know, it will be so cool and hip. Northwestern students were much more sophisticated than I was, but as it turned out, very conservative. By the end of my time there [the late 1960s], they had their little core group of demonstrators against the Vietnam war, but not much more. The '60s didn't come to the Midwest until about 1970, and I graduated in '69."

Patricia wanted to be a professional actress, and initially she was very lucky. "Just as I graduated from college, they were auditioning for the Chicago troupe for *Hair*. I went down [to Chicago] and got in line with all these hippies, and I got in! I was in *Hair* in Chicago for a year. It was a thrill, but it had a downside, too. All of a sudden, it was sex, drugs, and rock 'n' roll, and that was hard for me." Patricia yearned for a wild, exciting life, but when presented with the realities, she found that it was not quite what she was looking for.

After *Hair* completed its run, Patricia moved to New York City, where she struggled for many months. Finally, she got a part in the cast of a road tour of *Jesus Christ Superstar,* but when that ended, she came back to New York City and struggled some more. Patricia stuck it out as an actress for several years, working some, but not really making it big.

Her love life during these years was also problematic. "In show business most men are homosexual," Patricia explained, "and I fell in love with a gay guy. We had a nice relationship, but it ended up being very complicated, of course. About this time, I also met my husband-to-be, and by then, I really just wanted to concentrate on our relationship, marriage, and a family."

Patricia was a fascinating collection of contrasting qualities. On one hand, she was reserved and shy; on the other, she was straightforward, assertive, and strong. Part of her was clearly conservative and restrained, while another part seemed to be radical, almost wild. I was wondering how she managed to integrate these qualities, when she shocked me with yet another stunning dimension of her life.

Curiously, we had talked for almost an hour before, to my astonishment, she told me that she was a widow and had been since her children, who were now in their late teens, were very young. Despite our long conversation about her own mother's widowhood, she revealed that her own husband had died only after I pointedly asked her about him. Yet, not surprisingly, when I pressed her for details, Patricia was straightforward, informative, and thoughtful.

"Yes, I'm a widow," she said. "My daughter was two when

her father died. My son was seven. My husband died fifteen years ago. He was sick for a year with lymphoma, then it went into remission. Then a month later it turned into one of the worst types of lymphoma you can have. He was in the hospital for another month and then he died. He was forty."

She paused for a moment and then added quietly, "It's really bizarre to have this happen twice in my life." She went on and told me more about her husband, their life together, and his early and tragic death.

"My husband's name was Robert Phillips, and he was a stock-broker. Unfortunately, when I lost my husband, my mother was already deceased. She died of a massive stroke shortly after Robert and I were married.

"My husband and I met at a Buddhist meeting at a mutual friend's house. We were both trying to practice Buddhism at the time. Actually, I was sort of turned off by him initially. He was very aggressive and really pursued me. Robert and I were lucky enough to be in a situation where we were thrown together frequently because of the Buddhism. One day I looked into his eyes and I 'saw' him; I happened to see his eyes in the right manner—that's the only way I can explain it.

"We went out for a few months, lived together for a year, then got married when he was thirty and I was twenty-nine. We were married in 1976. Our son was born in 1979, and our daughter was born in 1984. Altogether, we were married for about ten years." Patricia confessed that she always worried the relationship somehow would not last. "I always had that fear," she said. "I just tried to put it down. Robert was sensitive to my fears. He would promise that nothing would come between us. But at one point, I realized there was no way he could promise me that.

"At the end, I was sitting next to him in the hospital, and the doctor called on the telephone and told me that Robert probably would not live for more than two weeks. I couldn't really hold my emotions then too well and I started to cry. So Robert and I talked about what the doctor had said, and Robert just said, 'So let's just have two good weeks. Let's just be together for two weeks.'

"The night he died, he was on morphine and in a coma, but I was able to say to him, 'It's all right, you can go now.' I feel very strongly that he heard me and he was able to let go, because he left then."

I asked Patricia which was worse, losing her father or losing her husband. As soon as I spoke the words, I realized that this was an insensitive question, but Patricia answered with great intelligence and dignity.

"It's not comparable," she said. "I was only two when my father died; I didn't know my father. When a young child loses a parent, he or she has no idea of what the loss means. I see it through my children. I'm so disappointed for them—that they didn't have their father. I know what their loss is because I had that same loss."

As Patricia said these words, I sensed that she was speaking as much for herself as for her daughter. Yet when she talked about losing her husband, her emotions were much more on the surface and much stronger.

"It was devastating to me to lose my husband because I really loved him. It's not something you get over," Patricia said. "I can function, but I'm still deeply distraught. I can't believe he's not here."

Patricia revealed that her strong feelings also had a practical dimension. As with many widows, Patricia resented that all decision making was left up to her. "I know that everything goes my way; I didn't have to argue with anybody. So many times I would just love to sit down and make a joint decision."

Patricia also missed her mother intensely. "Still, I think I learned a lot from my mother," she says, referring particularly to her mother's enormous losses. "She was just a lovely, angelic person, very open and accepting of anyone who would come into her life. And very strong. Never bitter. I saw her crying sometimes, but that was rare. She had experienced incredible tragedies, but she was always there for her children and her husband. She was a great mother and she would have been a wonderful grandmother."

At the time of our interview, it had been twenty-five years since Patricia and Robert had married and more than fifteen since he had died. During those years, Patricia had settled into a life that was focused primarily on her children. She was teaching preschool, which she enjoyed, but basically considered it only a convenient neighborhood job. Her career as an actress was long over.

Unlike her mother, Patricia had not married again. Whether it is because of her innate reserve or her wobbly self-confidence, Patricia attributed the lack of men in her life to her shyness. "I am very uncomfortable [around men]," she says. "I don't know how to flirt. I'm comfortable with my friends' husbands, but I'm terrible at parties. I just feel like the biggest wallflower."

This was a stunning statement to me, coming from a woman as pretty and personable as Patricia. Still, as I had noticed almost from the moment we met, Patricia had multiple dimensions to her personality. Somewhere inside her was that young girl who had managed to leave a small Southern town, graduate from a major university, and spend years working in the theater in New York City.

Despite her modesty, I felt the presence of that spunky girl and wondered if she did not suffer from the very thing she so regretted that her daughter also missed: the unconditional love of her father. The strong, independent soul was right there, and yet she seemed not to see it. And then she made a startling admission.

"I don't want to take care of anybody," she confessed. "I've taken care of two children. But it's no fun to be a single mom. I love my children, they are wonderful, and I'm so happy that they're here. But it really is difficult to be alone with children."

"Luckily," she concludes, "Robert left me in a position where I'm financially independent. I don't have to have more than this apartment. And then there's the closet issue. I don't know if I could share a closet."

DEATH MOST PAINFUL

If a child's father dies by his own hand—if he chooses to abandon his daughter in this most final way—the loss is inexpressibly painful. The operative word here, of course, is *choose*. When a father dies of illness or accident, the child knows (eventually, at some level) that her father did not choose to leave her. With divorce, he may be choosing to leave, but he is still, in theory, available to her. With suicide, he chooses to cut himself off with utter finality. In a sense, suicide is the ultimate rejection.

Suicide also engenders feelings of guilt, shame, and denial, with denial, not surprisingly, appearing to be the most prevalent. Indeed, denial is the hallmark of suicide and comes into play almost immediately after the death is discovered. Stories of suicide are always disturbing, and Catherine's history is both particularly moving as well as particularly hopeful.

◡∴ CATHERINE ∻

Catherine lives in a comfortable middle-class suburb on Long Island about one hour by train from Manhattan. I knew her brother casually, and when I told him I was working on a book about women and father loss, he told me that his dad had died when he was young and suggested that I talk with his sister. She agreed to be interviewed with alacrity and enthusiasm, and even over the telephone, she seemed open and easy. I knew that she was in her mid-fifties, so when she picked me up at the train station, I was also taken with how young and attractive she was: trim, shapely, with longish dark hair. By the time we settled down in her comfortable, orderly kitchen for our interview, I could already see that Catherine herself was as comfortable and orderly as her home and seemed to manage it all with tremendous energy and aplomb.

Catherine was born shortly after World War II. Her dad, Anthony, was a New Yorker of Italian descent who had grown up in the Bronx. He had been a GI stationed in England during World War II and had met Catherine's mother, Emily, while he was stationed there.

Catherine's mother had grown up in a tiny town in rural England. Her own father had died when she was a young girl, the result of wounds he had endured while fighting in France during World War I. When Emily married Anthony, she not only agreed to go with him back to his home in New York City; she converted from Anglicanism to Roman Catholicism, a decision that would strongly color her own life as well as the lives of her children and grandchildren.

Catherine was the eldest of four children and the only girl. Her three brothers were two, four, and six years younger. She had spent most of her childhood in New York City. In the late 1950s, her parents, like many postwar couples, decided to move their family out of the city into the calm and security of the suburbs. The comfortable kitchen where we sat talking was just two blocks from where Catherine had lived as a teenager.

"How old were you when your father died?" I asked.

"Thirteen," Catherine answered in a markedly assertive way.

"Oh, so you remember him well," I said happily, since so many of the women I had interviewed were very young when their fathers had died and did not have memories of their dads.

"Wrong!" she answered, again strongly. "My brother didn't tell you, did he?" she asked without hesitating, then continued without waiting for me to answer. "My father committed suicide. He shot himself with a rifle, right in our living room. I found him when I came home from school." She told me this in a straightforward, calm way, but I could tell her manner masked great emotion.

For my part, I was completely shocked by her revelation, and upset, which clearly she sensed. She kept on talking, almost to calm me, I felt.

"We'd had this new house for about a year. I came home from school and I had a key to the house and so I opened the front door, and there he was on the couch."

"It's funny—not funny ha-ha funny—just peculiar," she went on. "We were taught certain manners when we were kids. Say please or thank you—and we were taught never to just walk into somebody's house without being invited. We were told we should always knock on the door.

"The lady next door had six children. It was 1960, the doors were never locked, the kids were always in and out, but their front door was always closed. So I ran next door to get help, and I knocked on her door. I didn't push the door open or barge in or scream. I knocked and waited for someone to respond. And when I think about that, I laugh to myself in a way, because it's just so ingrained in us about how to behave."

After this memory, Catherine's impressions became sketchy and almost dreamlike. She remembered that the neighbor did finally come to the door and that she immediately called the police. She also remembered that her mother, who was a teacher at a local Catholic school, was dropped off by a colleague who had driven her to and from school every day. Catherine watched from the neighbor's window as the police intercepted her mother before she could enter her house.

Finally, although she did not remember her father's funeral, she did recall her grandmother (her father's mother) taking her aside and asking her what her father looked like when she found him. Catherine was shocked and upset by this. She understood immediately that the family had not told his mother that he had killed himself. She also intuited that she should keep up the charade, clearly a huge responsibility for an already distraught and traumatized thirteen-year-old girl.

"Many, many years passed," Catherine concluded, "and nobody ever talked about it. Nobody said a thing."

Neither of us spoke for a minute or two.

"So, you asked me if I remembered my dad," Catherine continued finally. "That's the thing that resulted from all of this: I don't. It was such a shock, such a trauma. Plus afterwards, there was this atmosphere of silence. As a result, I really have no concrete memories of my father. I have some feelings, some sensations. I don't know how to explain it. But there's not a memory that I can say, 'Oh, yes, that day we picked flowers.' Not that kind of a memory. Still, I have very good feelings about him. I know I miss him. I feel I miss him, but I have no memories to go on. Oddly, my brothers do have memories [of him], but they didn't know that [he killed himself] until much later."

Like many fatherless daughters, Catherine's life had two distinct parts to it: the time before her father died and the time afterward. Because of the trauma of his violent death—and the devastating effect on Catherine of finding him—the first thirteen years of her life were wiped clean from her mind. The time afterward took shape remarkably quickly, solidified, and then, fortunately for Catherine and her family, remained stable.

"I knew that I was loved," Catherine said, "and that's probably why I do as well as I do, because I had that baseline, and that continued right through my adulthood. But my mother was also strict, especially with regard to her Catholicism and the Church's rules. You couldn't eat meat on Fridays. There was no birth control. And abortion! I never heard of it [until I was an adult]. My mother told me nothing about sex, only that sex was to have children. That was it.

"Suicide in the Catholic Church is a mortal sin. Back then, there was a kind of a shame thing [surrounding suicide]. I knew there was something wrong because I was not supposed to talk about it."

Catherine's life settled into a predictable form surprisingly quickly. Interestingly, they remained in the house where her father had died, and her mother lived in the house for the rest of her life. Catherine spoke of her mother with great affection and attributes the fact that their family remained stable to her mother's English stiff-upper-lip strength and religious faith. She never got hysterical; she was the rock, always there. She taught school, but she never remarried and never had another man in her life.

Catherine married her high school boyfriend at age nineteen, perhaps in an effort to enhance a sense of security. Fortunately, unlike many women of her generation, and certainly many fatherless daughters, she was able to establish and maintain a strong marriage and is still married to her husband, Todd.

"I was signed up [to go to college] and I did go, for about a day, I think," Catherine explained. "I was in a car accident early in the school year. It was just a little fender bender, but for some reason I personally was a wreck, and I just quit right then. I think that's probably the only thing I ever quit in my life. Actually, I ended up going back [to college] years later, after I had my kids, which made it a little more difficult, but it was probably just the [right] time for me to go."

Catherine ended up getting a bachelor's degree in psychology and a master's in psychiatric social work. She and Todd have two sons and have lived a close family life. In a way, I sensed that Catherine didn't want to talk too much about her marriage, but she allowed that they had had their rocky times.

"I have to tell you, the one thing that I would think of all the time is that because my father died when he was only thirty-eight, it was very natural for me to think that Todd would die young also," Catherine said. "Plus his dad died when he was only fifty-nine. And he smokes; he drives me nuts! I have always prayed that the kids would grow up before anything happened to anybody! That feeling was always very present for me."

"Have I finished mourning my father?" Catherine said as we finished our talk. "Quite frankly, probably not. I don't know if you ever finish. You know, I was so scared, absolutely scared. I didn't know what was going on. Nobody was talking to me about it, and so, boom! I just kept going."

"Sadness," Catherine said at last. "That's the feeling that comes up when I think of him. Just sadness. That's all."

WHEN A FATHER LEAVES

As Victoria Secunda says in her book *Women and Their Fathers*, "Divorce is the closest thing to the death of a parent that a child can experience. Unlike death (except for suicide), however, it involves choice. And no matter how patiently parents explain to children that they are loved by both of them, no matter how ardently they try to reassure them that Daddy is not leaving them—only the marriage—

on some level children can't help believing that Daddy chose to leave them too."

Not surprisingly, children of divorce go through processes of grief and mourning that are in many ways similar to those of bereaved children. Beverley Raphael in *The Anatomy of Bereavement* confirms the presence of grief, but notes that in addition to mourning the breakup (or death) of their family, they are burdened with emotional complexities of another kind because the parent who has left is alive and may potentially be a part of that child's life. As Raphael puts it: "Many of the issues highlighted in relation to divorce are similar to those of bereavement by death. Yet the divorced parent remains, in fantasy or reality, a living force in the child's life in a way that is quite different from the situation after a death. The child here has to resolve the complex issues of this different relationship and the role it may play in the ongoing life of his family." The heartbreaking fact is, the resolution of these issues may take a lifetime.

For fatherless daughters, understanding her father's abandonment and resolving her emotional problems surrounding it take on a special color. As sociologist Judith Wallerstein found, girls "have a powerful need to create a protective, loving father, one who would never intentionally let them down. . . . Without any sense of contradiction, they are able to maintain a benign image of the loving father side by side with a history of repeated rejections and failures."

Jill's story is a classic one.

JILL

Jill opens the door of her Bohemian Victorian house (it's painted purple) in suburban New Jersey and greets me with an enthusiastic hug. She is a striking-looking woman with a mass of dark curly hair and black flashing eyes. Jill is in her forties and a divorcée, raising her two sons, ages nine and thirteen, on her own. Before her marriage, she had begun a career in public relations, and through several strokes of good luck and hard work, she is now an executive for a large PR agency and is able to work at home, an arrangement that suits her single-mom status perfectly.

"My understanding is that my father had an affair," is how Jill matter-of-factly explains her parents' divorce. Jill's dad, Eric, had been a successful Madison Avenue advertising executive who had managed to create the quintessential mid-twentieth-century dream life: a lovely and accomplished wife, three darling children (two sons, and Jill, the youngest), and a beautiful two-hundred-year-old farmhouse in Connecticut. They belonged to the local tennis club and a swanky golf club, but in the end, it didn't work.

"I have very few memories of him when I was really little because he worked all the time and he traveled so much," Jill said. "He was usually gone when we got up in the morning and he didn't come home until after I was in bed. When he would go on a business trip, he would always bring me a doll from whatever country he went to, so I had a wonderful doll collection. But I don't look back to my childhood and think: Oh, my Daddy was so great! He had no interest in his children. I don't talk about it very much, but I knew it and I internalized it."

Jill's parents divorced when she was nine and her brothers were eleven and thirteen. Until Jill was well into her twenties, her relationship with her dad was circumscribed, orderly, and cold. After the divorce, her father insisted on seeing each child separately, so Jill saw him about one weekend a month.

"I was put on a train, and arrived in Grand Central Station in New York City alone," Jill explained. "From the time I was very young, maybe twelve, he didn't even meet me at the train. Instead, I had to walk to his apartment, which was a few blocks away, by myself.

"My father is a very intimidating figure. He's not a sweet, loving, warm, enveloping sort of person. To look at him—he's about six-four—he exudes power and dominance. Plus, he drank. Because he was an alcoholic, spending the weekend with him was really unpleasant. I never, ever looked forward to going to see him. It was just something I had to do.

"Also, he was always very critical. He wasn't like some dads who might say, 'Oh, you're my favorite little girl and I can't wait to see you!' Instead, he would just get exasperated with me and would say things like, 'You're too fat' or 'I don't like how you pull your hair back from your face.'"

A year after Jill's parents divorced, her father married Barbara, a woman who had been his secretary at the advertising agency. "I don't want to say she wasn't a nice person, because in her way she was," Jill says with as much generosity as she can muster. "But she said from the start, 'I'm not your stepmother, I am your father's wife.' She had very little to do with us.

"I would say that the seventeen years my father was married to Barbara was probably the biggest transitional period of his life. A few years after they were married, in the early 1980s, he was forced out of his agency and had to retire when he was about fifty-two. When he lost his job, they moved to Florida, which is where he still lives.

"My dad went from being a very straight, buttoned-up guy in a navy blue suit who went out for three-martini lunches to being a hippie. After he lost his job, he quit smoking and drinking, and he became a vegetarian. When they started living in Florida, he got into yoga and meditation. Today he has a ponytail, a pierced ear, and a tattoo of a dragon on his shoulder.

"Up until I was about thirty, I did not have what I consider a relationship with my father. It was purely obligatory. However, when my father's marriage to Barbara fell apart, it apparently was a signal to him that the only people that he had in his life who were permanent were his children, and we were the people who he had neglected the most. When he came to New York to tell us all that he was getting divorced, he basically said to my brothers and me, 'Look, I'd like to ask you to give me one more shot at being your dad. I know I've made mistakes, but I really want to be the father that I've never been to you.'

"Well, frankly, my first reaction was 'fuck you.' But then I thought: Is it going to hurt me to give it one more shot? I decided that I had nothing to lose and everything to gain. There have been times in the past several years that it has been difficult, but on the whole, my dad has been terrific."

I found Jill's last comment fascinating. Throughout our entire interview, this was the first and only time she referred to her father as "my dad"; otherwise, for Jill, he was a rather chilly "my father." Still, the relationship between Jill and her father improved immensely and continues.

Aside from maturity on both their parts, the one factor that had the greatest effect on Jill's relationship with her father was her strong commitment to a career in a world he could relate to: public relations. Initially, Jill's dad had been very judgmental and belittling of her, largely because she had not been a top-notch student but also simply because she was a girl.

"One thing that my mother insisted upon in the divorce was that my father pay for all three of us to go to college," Jill explains. "During my freshman year, he called me and said, 'Listen, if you decide that you don't want to go to college anymore, I'll give you the rest of the money that I would have paid for you to finish.' I think the underlying message was, 'Hell, you're never going to make anything out of yourself, anyway, so why don't I just give you the money and let's call it a day.' A lot of it, I think, had to do with the fact that I was a girl. I don't think he had much respect for women."

About the same time Jill's father was divorcing Barbara and forging a new relationship with his children, Jill was also going through an upheaval, both personally and professionally. She had been living in California with the man she would eventually marry. However, the relationship wasn't really working at that point, and they moved back to New York, where Jill made some firm decisions for herself.

"I decided that I wasn't going to make it in the music business, a dream I'd nurtured for years," Jill explains. "Plus, I seemed to be good at being a secretary, so I figured that was my lot in life. So I decided I'd get a job as a secretary at the place that would pay me the most money.

"I was quickly hired by a man who I had worked for at a PR agency before moving to California. After I had been back [in New York] for about a week, he said, 'We need to talk with you about your career.' To my amazement, he saw something in me, and he helped me move from being a secretary to being an account executive."

From that moment on, Jill was promoted several times. Within a couple of years, she was offered a large salary to develop the public relations division of a small advertising company. "I think that blew my father away," says Jill. "I finally earned his respect."

Nevertheless, Jill's father had real problems with her personal decisions, particularly her choice of husband. But in an effort to be supportive, he remained neutral and respectful. "He could have so easily said rotten things about my husband, but he never did that. His bottom line was 'I just want you to be happy.'"

Jill is the first person to admit that her relationships with men were problematic long before she met and married her husband, Steven. Although she had had a number of casual sexual relationships, Jill didn't have a serious boyfriend until she went to London during her junior year in college. There, she got together with Mike, who, like Jill, was very into music. "We got to be friends very quickly and then fell in love," Jill says gently. "It was very magical." Although the relationship eventually ended, Mike and Jill remain good friends to this day.

Jill got to know her husband over the telephone because he was working at a job similar to Jill's at a recording studio often used by the agency where Jill worked. "We talked three or four times a day for a year, but we both were shy, so we never went out." At one point, Jill became sick with mono and was out of work for six weeks. During that time, Steven sent her several sweet little presents. Finally, he asked her for a date—on her birthday no less—to go to a David Bowie concert.

"We had the worst time," Jill remembers. "The concert stunk. Then, on the way home, we got stuck in traffic, and then I was nervous because I didn't want him to come up to my apartment because I specifically did not want to have sex with him. After that date, we decided in a sort of unspoken way that we were just better off as friends.

"A few months later, he invited my roommates and me to a

New Year's Eve party at his studio. His studio was right on the corner of 41st Street and Broadway, so it was a great place to watch the ball drop at midnight. I don't know what happened that night, but suddenly we were a couple. I think it had a lot to do with somebody paying attention to me for me. From the start, Steven seemed to adore me, and I really liked that!"

Although Jill and her father were beginning to forge a more understanding relationship, Jill's father, despite his hands-off attitude toward her personal life, was not pleased with the match, primarily because of Steven's professional life and his apparent lack of qualifications as a breadwinner. Steven was up in the air about his own career. He wanted to be a musician or a music producer, and he apparently had neither the sufficient talent nor the sufficient drive. Moreover, unlike Jill, who at a certain point in her life (around age thirty) accepted what she perceived as reality, Steven hopped from job to job. Nevertheless, Steven and Jill were married in a lovely ceremony in Central Park when they were both thirty-two.

Within a few months of their marriage, Jill became pregnant. Her father's response to the birth of her first son (and of Jill and Steven's second son four years later) was much the same as it had been for his own children: a barely disguised lack of interest. Nevertheless, although he did not cuddle and play with the children, he showed his affection by starting a college fund for the boys.

He never could accept Steven or support the marriage. Throughout their fifteen-year union, Jill worked full-time and was always the primary breadwinner, and that situation galled her father. As Jill puts it, "In many ways, I almost fulfilled the male role. I'm the primary breadwinner as well as the caretaker. I always have felt that I've had a very strong male side. This is taking nothing away from Steven."

But, of course, it said a great deal about Steven, who continued to have real problems finding work, keeping jobs, and accepting adult responsibilities. As the years went by, Eric became more and more distressed with Jill's situation and finally let her know that he was arranging his finances in such a way that Steven could have no access to Jill's or her children's potential inheritance. At first, Jill was upset with her father's decision, but deep down she knew the marriage wasn't what it should be and it should probably end.

Despite what Jill describes as "the little girl inside of me who says, 'Don't leave me,'" Jill ultimately had had enough and insisted that Steven leave their home. Although her relationship with her father remained stable, interestingly it was her mother's example that really sustained her through her divorce. Thirty years before, after fifteen years of living a seemingly ideal life as a housewife and mother, Jill's mom had had the rug pulled out from under her. But she pulled herself up, got a good job (not surprisingly in public relations), raised three successful children on her own, and ultimately became a highly respected writer. Today she has a wonderful life filled with a devoted companion, her children, her grandchildren, her friends, and frequent travel.

"If there's one thing that came out of my parents' divorce," Jill says, "it was that my mother finally had a happy, fulfilled life, which in turn was an inspiration for me. She turned her lemons into lemonade. Her example allowed me to be who I am. I can see that I've ended up being more like my father in a business sense, but I like to think deep down that I'm much more like my mother.

"I love my father, I care about my father, I want him to be happy, and I want him in my life. Sometimes I wish that he could be just a traditional easygoing daddy, but I guess I don't know what a daddy is. It's kind of weird sometimes. He'll call and leave a message saying, 'Hi, it's your daddy,' and I'll just sit there, thinking: 'Who *are* you?'"

SIMPLY FADING AWAY

During the years when I was working on this book, when I would meet new people at a party or discuss my work with old friends, invariably, a woman would say something like: "I have a father, but I might as well have been fatherless." Or, "My dad was never home!" Or, "I think my father loved me, but we really didn't have much of a relationship." It became obvious that this fading away of the presence of the father in a girl's life is very common. For many women, even if their dads were physically present throughout their childhood and adolescence, somehow they were emotionally missing in action.

Interestingly, the effects of a father's emotional absence on his daughter are similar to the effects of a father's death or desertion. As Sonia, a woman now in her late sixties, confessed, "I am sad and somewhat angry that my father had so little to do with my life and upbringing. Instead of giving thoughtful advice, he always spoke to me in aphorisms. 'Don't count your chickens before they hatch. People in glass houses shouldn't throw stones. We'll cross that bridge when we come to it.' This sounds funny now, but when I was growing up, his behavior toward me was hurtful and infuriating." Although Sonia has led a happy, productive life, which includes a strong marriage, children, and a successful career as a teacher, she explains that she is sad and angry that her father could not emotionally be part of her life.

Over the last twenty years, fatherlessness has become more and more commonplace. Today nearly one-third of babies are born to unmarried mothers. Add to this the high rate of divorced parents (and women remain the primary caregivers) and lesbian couples (who either adopt or arrange to have one partner give birth), and the number of fatherless homes continues to rise.

For women who lose their fathers through death, the paramount, everlasting feeling is sadness tinged with yearning and regret. Elements of guilt, shame, and anger are also present, but the prevailing emotion is sadness. Women who lose their fathers through abandonment usually feel rage. And women like Sonia who feel that their fathers were never truly present in their lives are often left with a melancholy mixture of both anger and remorse. How intensely fatherless daughters experience these emotions often depends on how old they were when it became clear to them that Daddy was gone.

4. THE TIME IN A GIRL'S LIFE

Loss of Daddy can stall the resolution of the Oedipal triangle: Her idealization of her father can become frozen in time, like an insect trapped in amber.

—Victoria Secunda, *Women and Their Fathers*

A girl's age at the time of her father's death or desertion is pivotal to how well she understands the loss and how well she will cope with the subsequent changes in her life. A little girl whose daddy dies in war when she is an infant will have a decidedly different father-loss experience from a girl whose father dies of a heart attack when she is eleven. A three-year-old girl whose papa disappears from home but continues to show up erratically will view her situation from a decidedly different perspective than a thirteen-year-old teen whose father runs off with his secretary and essentially cuts himself off from his family forever. Many other factors—from her mother's behavior to her own personality—will also color a fatherless daughter's experiences.

STAGES OF CHILD DEVELOPMENT

Professionals in the field of child development and psychology, from Sigmund Freud to Jean Piaget, Bruno Bettelheim, and Erik Erikson, generally break down child development into a number of similar stages of development. Although the experts vary to some extent, a simple but useful breakdown is as follows:

- Infancy and babyhood (younger than age three)
- Preschool (three to five years old)
- School age (six to nine years old)
- Preadolescence (ten to thirteen years old)
- Adolescence (fourteen years old to adulthood)

Freud famously broke down these stages into psychosexual terms. Specifically, he saw children developing through the:

- Oral stage (younger than eighteen months old)
- Anal stage (eighteen months old to three years old)
- Phallic stage (four to five years old)
- Latency (six years old to puberty)
- Genital stage (puberty to adulthood)

Briefly, the oral stage, symbolized by the mouth, is the period when an infant is nursing and the mother's breast is the source of food, which, symbolically for the baby, is love. The anal stage focuses on the anus and is the period involved with toilet training, or when children learn what is deemed appropriate with regard to excretion. According to Freud, the personality either develops into the anal-expulsive personality or the anal-retentive personality. That is, if the parent is too lenient, the child will develop into a careless, defiant, sloppy adult; if the parent is too restrictive, the child will develop into an obsessively clean and orderly adult who may be stingy, withholding, conservative, and passive-aggressive, among other qualities. Both the oral and the anal stages occur before the age of three.

The phallic stage, which takes place at about age four or five, is considered by most other experts in psychology to be one of the most challenging phases of child development. The pivotal event in the phallic stage is the child's interest in and attraction to the parent of the opposite sex coupled with envy, jealousy, and fear of the parent of the same sex.

In boys, the situation is called the Oedipus complex, taken from the Greek myth of Oedipus, who killed his father and married his mother. In girls, the circumstances are referred to as the Electra complex, again named for a Greek mythological character, Electra, who avenged the murder of her father by her mother. For boys, this stage involves the problem of castration anxiety, which results from fear of punishment from their fathers over their love for their mothers. For girls, it is even more complicated.

By nature, all babies are fixated on the mother. In the phallic stage, for boys, the fixation on the mother (the parent of the opposite sex) merely becomes more intense, while the child identifies his maleness with his father. For girls, the sexual fixation must shift completely from the mother (who was the primary love object during the child's infancy) to the father (the parent of the opposite sex). At the same time, the child must define her femaleness by maintaining her identity with the mother.

Today many modern psychologists question Freud's theories, particularly the concept of penis envy in women, which, according to Freud, comes into play during the phallic stage. However, most psychologists accept the basic dynamics for both boys and girls. They also agree that if a child for any reason (such as father loss) fails to negotiate the shifts and maturing processes of the phallic stage, the results can profoundly affect development.

According to Freud, from age six to puberty, children enter a stage called latency, where sexual feelings are suppressed and children develop other aspects of themselves physically, intellectually, and emotionally. This phase is the heart of childhood. During these years, children learn how to adjust to their social world inside and outside the home. At the moment of puberty, when children become physically capable of reproduction, they enter the genital stage, which features a renewed interest in sexual desire as well as intensified interest in—and often conflict with—the parent of the opposite sex. According to Freud, a child may experience difficulties at this stage if he or she was damaged or deprived during the earlier oral, anal, and phallic stages, or, indeed, if he or she is traumatized at this point.

FATHER LOSS AND THE DEVELOPING CHILD

According to many experts, the stages of a child's intellectual and emotional development appear to be related to major developments in brain growth. The human brain is not fully developed until late adolescence; therefore, until children reach at least the age of fifteen, they are not capable of reasoning as adults. The death of a parent or the breakup of their parents' marriage are among the most traumatic emotional issues that children can face, and how children respond to such traumas depends on the level of maturity they have achieved.

Many psychologists also believe that girls tend to mature more quickly than boys. At first glance, girls seem to adjust more quickly and initially exhibit fewer problems than boys do when they respond to father loss, either through death or abandonment. However, Judith Wallerstein, as part of her landmark study of children of divorce, identified a syndrome in girls called the "sleeper effect," which is characterized by a high level of anxiety and fear over potential betrayal and abandonment, and is often accompanied by anxiety and depression.

In Wallerstein's study, girls initially appeared to handle their parents' divorces with relative maturity and calm, while their brothers (or the boys in Wallerstein's study) acted out their pain by doing drugs, getting in trouble with the law, failing at school, and exhibiting other troubling behaviors. As Wallerstein put it, "Many girls may seem relatively well adjusted even through high school and then—wham! Just as they undertake the passage to adulthood and their own first serious relationships, they encounter the sleeper effect."

Here is a brief look at how girls tend to handle father loss, not only at the moment of their loss but also as they mature.

Beautiful Baby Girls (younger than age three)

Until the age of about ten months, it is difficult to assess how much a newborn can perceive and/or respond to a loss. Certainly, infants react with distress to the loss of a primary caregiver, which is usually the mother. This would include not only her departure but also possibly the mother's distress if her husband died or left the home. An infant would respond by crying, sleeping, or eating poorly, or generally being upset and cranky.

From ten months to two years of age, babies can perceive, reason to some extent, and respond to change. If they sense agitation in the home, they may have temper tantrums, appear apathetic, or revert to babyish things they have outgrown, like thumb sucking. Older babies, between the ages of eighteen months and two years, may even notice that Daddy is gone and go around looking for him, pointing to his chair or bed, or even crying if they can't find him.

Girls who lose their fathers when they are babies do not remember them in any way, at least consciously, and their memories or feelings about their father depend to a large extent on their mother's behavior. If a girl's father died and her mother kept pictures of him in the home, spoke lovingly of him, and encouraged her daughter to have a relationship with his family, then the daughter will obviously have good feelings about her dad. If the mother did not cultivate warm memories in her daughter because, for example, she could not deal with her own pain or she remarried quickly, believing that she should move on, then the daughter will probably have fearful feelings about her father.

If her father deserted the family, very often her mother will at best banish all evidence of him from the home, and, at worst, will speak negatively of him and his family. If her father maintains some connection with his daughter, she will most likely have a rather detached, uncertain attitude toward him.

Based on my interviews, however, the daughters who lost their fathers before the age of three, although they had no real memories of him, were strongly attached to him.

Daddy's Little Girl (three to five years old)

At this stage, girls who were fortunate to have had the attention of a loving dad recall being the proverbial apple of his eye. A little girl will usually be potty trained (that is, she will have negotiated the oral and anal stages) by this time and will have begun to express herself verbally. Experts believe that most children at this point cannot perceive or comprehend such sophisticated concepts as death or divorce. However, a three- or four-year-old girl will understand that her father is gone and will respond to the situation in a number of ways. For example, she may appear confused and bewildered, or she may regress to more babyish behaviors such as clinging, whining, asking for a bottle or pacifier, bed-wetting, or becoming hysterical when her mother leaves. She may also express her feelings through play, such as by hiding a doll, or through imitating adult behavior by crying or screaming. Sometimes a little girl may appear not to care that her father is gone, although this probably indicates that she doesn't understand what has happened. She may form strong attachments to other adults, such as a teacher or an aunt.

Death can be a particularly problematic subject. Often younger children are either not told of the death, or it is explained to them in euphemisms. Children, especially of this age, tend to be literal minded, so if a three-year-old girl is told, "Daddy is asleep," or "Daddy has gone to heaven," or simply "Daddy is lost," she will assume that eventually her father will wake up or return or be found. A child of this age is not intellectually or emotionally mature enough to make the leap from euphemism to reality.

Preschool children are often steeped in magical thinking. According to Swiss psychologist Jean Piaget, they are preoperational or prelogical because they do not yet use logic. Instead, they use magical and egocentric thinking to make sense of the world around them. Egocentric thinking does not mean that the child is selfish. It just means that she can't see things from anyone else's perspective.

If a young girl sees that her mother is sad, she will give her her favorite doll. She is offering her mother what comforts her most in the world and can't imagine why it wouldn't do the same for her mother. She is apt to think it rains because she is sad, or that her father died because she didn't eat her vegetables. In William C. Kroen's book, *Helping Children Cope with the Loss of a Loved One,* he states, "The death of a loved one—especially a parent—can be so traumatic and bewildering that the child resorts to 'magical thinking.' They start to believe that their words and actions have tremendous powers. They recall a tantrum or other incident of disruptive behavior that made the parent angry or distressed. They wonder if their words or actions actually caused the death."

The nineteenth-century English poet Francis Thompson put it this way: To be a child "is to turn pumpkins into coaches, and mice into horses, lowness into loftiness and nothing into everything." But the dark side of this process is that when something goes wrong and children experience a major loss, they think that it's their fault and that they can fix it. Very young children often try to test reality; they attempt to figure out and assimilate what is real, what is not real, but since they are still living in their own little prelogical world, this is not so easy and can lead to major confusion.

For girls who lose their fathers at this age, many of the oedipal problems their peers are working through never get resolved. This, too, can lead to big problems with emotional intimacy and sex as they start to mature.

"Those affected most strongly were girls who had lost fathers before age five, whether through divorce or death," claims Claudette Wassil-Grimm in her book *Where's Daddy?* "The daughters of divorce had more aggressive behavior, constantly sought attention from adults, and were physically aggressive to both male and female peers. The girls whose fathers had died before age five were extremely reticent around male adults, shied away from physical contact with them, and rarely smiled."

Victoria Secunda, in her study *Women and Their Fathers,* also found that girls who lost their dads at this period of development, particularly through divorce, had the toughest time: "Most researchers agree that divorce is hardest on very young children because the experience is so deeply embedded in their identities so early. Self-blame is one way children exert some sense of control over events. And the younger the child at the time of divorce, the more tenacious will be this guilt."

So whether a young girl loses her father to death or divorce, her reaction will be pretty much the same. This fatherless daughter may grow up to look like an adult, but emotionally she may not reach a full and happy maturity. She believes that she did something wrong, and if she can just find that magic potion, maybe she can fix it.

❧ BETSY ❧

Betsy Harris's father, Lieutenant Commander Andrew Earl Harris, was a naval officer during the period of the famous Bataan and Corregidor battles waged in the Pacific early in World War II. He was one of the thousands who lost their lives there in the early summer of 1942. His death shaped his daughter's life and continues to do so to this day.

Betsy Field Harris was born on March 24, 1939, in Annapolis, Maryland, where her dad, known affectionately as Squire, was teaching at the Naval Academy. In the 1930s, all midshipmen did a teaching stint at the academy, and Betsy's dad, himself a graduate of the Naval Academy (Class of '25), was no exception.

Born in 1900, Squire Harris had begun his education at the University of Kentucky with the idea of becoming a "gentleman farmer" like his father. However, his older brother, Field, had gone to Annapolis, and since Squire admired and looked up to his brother, he ended up there, too.

Not long after his graduation, Squire began seeing Betsy's mother, Lucia, who also hailed from central Kentucky but at the time was a student at Wellesley College in Massachusetts. That summer, Squire and Lucia began a courtship that would last for almost ten years. Finally, after years of an on-again, off-again relationship and several proposals, Squire gave Lucia an ultimatum: marry him now, or he was going to look for someone else. He very much wanted a family. This time, Lucia agreed, and they were married February 24, 1934, when Squire was thirty-four and Lucia was twenty-eight. Despite Lucia's previous resistance, the marriage turned out to be a great success.

Still, the life of the wife of a career navy man was not easy. Squire was transferred virtually every year of their marriage. Also, although they had a comfortable life in the United States, when Squire was assigned to China in the late 1930s, they were frequently separated (though initially the family accompanied him). Squire and Lucia had their first child, a boy, Waller, in 1936, while they were stationed in San Diego. Shortly thereafter, they were transferred to Annapolis, where Betsy was born in 1939. Betsy was just an infant when they were sent to China, and they remained there for about fifteen months until November 1940, when the wives and children of American servicemen and other civilians were ordered to leave.

While in China, Squire Harris commanded a gunboat, the *Guam,* on the Yangtze River, and continued his command after his family left for the United States. Betsy researched her dad's life through his private letters, military papers, and by attending several reunions of the Asiatic fleet. She tells her story with feeling.

"I know a good deal about what happened, because in recent years I got to know several men who served with him, particularly a man who served as his executive officer on the *Guam* for a number of months, named Kemp Tolley. Kemp Tolley, one of the premier historians of the U.S. Navy wrote a very interesting account of the *Guam* for *Shipmate,* the Naval Academy alumni magazine.

"My father reached the harbor at Shanghai in November 1941. Kemp Tolley was the second most senior naval officer available, so he navigated the gunboat *Oahu,* and my father navigated the *Luzon,* then the flagship of the Yangtze Patrol, and they both departed for the Philippines through a typhoon. These boats were not geared for the open sea, but somehow they managed to get to Manila.

"At that point, my dad moved on to Corregidor, where General MacArthur had his headquarters. By late 1941, MacArthur was leading the armed forces in the Pacific. He wasn't popular— he was an army man, not a navy man. At any rate, my father, along with a lot of other navy people and marines, ended up working on Corregidor for MacArthur.

"Corregidor is an island in Manila harbor which was called 'the Rock.' It was supposed to be invincible in that it blocked the enemy from coming into Manila, but that belief proved to be wishful thinking.

"My father arrived there in late November 1941, and, of course, the Japanese bombed Pearl Harbor on December 7, 1941, less than two weeks later. From that point on, my dad was reported missing in action, and my mother had no idea where he was.

"Then, purely coincidentally, my mother saw a photograph of him in *Life* magazine in April 1942. Of course, in the 1940s and especially during World War II, *Life* magazine was like television is today: the primary source of information, particularly visual information. Apparently the moment my mother saw this picture, she said, 'I know that's Squire.' And sure enough, it was.

"A couple of *Life* photographers had taken many photos, including this one of men working in the huge Manila tunnel on Corregidor which was used to store armaments, but ultimately it became the central headquarters on Corregidor. Since December 1941, the Japanese had been bombing the island relentlessly, and this tunnel had turned out to be the safest refuge.

"Corregidor fell in May 1942, and my father, along with thousands of others, was captured by the Japanese. He ended up in a prisoner-of-war camp on Luzan Island, where he contracted malaria and died in late August 1942. His remains were eventually shipped back to Kentucky, where he was buried in my mother's family plot in Richmond. She now rests beside him.

"In late 1940, shortly after we left for the United States, my father wrote both my brother and me a long letter filled with expressions of his love for us and some heart-felt advice concerning how we should live our lives. It is almost as though he knew he would not make it through the war, or perhaps, more realistically, he knew that given the volatile situation he was in, the chances were good he would not return. The letters must have been very difficult for him to write.

"I consider my letter from my dad my most precious possession. It is one of the few expressions I have of my father made directly to me. In his letter to me, he urged me to listen to my mother because he knew that her advice would be good because he always respected what she had to say. He also said that he hoped I would be able to find someone sometime that I could love as much as he had loved and adored my mother.

"And he also said something that has been useful to me all my life: 'Never assume that the world owes you a living,' he said. 'Do your part.'

"After my father's death, we stayed at my grandmother's

house in Richmond, Kentucky, for the remainder of the war. My grandmother died in 1947, and late in 1947, when I was eight, we sold the house and moved to Ocala, Florida, to be nearer my mother's sister and her husband.

"Not long after our move, my mother began teaching in the public schools, a program funded by the local ministerial association, and we settled into life in this small, Southern town. My mother ended up living for another twenty years, but I don't think these were particularly happy years for her. She died in 1968 at the relatively young age of sixty-one of a heart attack. I don't think she ever really recovered from my father's death."

Despite Betsy's appreciation for her father's achievements, her own life mirrored her mother's to a great extent. After finishing high school in Ocala, Florida, Betsy went to Wellesley. Then she moved to New York City, where she taught English literature in the public schools for the next thirty years. Somewhat regretfully, she never married.

Betsy confirms her strong attachment to her mother in a short biography for her fortieth Wellesley reunion: "The strongest influence in my life was that of my mother. I went to Wellesley because of her, became a teacher because of her, and even rebelled against marriage because of my reluctance to assume the burden of care-taking after years of supporting and nurturing this single parent. The fear of losing my remaining parent and desiring to please her governed my life through college and my first teaching experiences. Anger against men because of my father's absence from his family, including me, further militated against my commitment to a man in marriage or a living-together arrangement."

As Betsy got deeper into middle age, she felt a need to know more about her father. In the late 1980s, she spent a year teaching English to young Chinese students in rural China, where she had lived as an infant and where her father had served in the navy from 1939 to 1941. Later, she visited Japan in an effort to understand and accept a people and a culture that were responsible for the death of her father.

In the early- to mid-1990s, Betsy began attending reunions of the World War II Asiatic fleet. At these reunions, she met men who had known her dad and who were only too happy to tell her more about him. One of these men was Rear Admiral Kemp Tolley.

"Through Admiral Tolley, I got to know a different father from the one I thought I knew," Betsy says. "As it turned out, Admiral Tolley didn't particularly like my dad. My dad, according to Kemp, was rather humorless and a strict follower of the rules; a responsible and rather formal naval officer who hated the war and wanted nothing more than to get home to his wife and children. Admiral Tolley believed that he would do his duty because he was trained to do so and believed he was honor-bound to fight. However, unlike Tolley, he was not thrilled by the prospect of war.

"My brother and I grew up believing that our dad was a hero, and indeed he was. But, perhaps to Kemp Tolley's surprise, I liked the 'softer' man he described better than I would have a hard-nosed military type. What's more, I also began to feel that I could relate to him better knowing about this side of him. He seemed more human to me. I also realized that he probably knew he would die, and that the pain of leaving his beloved wife and his two small children must have broken his heart."

In Betsy's family, no conscious secrets were kept about her father. Indeed, Betsy and her brother were encouraged to talk about their father. Betsy retains close ties with members of her dad's family to this day.

But it wasn't until Betsy was an adult and had researched her father's life on her own that she was able to fully appreciate him and to understand herself in relation to him. As is often the case with fatherless daughters, Betsy was deeply influenced by her mother. By getting to know her dad, Betsy was able to free herself from the tight hold of her mother and integrate her dad's truth into her life.

Pigtails and Ponies (six to nine years old)

This latency period is the height of childhood. At this stage, a little girl will have negotiated (or not) the Electra stage, and will have suppressed her sexual interest in her father and her budding conflicting feelings about her mother. She will be interested in the outside world. She will begin to have more and more friends, she'll be concerned with school, and she will probably develop other outside interests such as ballet dancing, sports, horseback riding, and dolls.

Intellectually, her thought processes will become more and more complex, organized, and logical. She will show the ability to perform multiple tasks, think logically, and solve problems. On an emotional level, little girls at this age remain strongly egocentric. They may have a tendency to focus attention on one aspect of an object or subject while ignoring others. According to Piaget's theory of the stages of development, this child is now moving out of the prelogical (preoperational) phase into concrete operations. She begins to use logical rules, but she only applies them to people and things in the physical (concrete) world. Abstract ideas such as justice and truth are not part of her lexicon yet.

Magical thinking may well still be a big part of her life: "If I wear the silver bracelet Uncle Joe gave me for Christmas every day, nothing bad can happen to me." Reality is not firmly in place: "Maybe Dad will come home if I get all A's." Her perceptions dominate her judgment: "I know I'm fat and ugly even though everybody tells me how pretty I am." In the realm of morals and ethical behavior, she has not embraced the principles that underlie a strong character yet; nor has she developed her own set of rules. Her behavior is mostly dictated by the simple do's and don'ts imposed on her by the authority figures in her life.

Children of this age understand the concept of death and know that death is permanent and real. They can also understand (sort of) the concept of divorce, or at least understand that Mommy and Daddy are no longer living together, and if the separation followed months of acrimony, that Mommy and Daddy no longer love each other.

However, they don't understand what the loss means to their life.

They may respond to the loss by denying it, or idealizing the lost father, especially if he has died: Daddy was the best man in the whole world. Guilt may also play a part in the child's reaction, and this guilt is often linked to denial, especially if the child appears indifferent to her loss.

When a child at this stage fails to acknowledge and grieve for the lost father, whether by death or divorce, she is most likely riddled with fear and feels terribly vulnerable. She may try to hide her fears from her mother, her siblings, and her friends, and as a result, her false indifference may go unnoticed. She may find comfort in taking care of the people around her, especially younger siblings, turning into a little mommy, which provides the illusion that she has some control over her life. Or, conversely, she may become clingy, worried about her health, and refuse to go to school.

Some children who lose a father keep trying to find him. They think they saw him at the foot of their bed one night, or spotted him in the crowd at the mall on Saturday, or by the lake in the woods in back of their house. Girls who lose their father during this period of childhood often grow up to be nice, well behaved, but rather indifferent. At least they appear that way. But they may be terribly frightened and don't have the tools to fix their problem.

Preadolescence (ten to thirteen years old)

This is a very tricky period in child development, a transitional phase full of complexities and confusion, and girls come to it in a broad range of ways. A ten-year-old girl can be physically developed with breasts, a regular menstrual period, and a budding sexual interest in boys, or she can still wear her hair in braids and insist on beating her brother in races on their bikes. Or she may well be both!

At this time, children begin to explore their independence and their developing identities. Their thought processes are more logical and sound but more abstract. Preadolescents physically mature at astonishingly different rates. Some are disconcerted by early physical signs of puberty, such as budding breasts or evidence of pubic hair, whereas others are worried because they do not seem to be maturing quickly enough. In any case, children vary widely in how they develop physically, intellectually, and emotionally at this stage, and most experts agree that girls often develop and mature more quickly than boys.

Death of a loved one, especially a parent, is perceived as something that makes children different, and it often arouses feelings of embarrassment and even shame. This was something I experienced profoundly and did not outgrow until I was well into adulthood. As I was writing this book, one of my oldest childhood friends, Barbara, told me that she remembered our Sunday school teacher telling the other children that my dad had died and how terrible she felt. Her memory reminded me that on the day my dad died, this same Sunday school teacher had asked me how my dad was feeling and I had lied to her, saying that he was fine when I knew he was very, very sick. I was afraid that I would upset her (or myself!) and I was embarrassed.

Preadolescents may not show any outward signs of grief; they may not cry or act upset, giving the appearance that they don't care. In fact, they are in terrible pain, but they are confused and unsure about how to behave. In addition, they may display anger, moodiness, aggressiveness, rebellion, fear of their own mortality, fear of abandonment, and various physical pains, including problems with sleeping and eating. They may not want to go to school.

This is a very troubling time for a girl to lose her father. She is still so young that she doesn't fully comprehend emotionally what has transpired, regardless of whether her father has died or her parents have separated and her father is no longer a part of her life. She is about to embark on adolescence, or what Freud called the genital phase, and her father is not there to help her negotiate this hurdle.

Adolescence (fourteen years old to adulthood)

Losing a parent as an adolescent is characterized by a special sort of intensity. Teens are shocked, and they tend to repress not only their grief but their anger and even their disbelief. This is true whether their parents divorce or their dad dies. Teens want to appear cool and in control; they are also often cynical and depressed about life in general, so they can easily fall into acting out, quarreling with family and friends, doing poorly in school, drinking and using drugs, or indulging in inappropriate or unhealthy relationships.

Many classic teenage problems are exacerbated if a father is lost, either through death or divorce, during adolescence. For example, normal teenage moodiness, characterized by sadness, boredom, and lack of enthusiasm, may mask serious depression. A classic teenage refusal to discuss deep feelings could be part of the normal process of emotional separation or indicate significant loneliness and despair.

Most teenagers are preoccupied with sex, and certainly sexual fantasies are normal, but many adolescent girls, especially those whose parents have divorced, may begin indulging in irresponsible, promiscuous, risky sexual behaviors. These are not only dangerous but signal feelings of low self-esteem or other problems. Adolescents who feel hopeful about their future—for example, who do well in school and who plan to go to college or have a career—are more likely to avoid risky sexual behaviors; they have too much to lose. Finally, teenage girls are notoriously overly concerned with appearance, but fatherless daughters may become compulsive about their weight, clothes, hair, and makeup.

Teens often struggle with the big philosophical questions: Who am I? Why am I here? The later adolescent years, in particular, are times of idealism. Teens often adopt political positions that counter those of their parents and defend them with great enthusiasm. What would be more cause for worry is a teen who is convinced of the meaninglessness of the world and who feels that she has no role and no future. Suicide is the third most common cause of death in teens, after unintentional injuries and homicide. If a major loss has been endured in the family, a father-loss daughter may be more susceptible.

If a parent dies or disappears during these turbulent years, it can leave a teenager with strong feelings of things left unsaid or undone. An ongoing struggle between a father and a daughter that is left unresolved upon the death of the father leaves the daughter racked with guilt about not listening to her dad, about things she said, and about not spending more time with him when he was present.

Conventional wisdom holds that all adolescents rebel, feel miserable much of the time, and engage in dangerous behaviors. However, studies show that many adolescents accept their parents' core values and value their parents' advice. They work hard at school and avoid foolish risks. Some amount of friction is to be expected as adolescents struggle to become more emotionally independent, but it is not always a time filled with drama. However, if a father dies or parents divorce during the teen years, serious problems can arise.

Despite all these warnings, girls who lose their dad after they have jumped over the hurdle of puberty tend to have fewer long-term problems. By their late teens, most girls have achieved physical and intellectual maturity. They have internalized that their father has died, or that their parents' problematic marriage has come to an end. They may be upset; they may act out—perhaps to a greater degree than if they had not endured a trauma—but ultimately (usually by their late twenties) most of these girls will have settled into a relatively calm adulthood.

∽ THE KENNEDY SISTERS ∾

Sheila had no doubt what the telephone call meant. It was a late afternoon in early June, and Sheila, seventeen, and her sister Trish, just fifteen, were sitting at the dining room table, studying for their final exams. A nurse from the hospital where their dad had been for almost two weeks recovering from a heart attack was on the other end of the line.

"Is your mother there?" the nurse asked.

"No," Sheila said, "she's on her way to the hospital."

"Good," the nurse replied, and then hung up.

It wasn't simply the nurse's curtness that troubled Sheila. It was the fact that there was something else in the nurse's voice, something "funny," as Sheila put it. She didn't sound angry or frazzled, just anxious.

Sheila feared the worst. Everyone kept saying that her dad couldn't possibly *not* get well. But even though Sheila had never experienced the death of a close family member before, she had a feeling that the news was not good.

"I said to Trish that I was afraid Dad may have died," Sheila explained. "But she just said 'No way' like I was crazy or something. I believed her because I wanted to. But we were both wrong."

The Kennedy sisters are from a large Irish family in Baltimore. The girls I interviewed were at different stages of development when their father died: Sheila, at seventeen, was well on her way to adulthood; Trish, just fifteen, was at the height of adolescence; and Allison, age seven, was still a child.

Although Frank Kennedy had married at the somewhat late age of thirty-six, he and his wife, Annie, had seven children in ten years—five girls and two boys—then, after a gap of seven years, they had another baby, Allison. Not only was the family large, it was poor. Frank worked as a linotype operator, and feeding ten people on his salary was tough.

At the time of Frank's death, the five eldest Kennedy children had already graduated from high school, although three of the five still lived at home. Kathleen, the eldest girl, had cerebral palsy and needed a fair amount of care. The two Kennedy boys, Dan and Jim, both in their early twenties at the time of their dad's death, were going to college and working part-time. Two other sisters were in their early twenties and were also away at college.

Sheila was the quintessential middle child, the go-along-to-get-along kid who tried to appease everybody. As the sixth of the eight children, she was at once the youngest of the older children and the oldest of the younger ones. At the time of her dad's illness and death, she found herself more or less in charge of the household.

"It was late May," Sheila explains. "My parents had just celebrated their twenty-fifth wedding anniversary, and it had been a big celebration. A couple days afterwards, my father began complaining of pain in his arm. He went to work on a Friday, and Trish and I were home from school because we had exams that day or something.

"The phone rang, and someone from my father's workplace said, 'Your father is in the hospital.' We didn't have a car, and he worked very far away from us, and we would have needed two buses to get there. Finally, my aunt drove my mother and me to the hospital. It was his first heart attack, but it was a serious one.

"The people at the hospital said, 'Just hold tight and pray,' and he was up and down for two weeks. He improved, he didn't improve; he improved, he relapsed. Finally, they put in a pacemaker. It was hard because we had a long way to go to visit him, but by the end, I think everyone in the family had a chance to visit with him—except Allison. And he seemed to be improving.

"It was two weeks to the day after the attack, and my mother was on her way to visit him. Once again, I got a phone call in the morning. They asked where my mom was; I said she was on the way, and they just hung up. Then we just waited. Several hours passed, and by the time my mother got home, Allison was home from school.

"I remember vividly when my mother walked in the door. This sound came out of her! It was indescribable. I had never heard my mother sound like that! It was just this deep moan. Like a wail from deep inside. She was just breaking.

"I pulled Allison out of the house as fast as I could, and we went for a very long walk. When we got back, I took Allison upstairs and told her what had happened. She was so little. I remember telling her that Dad's heart was sick and it couldn't keep working and that he wouldn't be around anymore. I don't know how much she remembered. She was very close to him.

"The funeral was one of the most tremendous experiences. We had a combined wake and funeral mass, which started early in the morning and lasted all day, and they actually had to have police come in to take care of the crowd. I didn't know that my father knew that many people.

"My dad was a very funny man, so there were a lot of funny stories. It was really uplifting. They said good things about him, and it was very encouraging for me as a teenager to hear people admire my father."

Although the Kennedy sisters came from a working-class family with little money, all three girls were artistic and all three pursued careers in the arts. Sheila was a violinist who ultimately ended up teaching music to high school students. Trish was a painter; she studied art in college and spent a decade as a production manager in a publishing house (a career surprisingly similar to her father's as a linotype operator) before going to law school. Allison was a poet. Each girl came to see that her father had influenced her career choices but perhaps not quite in the way he might have wished.

"I was in the middle of who knows what when my father died," Sheila says. "I remember my father didn't approve of my pursuing a music career. It wasn't safe; it wasn't secure. He said that if I wanted to do something like that, I would have to learn to type, which is funny because I did work my way through college by being a secretary. But I don't know, had he lived, whether I would have been able to major in music."

By all accounts, Frank Kennedy, despite his friendly nature and great sense of humor, was a firm authoritarian, especially with regard to his daughters. Plus, according to both Sheila and her sister Trish, he had a short fuse. Still, Sheila went on to get a master's degree in music (violin) from the University of Massachusetts. After a number of disappointments, Sheila accepted that she wasn't going to make a living in the competitive world of classical music. But she did learn that she was a fine music teacher and she adored teaching. She married a black man and had a child. Sheila seems to have done all these things with great ease and confidence, but she feels certain these choices would not have been so easy to make had her father been alive.

Still, Sheila believes that perhaps her father had a greater influence on her in some ways than her mother did: "I think in many ways, I'm very similar to my father. I'm much more aggressive than my mother, and I want to fix things. I'm also very fast, like he was. When I think about it, he had an enormous influence on me."

Sheila's sister Trish feels much the same but expresses it in a very different way. Trish and Sheila are close in age but are very different in temperament. "I sort of take the more positive view and just kind of go along to get along," says Sheila. "Trish was a door slammer."

"I had just turned fifteen when my dad died," Trish explains.

"It's funny, but I literally didn't grieve my father's death until my father-in-law died seventeen years later. I really feel like I suppressed a lot of the grief.

"When I was growing up, I really loved my father. I thought he was funny. When I was younger, I was kind of a lonely kid, and when I was ten or eleven, he would take me into town on the train to the big library in Baltimore. It was like he was giving me treasures. He would just sit in the library and let me take as much time as I wanted. I'd plow through the books and I'd bring home these treasures.

"He would never think of not protecting us. We didn't have a car, but he would walk with us anywhere we wanted or needed to go. He'd take me to the library; we babysat, so he would walk us to our jobs. When we had part-time jobs at the local drugstore or the rectory, he would walk over and pick us up. If we were late, he would just wait.

"I also remember he would take Sheila and me for walks in a beautiful park in Baltimore. These memories are real treasures in my memory bank. He wasn't demonstrative, never hugging and kissing us, didn't say, 'I love you.' But he showed his love in all these other ways.

"As I was getting into my teen years, I was challenging stuff. I didn't want to go to church—that was a big thing, very Irish Catholic. And we wouldn't have big fights about it, because to him it was not even a point for discussion. And I was having some problems with him; I was questioning him; I was thinking maybe he was not as perfect as I had once thought. And then when he died, I couldn't believe it!

"I don't know how to describe it; it was like, 'This person can't *not* be here.' And I think I squashed any feelings I had, and I didn't feel like I could really cry about it. I actually postured like I just had no feelings for my father.

"A year after my husband, Chris, and I got married, my father-in-law died. When his father died, it was like a trigger for me. All of these feelings just came flooding out of me, seventeen years after my dad's death. It was a kind of delayed grief, but it finally happened, and that's good. I actually really did love my father-in-law—he was a very, very sweet man—but I didn't know him all that well. I knew that the intensity of my feelings of grief over his death were really leftover feelings for my dad. I felt like I was kind of reliving my grief for my own father. I had a flood of all of these positive memories about my dad that I had really, truly set aside.

"The reality was that at fifteen I just didn't deal with it. I think that losing a parent is such a deep loss, and it gives you such a sense of the temporary quality of life. Somehow you feel you can't ever be as happy as you were before. You learn that life is real and people are going to die, and you can't plan every last aspect of your life because life might hurl something at you that you think will never happen. Some terrible thing can just leap out at you, which is how I felt with my father.

"After my father-in-law died, I went to my dad's grave. I had gone on an Outward Bound trip; they gave us these three pretty stones and a pin. They represented accomplishments, and I put them at his grave site under the dirt. Also, my husband and I took a hike in the park where my father had often brought Sheila and me. I framed a picture that I found of my dad and me. So those were the things I did to come to terms with my grief.

"I think there is something about losing your father, losing a parent, at a certain point in your life, you feel changed. It's a generational shift. Part of you steps into a role that you think: Wait, I have nobody now who is going to tell me what I should do or how I should do something. It's a sense of stepping up. The problem with losing a parent when you're a child is that you have no skills to help you step up."

Both Sheila and Trish have loving memories of their father that are couched in reality. Although both women remember their dad with affection, as Trish put it, "Sheila and I feel like we bore a lot of the real bad stuff, too." Both women talk about his temper and his rigidity, particularly about the girls' studies and their potential careers. They feel that he would have blocked their wishes of studying music (Sheila) or art (Trish), and that they would have probably ultimately succumbed to his demands. Allison's experience was very different.

"He was so sweet with her," Trish remembers. "He was so much older when he had her. It was almost like she was this little only child because she was so much younger. A special gentleness and sweetness came through from him for her.

"When he was in the hospital, he wrote a letter to her," Trish continues. "I think it was because she wasn't allowed to visit him there. A nurse apparently said, 'Now you sit down and write this letter to your kid.' And he did it, and I'm so glad he did. I know she treasures it."

All three sisters, including Allison herself, agree that Allison grew up like an only child. Not surprisingly, she was very attached to her mother, and as Sheila says, "She had Mom all to herself in many ways."

"I remember him a little bit," Allison says of her dad. "He really liked trains. He met my mother on a train platform. We were always taking the train into the city. He took public transportation or walked everywhere. I remember going downtown with him and riding in a glass elevator. I think we had ice cream. I know that we played Scrabble together, which is really kind of crazy.

"He wrote me this letter. He wrote me from his deathbed basically saying, 'I will be out of the hospital soon and we can play Scrabble again.' It's a gorgeous letter."

Unlike her sisters, who have concrete memories of their dad, Allison basically feels that much of her experience resulted from the fact that her father was absent during most of her growing-up years.

She went to public school rather than to Catholic school. "It never would have happened had he been alive," Sheila confirms. Allison also went to the University of Michigan for undergraduate school and even spent her junior year in Scotland. Allison is now in her early thirties and earns her living as an editor for a nonprofit organization, and, perhaps most importantly, is a much-published poet.

"I can't help but think, had he been alive, he would have affected my choices in life," says Allison. "My mother constantly asks me: 'What are you really gonna do with your writing? Are you gonna teach?' But she doesn't really put any muscle behind it. But apparently he was very forceful."

Still, although Allison's father was with her for only seven years and she sometime fears he might have exerted tremendous pressure on her had he lived, his hardworking example is strong in her.

"I worked two jobs the whole time I was in college," Allison says, "and I had loans, aid, and scholarships. So I basically just pieced it all together, and I just made it work, because I knew it was going to work."

How old a girl is when her father dies or leaves plays an exceedingly important role in how she matures. By understanding her level of maturity at the time of her father's loss, a fatherless daughter can better comprehend her immediate reaction to his death or departure; in addition, she can better come to terms with how his loss may affect the rest of her life. Of course, factors other than age and maturity come into play. A three-year-old little girl whose Daddy dies (and who, as a result of her relative development, may be terribly vulnerable) may recover quite well if she is surrounded by loving and concerned relatives who help her through her loss. A twelve-year-old preteen whose father leaves the home may go through a wild, rebellious adolescence only to come out the other side a mature and balanced young woman if some important person in her life offers patience, love, and understanding. Very often that other person is her mother.

5. THE MOM FACTOR AND OTHER FAMILY MATTERS

Me, I never knew the love of a father after the age of eight. My mother came in one morning with tears of nobility in her eyes and told me he was gone for good. I hate her for that.

—Sylvia Plath, fatherless daughter, from her diaries

My mother, to the nth degree, made lemonade out of her lemons.

—Jill, daughter of divorce

I often call my ninety-six-year-old mother first thing in the morning. One morning recently I called her at 8:30 A.M., and when she answered, she asked, "Did you call me a few minutes ago and hang up?"

"No," I said. "Why?"

"Well, somebody called and hung up. I thought it might be you."

"Maybe you have a boyfriend, Mom," I said half joking.

"Boy, I wish I did," she said, also half joking. (By the way, my mother has all her marbles, as they say, and lives in a very nice assisted care community in Cleveland, Ohio.) "I'd like to escape from here. If I had a boyfriend, he could take me out once in a while."

She paused for a minute, and then she said, "Actually, I'd rather have a car. I could escape in a car, too, and cars are a lot easier to take care of."

I laughed. The story is vintage "Mom."

On this particular day, I had called her to confirm a memory I have of her taking care of my father, who, as I recall, was sick in bed with the chicken pox. (I also have many memories of her taking care of him several years later during his last illness.) I must have been three or four years old, and my dad, who apparently was sick as a dog, was about forty. I can see her running up and down the upstairs hall wearing a slinky blue nightgown. She must have been giving him a sponge bath or his medication. So, she was involved in a very practical endeavor (giving medicine to my sick father), but performing it in a decidedly impractical way (in a slinky negligee). Somehow this, too, is vintage Mom. (I also have another memory of her cooking fried chicken in her slip.)

In fact, I have many memories of my mother doing impulsive things, especially after my father's death. She seemed to sometimes act on the fly, taking risks, perhaps trying to escape. For example, two months after my dad died, she piled us (four children under age fourteen) into our 1953 Chevy and drove from Cleveland to Philadelphia, where she dropped my younger brothers off with her sister, and then she drove my older brother and me on to Washington, D.C., to see the sights in the capital. On the way back, she ran out of money (a constant theme in our family), and we drove and drove with the gasoline needle pointing toward empty, praying that we wouldn't run out of gas, particularly in one of those tunnels along the Pennsylvania Turnpike.

Again, this is vintage Mom. Actually, we didn't have very many vacations after my father died, and none as a family after this adventure to Washington. Each child was occasionally given holidays or special outings separately—my mother sent my brother Herb to camp, took my brother Bo to the Baseball Hall of Fame in Cooperstown, and permitted me as a young teen to visit my cousin in New York City. She managed to do something for each one of us.

My mother seems to have gotten through her widowhood using the defense of denial to its best effect. She simply refused to see—or at least to face up to—certain circumstances. If she had opened her eyes wide and taken a close look at her situation—a single woman with virtually no money trying to raise four children on her own—I suspect she would have thrown up her hands and given up. Actually, I know that she sometimes did feel that way and for years suffered from severe migraine headaches that were clear symptoms of her stress. However, most of the time she put her head down and kept on going, driving and driving even though the gas tank was frequently pretty close to empty.

This sounds like I have nothing but positive feelings about my mother, but the fact is that I was sometimes very angry with her throughout my adolescence and for years afterward. We locked horns frequently and still do on occasion. Indeed, my mother was concerned about my writing this book because I think she was afraid I might take her to task about certain things (like cooking fried chicken in her slip).

However, as I researched this book, my respect for my mother grew steadily and tremendously. Unlike many of the mothers of the fatherless daughters I interviewed—mothers who were, I'm sorry to say, often paralyzed, ineffectual, or, indeed, drunk—my own mother always behaved in a brave, forthright, effective way. I never saw her weep. Although she found a full-time job within a year of my father's death (and continued to work for the next twenty years, until my youngest brother was finished with college), she always had dinner on the table and even managed to do other astonishing things, like wallpaper the dining room and teach me to drive. She also remained genuinely responsible toward her children, her parents, other family members, and her friends. Sometimes she was self-centered, sometimes she seemed uncaring, sometimes her denial tactics had negative effects, but as I've fortunately been able to tell her, when all was said and done, she got an A in mothering.

THE MOM PARADOX

"If it's not one thing, it's your mother!" Despite its humor, this old joke has a bit of an edge for fatherless daughters. When a father dies or deserts his family, Mom becomes the central and often the only source of security for her children. She must now act as both the father and the mother in every way: physically, emotionally, socially, and very often economically.

The ways in which a mother's new authority can affect a fatherless daughter are infinite. For starters, what were the circumstances? Was she widowed? If so, was her husband's death sudden or the result of a long illness? If she was divorced, was she deserted by her husband or did she choose to leave the marriage?

Is the family left well off or struggling financially? Is the divorced father paying child support? Is he paying it regularly and on time? Must the mother find a job after years of being a stay-at-home wife or perhaps having never worked before? Does she already have an income-earning career or can she develop one?

How many other children are there? Are the other children boys or girls? Where does the daughter fit into the birth order? Are there other relatives who live in the home or nearby to help with child care?

Did Mom remarry? If so, how quickly after she was widowed or divorced? How does the stepfather treat Mom? How does he behave toward her children?

What is Mom's personality like? Is she a positive, assertive woman or is she a fearful, passive person? Is she generous or self-centered? Is she cheerful or chronically unhappy?

Is Mom sincerely interested in her daughter's welfare and development? Does she understand her daughter and relate to her well? Is she jealous or competitive with her daughter, sexually or otherwise? Is she overly involved and suffocating or so caught up in her own problems that she ignores her daughter's needs completely?

Regardless of how these questions are answered, after a father's death or departure from the family, Mom has all the power. At the same time, paradoxically, as an overwhelmed widow or divorcée, she may have very little time or energy to use that power effectively or to even think about it. A daughter, depending on her age, may come to resent her mother's power while yearning for her attention and affection.

Widowed Moms Versus Divorced Moms

It's never easy to be a single parent, and perhaps even less so when the choice is not your own. For a widow, at least during the early months after the death of her husband, her lot in life may be a bit easier than for a divorcée. If her spouse has died after a long illness, she may feel a sense of relief. Granted, this feeling may be coupled with a tinge of guilt, but she will quickly be reassured that her feelings are natural. If her husband's death is sudden and shocking, such as the result of an accident, she will probably have plenty of emotional support from other family members and friends. Society tends to give widows more support for their grief than it gives divorcées.

The end of a marriage will probably bring a divorcée less sympathy from the world at large. Even if her husband has left her for another woman, the breakup is frequently seen, at least in part, as her fault.

Regardless of whether a mother is widowed or recently divorced, her competence as a mother will probably decline, at least in the early months after the loss. A widow's sadness, grief, and fear for her family may paralyze her. A divorcée's emotional and legal turmoil may distract and deplete her completely. In both cases, the mother may be depressed.

The primary difference between a widowed mother and a divorced mother will very likely be her attitude toward her husband. A widow will very likely revere her husband and speak well of him, perhaps even elevate him to God-like stature, especially if he has died in heroic circumstances, such as during wartime. In her grief, she may obsess about him or she may not be able to discuss him at all. In either case, her daughter will feel shut out and alone.

An abandoned wife or divorcée may be extremely negative about her husband, even if she instigated the divorce, and these negative feelings often hang on for years. Very often, she will speak disparagingly of him. Whereas a widowed mother might advise her daughter to establish a career because she may lose her husband (that is, he might die), the deserted mother will advise her daughter to establish a career because husbands sometimes leave. The attitude toward and message about men is quite different.

Regardless of whether a girl lost her father to death or divorce, regardless of whether the mother adored or loathed her husband, regardless of how the daughter felt about her father (and most fatherless daughters adore their absent dads), many fatherless daughters intensely dislike their mothers. The poet Sylvia Plath, who famously expressed incredible rage toward her dead father in her poem "Daddy," was equally hostile toward her mother. In her diaries, she wrote: "Me, I never knew the love of a father after the age of eight. My mother came in one morning with tears of nobility in her eyes and told me he was gone for good. I hate her for that."

To me, this is a fascinating paradox. Mom is the person absorbing the most grief or rejection and the most responsibility, yet she often receives the greatest criticism (at best) or hate from her daughter. Indeed, in some cases, Mom may be the recipient of negative feelings that should be directed toward an abandoning father.

The Bad Mother

The mothers of a few of the women I interviewed were truly "bad" mothers. They were self-centered, irresponsible, and rejecting of their children, often exposing them to dangerous people and situations. Lauren, the oldest of three children, now a fabric designer in her late fifties, describes the nightmare of growing up with her mother.

"My mom married probably six months after my father died. She'd been advertising for a babysitter and had transposed the girl's number, and somehow the number she called was this man's. He had four children, three that lived with him. I guess they hit it off on the phone. She must have felt like somebody was coming to save her.

"She was only twenty-five when my father died. They had just built a house in a community of couples with young children on Long Island. I think she felt terribly depressed. She may not have actually married this man until a year or two after she met him, but he and his three younger kids moved in with us right away. It was a nightmare. He sexually abused my sister and me. I don't know if he hurt my brother; my brother would never talk about it. Later there was a big trial about this and my mother finally came to her senses.

"Not long after the trial, she got together with another guy, and we moved to a farm in upstate New York. For me the whole thing was pretty traumatic. Not only had I lost my father, there was this other awful man living in our house, and my mom seemed to be completely oblivious to what was going on. It was just horrible and it has left an indelible imprint on me, especially when it comes to my relationship with men."

The Problem of Alcohol

Problems with alcoholism came up with startling frequency among the mothers of the fatherless daughters I interviewed. It colored the lives of women of every class and condition, from the gentle farm-town mother of ten who played the organ at her church on Sunday, to the tough-as-nails working-class mother from upstate New York, to the wealthy Connecticut matron who drank herself to sleep with old-fashioneds every night, to the Wellesley graduate who taught school during the day but got drunk every night.

Katie, whose dad died suddenly when she was fifteen, leaving a family of nine children under the age of eighteen and little money, tells the story of her mother's struggles with particular poignancy.

"When Dad died, I think my mom was still mourning my baby sister, who had died a few months before when she was just three weeks old. It must have just all been too much for her, and so she started drinking a lot. My parents had always been social drinkers. Dad would stop off at the tavern after work, but it was never a big deal. All of my relatives drank. We were from a big Irish Catholic family, and drinking was simply part of what they did. But after Dad died, my mother really started drinking a lot, and it wasn't long before she became a real alcoholic.

"I think she suffered from depression that really wasn't diagnosed, and I think she was depressed the last twenty-five years of her life. Everybody we knew saw my mom as this happy-go-lucky person, but it was a façade. When she was around other people, she was real bubbly and happy, and everybody would think that she was the most wonderful person, but when others weren't around she drank and cried and drank and cried and drank and cried. Alcoholism was probably more of symptom of her depression than the cause, but as time went by, it became the cause."

For some fatherless daughters, alcoholism in the family preceded the death or departure of the father, and indeed, the father was often

alcoholic as well, and his problems with alcoholism may have contributed to his death or the breakdown of the marriage. In other cases, the
mother began drinking after her husband died or left as a way to cope
with her loneliness and depression.

"I just feel that the alcoholic thing in my family played a huge role,"
explains Daphne, whose dad died when she was eleven. "My mother
was an alcoholic—absolutely. She and my father always drank too
much. It was all socially acceptable drinking. Every single night when
my father came home from work, we all had dinner early, and then
she and my father would sit down in the kitchen and start drinking.

"Of course, as a result, this drive that I had to involve myself with
alcoholic men was absolutely unstoppable. Put me in a room full of
normal, healthy men, and I'd find the one alcoholic and go home with
him. Every time I met one, I said, 'Oh, the love of my life! Wow! Let's
go get drunk!' It was all so comfortable and familiar."

The effects of the alcoholism were strongly felt by the fatherless
daughters I interviewed. Often they had to be solely responsible for
themselves at a very early age or they frequently had to take on the
mothering role for younger siblings. Also, alcoholism often had serious
repercussions on a fatherless daughter's choice of a mate later in life.

The Great Mom

Jill, now a public relations executive and the mother of two teenage
boys, was devastated by her parents' divorce when she was nine. Her
father left the family for a younger woman. Her mother had to figure
out what to do after spending fifteen years as a suburban housewife.
As Jill says, "I'm sure she was very sad and humiliated, and I'm sure
she had no idea what to do, but amazingly, to the nth degree, she
made lemonade out of her lemons. Whatever my father couldn't give
me, my mother did ten times over. My mother has been there for me
every second of my life. She is not only an incredible mother, but she
is the best friend I've ever had and will ever have. And you don't get
that just every day.

"Suddenly she had to work and had to take care of these three
young children by herself. We lived in this big, old house, which
always had something going wrong with it. She had not worked at all

other than volunteer work through her entire marriage. The woman that became my best friend was born at forty."

Many fatherless daughters shared similar stories of exceptional mothers. Anne's mother was particularly special.

◡ ANNE ◡

The society page editor of a New England newspaper, Anne is a warm, welcoming woman with a twinkle in her eyes. I found her because a friend from Providence sent me an article that Anne had written for her paper on Mother's Day, praising her mother's behavior after the death of her father.

Married with an eleven-year-old son and a seven-year-old daughter, Anne had grown up in farming communities in the midwest. Her mother was from a German farming town in Wisconsin, and her dad from a similar town in Kansas. Her dad had been ambitious and smart, managing to work his way through the University of Kansas during the height of the Depression. Anne was their only child, and by the time she was in sixth grade, they lived in a Chicago suburb in the "shadow of the Crackerjack factor," as she puts it.

Anne's dad had been sick for years with a hole in his heart, which was diagnosed in the early 1950s. Today it would be an almost routine problem to repair; fifty years ago, it was unfixable. James and Agnes's marriage had not been without sorrow. They had had one other child who had died before Anne was born. Anne's mother had told her that after the baby had died, Jim had quit his job as a chemist and taken her on a cross-country car trip to look for work someplace else so that they could just get away from the memories. They wandered in California for a few months but eventually ended back in Chicago.

Jim died on July 12, 1963, just a few days after the family had taken a road trip to Kansas to visit Jim's parents. They had to take lots of back roads to get there, and Anne's mom had had to drive because her father was just too tired. "He lay in the back seat, kind of propped up there and not feeling good for most of the trip," Anne said. "And when we got home, he went right to the hospital, and that was kind of it." Jim was fifty-one.

"I remember going to the funeral and listening to the hymn 'Rock of Ages' that they played. I remember crying, being sad. I don't remember much else though. I think I was just numb. I couldn't imagine what was going to happen next. But I do remember thinking that this was not as catastrophic as it would have been if my mother had died."

Still, Anne has fond memories of her dad: "We did spend quite a bit of time together, because for a while my mother worked at night in a factory. In those days, everybody ate dinner at 5:30. I remember he would come home at quarter-to-five, and my mother would leave at quarter-to-five because her night job started at five. She wanted to earn enough money to buy us a color TV or something like that. That was her goal.

"So my dad would come home at quarter-to-five, and they would sort of meet in the driveway just like people are doing today to avoid having to pay for child care. Then he and I would hang out for the rest of the night. He had to do everything. He had to roll up my hair in curlers, fix dinner, put me to bed, everything. And he was great. I guess I just took all of that stuff for granted when it was happening."

After Anne's father's death, her mom really rallied. "My mother was a very streetwise person, but she wasn't highly educated; she had not graduated from high school. My father was the one who had gone to college and gotten a pretty good job, even though he didn't earn a ton of money. And then when he died, all of a sudden, we were concerned with the possibility that she was going to have to work all the time and she wouldn't be there when I came home from school. I was really appalled that I was going to have to deal with that. I remember my mother saying, 'Well, what do you think? We've got to have money. I can't just stay home.' I guess I had this vision that we'd get this Social Security money that you got when your father died and everything would be okay.

"'Oh, don't go back to work. Stay home and be here when I get home.' I begged her, and so she did. She was always there when I got home from school. She worked as a lens inspector in a big plant that made copy machines. The factory was behind our house, so she just walked across the field to work. It was very convenient.

"She just worked like a dog. I had more responsibility maybe for coming home after school and taking care of myself a little bit. I can't say that I felt like we were big partners in this, because she was doing everything. She was bringing home the bacon, and she was cooking everything. I can't remember having to do anything. I certainly didn't feel put upon. She even managed to pay for us to have a trip to Europe together. What she did was just amazing, I realize now when I look back on it. She was just always so spunky.

"She remarried about sixteen years later. And he lived about seven years and then he died of cancer. He was a nice enough man, but she wasn't too crazy about him after a while. They lived in Florida after she retired. He had been married to a friend of hers who had died of cancer, and she said to me before she married him, 'You know, Bee [his wife] never said a bad word about him.' And after she got married to him, she said to me, 'You know, Bee never said a good word about him.' I said, 'Mother, you said that Bee had never said a bad word about him.' She said, 'Bee never said a *word* about him.'"

"She dated a lot after Dad died, but my father had been turned into this saint after his death. His profile became much larger in death than it apparently was in life. I don't think anyone else ever measured up. She did like my husband though, because he was handy like my father.

"Years later, long after I was married, Mom's house burned down. My husband and I walked into our house one night, which was in the same town, and the phone was ringing. It was my mom's neighbor, who said, 'Where is your mother? Her house burned down.' So we called my mother, who was at my aunt's, and told her to come home, and we raced over there. The fire engines were all over the place, and everything was still smoking. My mother was hysterical, and I turned to her and said, 'Mother, think of it this way. Nothing else bad has ever happened to us in our life.' And she looked at me and said, 'What are you talking about? Your father died.'

"And I thought, she must have handled my dad's death pretty damned well, because my view was that this was the worst thing that had really ever happened to her. I realized right then that because of her, I'd gotten off pretty lightly. I think that the mother, and the way she deals with things, is the key to the whole situation when someone's father dies.

"I know my father did not want to die. I didn't feel like he had decided to abandon me or us. My mother told me that night that he died that I gave her a big hug, and I said, 'Oh Mom, what if it had been you?' And she said, 'Oh, my gosh. I guess she really does love me.' It was certainly clear even then that I had thought a real big catastrophe would have been if it had been her. She was the rock.

"I feel like it is really different for my kids. They know that we will both be there for them. We have a big cocoon that wasn't there for me. Even though somebody was making my bed and washing my clothes and doing all that stuff, the secure, loving family part was not there for me. I had to provide that for myself. Maybe I would have done it differently if my father had been there to say, 'You know, think about this, think about that.' But I didn't have him and so I had to make a lot of important decisions for myself. Mom was there for me, but her attitude was, 'I'll try to get you the money, Dear. Do what you want to do, and I hope you can figure something out.' I always worked, and I always managed to figure something out."

It's clear that Anne had an extraordinary mother. The quality of the mothering can have a huge effect on how a girl experiences the loss of her father. A lot of the women I've talked with have had major conflicts with their mothers. The mother was either too engulfing, or too critical, or not supportive. In any case, a lot of the women said the big problem was that there was no buffer between themselves and their mothers. Anne agreed with this, but said, "I think because my mother had never gone to college, she thought everything I did was wonderful. She was never jealous or resentful. She was just proud of me, so even though I grew up without a father, I really had all the support I needed."

The Good-Enough Mom

Most of the mothers of the fatherless daughters I interviewed, in fact, were "good enough." In the months immediately following her husband's death or departure, many of these moms were in shock and deeply depressed. Sometimes they were completely overwhelmed with their responsibilities and remained so for years. However, like me, the daughters of good-enough moms came to realize that their mothers did not only do the best they could, they did an excellent job.

Many fatherless daughters talked about their mother's emotional passivity. One woman explained: "My relationship with my mom is not great. I love my mother, but she's very passive, a subdued personality, and a little bit depressed. I often felt that she made me carry her anger for her. She would tell me things, I would get angry, but she wouldn't, because she couldn't deal with her feelings. I often felt that she was dumping feelings on me and that I was being used. I wanted her to be more of a parent to me. Still, I might have expected more than she could have given. She's a lovely woman. She's a very good person, but after my dad died, we just had fights and fights and fights. I realize now that she was grieving. She must have just been thrown for a loop, and her grief probably caused her to become so withdrawn. Our house was always a mess and she didn't even seem to notice."

Having grown up in a chaotic home myself, I was fascinated and amused to hear that other fatherless daughters had experienced similar situations. One of the most obvious indicators of an overwhelmed mom is a messy house. As one fatherless daughter, Mary, a woman now in her nineties, described it: "When I got to be in my, say, early teens, or even before that, I noticed a difference between our household and our friends' households. Everything seemed so quiet and so ordered and so proper and so stiff in everybody else's house. In our house, everybody was always busy and it was always pretty tough to find things.

"I remember being at my friend's house, Helen Kleffeger, and we went in the kitchen to get something to eat, and my God, everything was so *clean*. There was nothing showing; it was all so sanitary! Holy cow, I thought. What kind of place is this? Do people eat here? I never attributed that difference in our life to not having a father, but I think now that it probably was. My mother would have kept house better if my father had been around. I'm almost sure of that."

A Word About Money

Issues surrounding money and financial security come up frequently in the lives of many fatherless daughters. Most of the time, fatherless families are financially strapped. This was certainly true in my own family's case.

Many of the mothers turned out to be remarkably shrewd about money. As Karen, whose dad died when she was seventeen, said: "Mom got a Social Security check; a very small amount, I can't remember what it was. She kept half of it and she gave me the other half, and I always liked to be very careful with it. We were all struggling. My brothers and sisters all had jobs so we could make do. I had a lot of financial aid for college, and that really helped. I had great jobs in the summer as a secretary. I can thank my father for that. He insisted that I learn to type and take shorthand, so I was always able to support myself, and that has never stopped."

FATHERLESS DAUGHTERS AND THEIR SIBLINGS

The number of siblings a fatherless daughter has, the gender of those siblings, and the daughter's placement in the sibling hierarchy all play roles in how a girl reacts to the loss of her father. What was the dynamic among the siblings in relation to their father before his death or departure? Does the mother favor the fatherless daughter, or does she prefer her sons or the younger children? How did the fatherless daughter relate to her siblings as she was growing up? How does she relate to them in adulthood?

Next to the relationship between parent and child, the sibling relationship is certainly the longest and often the closest in most people's lives. In some sense, it is closer than the relationship between parents and children, since siblings belong to the same generation and share a perspective on their parents that parents simply cannot have. In the normal course of things, the relationship between siblings persists after the parents have grown old and died. Loyalty between siblings is one of the strongest social forces.

However, sibling relationships can also be fraught with tensions. Jealousy over parents' love and affection is a powerful emotion, leading to hatred at times. All siblings fight sometimes. In some families, however, the fighting between siblings reaches the level of physical or emotional abuse.

Genetically, siblings share on average half of their genes (except for identical twins, who share 100 percent of their genes), but the inborn differences among siblings are often very notable. One is easy as a baby; the other is tremendously challenging. One likes books; the other climbs trees and does cartwheels from morning to night. One seems eager to please; the other balks at authority.

When temperaments fit well together, the siblings can be a powerful team. When sibling temperaments clash, the children can find themselves living with companions with whom they have little in common.

Siblings help the child learn about sharing and cooperation. Children learn many skills directly from their older siblings. It's commonplace for a younger child to learn letters and numbers from her older sister, for example, and later to learn about boys and dating from an older sibling as well.

By watching siblings and how they get along with their parents, children can try out different behavior styles at a distance. They might decide, for example, to model certain behaviors on their older brother, but definitely to avoid other behaviors that result in parental disapproval or anger.

Over time, these lessons learned from siblings can have a powerful shaping force on the child's personality. Ask adults about how they grew up and what made them the way they are, and the discussion often turns to their siblings. Obviously the death or loss of a father changes the way siblings relate to each other and can exaggerate personality differences that otherwise may have been insignificant.

Beth was twelve, three years older than her brother, Danny, when their father ran off with another woman. She had always been the superachiever, and her little brother had had a tendency toward aggression.

"But after Dad left," she said, "Danny just became wild, uncontrollable. It was really sad, but at the time it was mostly scary. I still have scars on my thighs where he bit me through my jeans when we were having a fight in the backyard. Mom was pretty much out of it, angry, depressed, drinking much of the time, so we just had to work things out for ourselves. We are great friends now, but I've always felt that in some ways Dad's leaving was even harder on Danny than on me. I was older and out there trying to be a little star in school, and he was just a nine-year-old boy left without a dad, and for a long time without much of a mom. Thinking about it still makes me sad."

Siblings as Surrogate Parents

When the father in the family dies, siblings, especially the older ones, often become the surrogate parents for the younger children. The problem is that not only have these children lost the most or second most important person in their lives, they also lose their childhood.

Patty, the oldest of four children, who was fourteen when her father died, puts it this way: "You just have to suck it up. You have to be strong for your mom, so that's what I did. It was as if I was on automatic pilot. Somebody had to make sure there was enough food in the house. Somebody had to make sure that the dishes got done and that everybody had plenty of socks, and that person had to be me because nobody else was up to it. Mom was in shock at first, and the other kids were too little to be able to manage things (they were ten, six, and four), so I just had to take over. The hardest part was that this was at the time when I was beginning to notice the cute boys in my class, and my friends were all going to dancing school and parties with those boys, and I pretty much had to stay home and take care of everything. I never really got to be a teenager. I became a twenty-five-year-old fourteen-year-old practically overnight.

"And with my kids now . . . it wasn't until they were teenagers, actually, that I thought: You know, if something happens to me or my husband, people should be there for them. They shouldn't have to go through what I went through. My kids should not have to be there for their parents. Just the opposite. When I look back now, I think that even though I did most of the work, all of us were snapped into adulthood on some level while we were still children."

For Anita, it was a little different. She was the only girl in a family of five children, so her brothers became her charges and her mom was almost like her daughter. "I had to take over when Dad died. The boys didn't have a clue about what to do and Mom was a wreck. I didn't really mind so much, but it always felt as if I never really had a mother of my own. The biggest part of my job was taking care of her.

"As we look back on it now, she and I have so many different conversations about that time and about growing up. I remember there was a period when she'd ask me, 'Do you know about this?' like having your period and what to do about it, or sex or something like that, something a mother would explain to a daughter, and she was always surprised to hear that I had already learned about it through my friends. And it was just one of those 'Whoa, she's growing up and I haven't been a part of that' insights that she'd have but couldn't really do anything about."

Only Child/Only Daughter

Traditionally, only children have gotten a bad name. Not many years ago it was common for people to assume that an only child was sure to be hopelessly selfish and spoiled. Experts added to the list of only-child woes, claiming that these children were apt to be more aggressive, uncooperative, socially inept, less successful in marriage, than were children who had grown up with brothers and sisters.

But none of this is really true. Only children often grow up to be happy and well adjusted. In fact, being an only child has some advantages: They spend a lot of time interacting with adults, so they develop strong language skills, which serve them well in school and later in life. In theory, they enjoy their parents' undivided attention and never have to suffer the pain of sibling jealousy. And they often enjoy educational, cultural, and travel opportunities that children from large families might miss out on.

But only children—and in certain ways, especially only daughters—face some real challenges when coping with father loss.

For starters, she may have been Daddy's little girl, his unique and special child, maybe too special. Such an indulged child may well be overly spoiled, but also may feel a great deal of pressure to be perfect. Depending upon her age and level of emotional development, she may feel that her father's departure (even if he has died) is somehow her fault. In any case, she may experience her father's loss even more intensely than a girl who can potentially share her emotions with siblings. Her guilt, her fear, and her sadness may be intensified, and since she has no siblings, she could well be excessively lonely.

GRANDFATHERS AND OTHER FATHER SURROGATES

A few weeks after my father died, a very nice man from our church offered to take my older brother, Steve, to some event or other, possibly a football game. I recall my mother talking to him about how important it was for a boy to have some adult male influence in his life. I remember overhearing this conversation and thinking to myself: What about a girl? Doesn't she need male influence in her life? But I didn't say anything. Moreover, as well-meaning as this man's gesture was, it didn't take. My brother was no more interested in doing things with a strange man after our dad died than I would have been. Nobody can replace your dad.

Still, many of the women I interviewed have fond memories of men in their lives who stepped into surrogate father roles. These included grandfathers, uncles, family friends, neighbors, and later, loving fathers-in-law.

Alice, whose dad died when she was thirteen, has a number of comforting memories: "I had several different father figures in my life. I was really blessed, because right across the street where I grew up were Mr. and Mrs. Carter, who were friends of my parents. Mr. Carter became like a second father to me and to my brothers. All the kids used to go over to their house to swim in their pool. They also had a big tree in their backyard with a rope with a seat on the bottom, and you could climb up in the tree and swing like Tarzan. I got married at nineteen, and my father-in-law also became an influence in my life. Ah, what a doll! He was a very quiet man but had a good sense of humor, and you just got that feeling that he cared about you. For me, these surrogate dads were a big help in dealing with Dad's death."

Several of the women I interviewed spoke of the influence of grandfathers, usually their mothers' fathers. Very often, particularly when a woman was widowed and had young children, she would return to her parents' home.

I could relate strongly to this, because I, too, was strongly influenced by my grandfather. Although we didn't live with him, my grandparents lived down the street from us, only a few minutes away. They became very powerful influences in my life, and, I believe in the lives of my brothers. For me, however, I can't say that my grandfather became my father or even a father figure. He was always a quintessential and quite wonderful *grand*father.

Although he was affectionate and much loved by me, there was always a level of remove. We never fought, and even though he sometimes gently reprimanded me, he always left serious issues to my mother. I believe both he and my grandmother did not feel it was their place to intrude in the upbringing of their daughter's children. In any case, I never worked through any adolescent oedipal issues with my grandfather (or with anyone for that matter); that was simply not the nature of our relationship.

Still, several other fatherless daughters felt a bit differently about their grandfathers; these were usually women who had no memory of their fathers and developed fatherly relationships with their grandfathers at a younger age.

Cynthia, whose father died in a car accident when she was only five months old, grew up in her grandfather's house from infancy until her mother remarried when she was eight. Then in high school she returned to her grandfather's town for boarding school, and, again, was very much a part of his life.

"I was very close to him," Cynthia says. "I named my son after him, and it was a very special relationship. If anything, it almost felt in the household like they were my parents, my mother was my older sister, and my Aunt Betsy was another sister, and then there was me. In a way, I was the youngest in a family of three girls.

"My grandfather was an important man in our community and we knew everybody. He was a member of the country club, on the church finance committee, and owned an important business. All these things anchored me. We knew the neighbors, we knew people at work, and we knew the community. Actually, my best friend didn't have a father. I could really relate to that. I believe that was a divorce situation. This all seemed perfectly normal to me, and we were both pretty happy. We both had mothers that we thought the world of. That was the best part."

Pat, whose dad died in World War II, is grateful to her mother and her stepfather for encouraging her to spend time with her father's parents.

"In some respects, my grandparents took the place of my father," Pat says. "I knew something of his origins because I spent months at a clip living with my grandparents. They lived in Greenwich, Connecticut, in the same house that they had raised their own kids in. So again there was a little bit of a sense of continuity . . . my father used to sleep in this room."

Some fatherless daughters had deep relationships with their grandfathers, although not necessarily loving ones. Elizabeth, whose parents divorced when she was eight, and then her dad disappeared, remembers her mother's father this way: "My grandfather took care of us, but not emotionally. I learned how to manage my grandfather because he did help us financially. But you always had to pitch him. I'd meet with him and tell him that I needed money to pay for clothes or my AmEx bill or something, and he'd hand me three hundred dollars. He was always very generous, but he never gave you what you asked for, only what he felt like giving you. He didn't come to my college graduation; he paid for my education and he didn't even come to my graduation."

❧ ELIZABETH ❧

Elizabeth is a slim, attractive woman, with beautiful hair, lovely, casual clothes, and a great sense of style. She agreed to meet me for an interview in a two-hour window of time between dropping her toddler off at playgroup and picking up her kindergartener at school. From the start, I found her energy disconcerting. Although she appeared to have her life together—a husband, two children, a beautiful home—I sensed that her parents' divorce and her father's abandonment remained an unresolved issue in her life.

Her parents' marriage had been extremely problematic from the get-go. For starters, Elizabeth's grandfather (her mother's father) was a rich clothing manufacturer who ruled over the family, including his daughter's marriage, with an iron fist. Shortly after her parents' marriage, he arranged for Elizabeth's father to work for his company. Her father, however, was by training and by nature an artist, and it was clear to everyone that he hated selling men's clothes. Still, her parents thought they needed the money, although her grandfather footed much of the bill for their lavish lifestyle.

To complicate matters, Elizabeth's parents had severe sexual problems. Still, within the first five years of their marriage, they had two children, Elizabeth, and her brother, Ethan. But even the children did not hold the marriage together.

"My parents were married for twelve years," Elizabeth explains. "I think that somewhere near the end of it, my mom started realizing she was interested in women. My dad was also seeing other women."

It wasn't long before the marriage fell apart, and when Elizabeth was nine, her parents divorced. For the first couple of years after their split-up, her dad lived nearby and continued working for his father-in-law. He quickly began dating openly, and within two years decided to marry again. From the moment he remarried, he cut off contact with Elizabeth and her brother. From the time she was eleven until she was twenty-two, she had no contact with him at all.

Elizabeth still insists that her father was always her favorite parent, her hero. She describes her dad the way someone might talk about a boyfriend: "He looks like me . . . with curly hair. He's very fit . . . an incredible body. His body looks like he's twenty. He's really smart. He can learn anything from a book. He's not good at sitting still. He always has to be busy. If you're in his house, he's doing something. He's not hanging out with you. He's not social. He has trouble getting on the phone with me. He is very creative, very talented, very bright."

Elizabeth experienced her mother as angry and abusive: "Mom kept me dressed, she got me to school, she got me to ballet—she was emotionally ever-present, but she was away a lot, too. She was busy working." Her mother became a psychiatric social worker.

"She was my best friend on some levels. I always told people my problem wasn't my mom's sexuality, it was her personality. I hated some of her lovers. But that would have been true if they had been men, and I always knew that. Listening to her have an orgasm with another woman in her bedroom was not fun."

As it turned out, Elizabeth's father ended up moving to northern California with his second wife, Cleo, and living on a commune north of Eureka. He became a classic 1970s hippie. (Elizabeth's parents divorced in 1974; her dad remarried in 1976.) He began supporting himself by making jewelry and, apparently, living off the land.

"You know, he doesn't believe in the way our society lives.

He lives on a communal property. He has an outhouse. He recycles . . . he lives on the earth."

When pressed to talk about why she thinks her father essentially abandoned his family, Elizabeth says: "I have a lot of black holes in my life, and that's one of them. I don't know why. . . . He basically couldn't afford to pay my mother alimony or to take care of us. And . . . he was hiding out."

Shortly after Elizabeth finished college, she was traveling in California with a boyfriend and decided to visit her father.

"We had a decent visit with him," she says. "It wasn't terribly intimate, but I think he was just happy I was out there. He said that he kept trying to get my brother to come visit him, but my brother just wouldn't have anything to do with him."

After that visit, she and her dad remained in touch, but not close, and didn't meet again for several more years until she was about to get married.

"Soon after I met my husband, Tom, I went to a friend's wedding in California. So I called my father again, and I asked him if he'd be willing to meet with me. He came, but I got really angry with him because he brought his new wife, wife number three. At the time, I felt like, 'I don't want to deal with your wife. You and I have no relationship. Don't start bringing her into the picture. It's not about her.' We went for a drive. I started asking questions like, 'Why did you let my mom hit me? Why did you leave?' He really didn't have an answer.

"While I was visiting him, I fell in love with this piece [of jewelry] that he had made, called 'Kissy Face.' But he said, 'I can't give that to you. . . . I have to show it in LA,' or whatever. Instead, he sent me these ugly pieces he had made . . . my father's an incredible jeweler . . . but these things looked like his experiments that didn't work.

"Anyway, on my thirtieth birthday I got a package from him. I had to pick it up at the post office, and I was standing there, opening this box, and it was 'Kissy Face.' My father had sent it to me for my birthday. I just lost it in the middle of the post office."

Elizabeth is now in her late thirties, yet when she describes her relationship with her father, it still rings of a sort of adolescent infatuation, a romanticized ineffable longing.

"My relationship with him now is pretty good," she says, "and I've worked really hard at pursuing him. Everything I am is because of him. Because he wasn't around, I went on my own. I majored in writing; I minored in photography and design. I still do photography; I still write. I describe myself now as an artist, although it's taken me a long time, because I don't actually create on a day-to-day basis."

The reality is that Elizabeth is a wealthy suburban housewife and mother who seems a bit lost. "I'm a strong person," she says. "I'm a self-sufficient person. But I have abandonment issues." What's more, her mother and her grandfather are the people who wield the emotional clout.

"On my wedding day, I had a fight with my mother about who was going to walk me down the aisle, my mother or my grandfather. My father wasn't even there. I wanted my grandfather to walk me down the aisle because he was paying for the wedding, and he had basically been as much of a father as I could have had in the family. But she felt she had taken care of me, raised me, so it was her right. So they both walked me down the aisle. But it turned out to be a joke. My mom didn't tell them how to place the chairs when they created the aisle, so the aisle was very narrow, and they both ended up walking behind me, and I walked down the aisle alone.

"And I'm alone a lot still. That just seems to be the way things are. I guess everyone's alone when you get right down to it."

STEPFATHERS AND THE FATHERLESS DAUGHTER

My mother remarried in June 1966, more than nine years after my father died. Robert Mathews was a friend of friends, who had been recently widowed, and who had two children of his own: a daughter,

Gail, who was a year younger than I, and a son, Gregory, who was a year older than my youngest brother, Bo. I was blessed because Bob not only loved my mother, he cared about us children, too, and he was determined to blend our families. Also, where both my own parents had been indecisive, rash, and at times impulsive, my stepfather was rational, clear-thinking, and especially sensitive to the needs of teenaged children. He was not wealthy, but he was financially comfortable, and this gave my mother a sense of security she had never known in her adult life. Their marriage, which lasted for thirty-two years until his death in 1998, was a joy to them, and after an initial period of adjustment, a relief to us children.

Let me back up a bit. The initial period of adjustment that I refer to was not all that easy. My stepfather, as I said, was a very different sort of man from my own father, and in the beginning I didn't like him very much. However, I was twenty years old, in college, and actually lived at home with them for only a few months after their marriage. Once, a few weeks after their wedding, he yelled at me for typing late at night (back in the days when typewriters made lots of noise), and I remember being enraged. But I was able to slough it off. My younger brother, Bo, who was fifteen when they married and had no memory of our own dad, had many more difficulties adjusting to a new two-parent home. I don't think Bo spoke much for the first five years of their marriage!

Fortunately, we got along well with Bob's children from the beginning. During the Thanksgiving break of my sophomore year in college, my mother and Bob announced their engagement. Actually, they had been dating for several months, and both my mother and stepfather had spoken to each child about their tentative plans to marry. After dinner on Thanksgiving, they sat us all down in the living room and announced that they had formally decided to marry and would do so in the next few months.

They were going out that evening, and not long after their big, not-so-surprising announcement, they left us. My brothers and I and my stepsiblings didn't know each other very well yet. (Over the years, in part due to the age and placement of various grandchildren, interesting relationships have developed among us.) However, our parents had not been out the door five minutes before my quiet but thoughtful brother Herb said:

"You know, your dad doesn't really know our mother."

Whereupon my stepbrother Greg, in his distinctly laconic manner, answered, "Don't worry about it. Your mother doesn't really know our dad."

We all laughed, and a relationship was cemented that has lasted more than forty years.

For me, my mother's remarriage was a blessing. My stepfather gave her a wonderful life, and we have never had to worry about her or take care of her emotionally or financially. I have always referred to Bob as my stepfather, whereas I know many stepchildren refer to their stepparents as "my mother's husband" or "my father's wife." Although Bob did not replace my father, he gave us a great amount of fathering, especially given our somewhat advanced ages when they married. His marriage to my mother both liberated me and gave my life a certain balance and security, even though I had reached adulthood. As I said to him on more than one occasion: "If the worst thing that has ever happened to me was the death of my father, the best thing that happened to me was you."

Stepfathers: Myth and Reality

In his book *Life Without Father,* sociologist David Popenoe writes: "Biological fathers are more likely to be committed to the upbringing of their own children than are non-biological fathers. . . . Engaged biological fathers care profoundly and selflessly about their own children, and such fatherly love is not something that can be transferred easily or learned from a script."

I believe that this statement is true, and most of the fatherless daughters I interviewed concurred. For example, Kathleen, whose father died when she was two, said of her stepfather: "I grew up calling him Daddy. But there's always that under voice, where you'd say, 'You're not really my daddy.' He was a good dad; he just wasn't *my* dad." And Cynthia, whose dad died when she was an infant and whose mother remarried when she was eight, recalled: "My stepfather didn't bargain for me. He met my mother, and I came along as part of the package. I think that was just the reality. He did the best job he could with it."

Among the fatherless daughters I interviewed, less than one-third of them experienced life with a stepfather. Most of these fatherless daughters had lost their dads through death. (Of the 106 women I interviewed, 66 had lost their dads through death, while 40 were products of divorce. Of these 106 women, the mothers of only 29 of them remarried. Of the 40 who were products of divorce, only a few of their mothers remarried, and most of the daughters had no contact with their natural fathers. In fact, in two cases, the girls were unaware that they had been adopted until late childhood.)

Most of the mothers who remarried were younger (that is, still in their twenties or early thirties) when they remarried, and their children were usually preschool age. Among the few older mothers who remarried, their children were usually grown or at least out of the home in boarding school or college.

If older children were in the home, the remarriage often failed, sometimes quickly. A few mothers remarried too quickly after their husband's death or abandonment, and these marriages were almost always problematic if not disastrous. As one fatherless daughter described: "My brother went off to military school, and his roommate's father called my mother for a date. They sort of fell in love. They met in September, were married in December, and had their marriage annulled in March." In other cases, the children were so against the remarriage that the union fell apart under the weight of their disapproval.

These facts and figures more or less confirm the conventional wisdom stated by many sociologists that nonbiological fathers are not as committed to children as biological fathers. Still, I don't believe it's the entire truth, or, at least, that stepfathers are without influence or positive effect.

Speaking for myself, I came to respect and love my stepfather tremendously. Several other women expressed similar feelings of influence, respect, and love for their stepfathers.

Roni tells this lovely story of her relationship with her mother and her stepfather: "The only father that I really remember is my stepfather. My mother, my stepfather, and I went to a wedding for one of my stepfather's nieces. I noticed during the wedding that my mother was sitting at a different table and she looked distressed. I said to her, 'What's the matter?' She said, 'I have to tell you that today is the twentieth anniversary of your father's death, and it just got me thinking about what if he had lived. I was just reminiscing and thinking.'

"So, I said to her, 'Did you tell Abe?' (By the way, I always referred to my stepfather as my father, but I always called him Abe.)

"'Oh, I wouldn't do that,' she said. And I said, 'You know, Mom, I think he would understand. He knows you had another husband; he knows you had another life. You've been with him for a long time, and it's natural.'

"Later that night, I got a phone call from my stepfather, thanking me, because my mother did tell him. Apparently, she told him, 'I didn't want to tell you, but Roni said I should.' And he called me to thank me."

THE POWER OF MOM

Moms matter. In some ways, the way a girl's mother responds to the loss of her husband has a greater impact on her daughter's future life than does the loss itself. One middle-aged woman whose dad died when she was in her midteens, and who for a time felt tremendous anger toward her mother, said: "My mother must have done something right, because you learn your parenting skills from your parents, and as much as I can sit here and be critical of how Mom parented, she must have done something right, because I never loved anything more in my life than my kids. You get that from somewhere, and she must have shown us enough love so that we could love our own children so much. Somehow, in the midst of all the chaos that surrounded my dad's death and in the years that followed, she seems to have managed to show us the fundamentals of good parenting, if only on a subconscious level. It's just too bad that she couldn't have figured out a way to be happier in her own life."

PART III

AFTERSHOCK

———◆———

The Woman She Becomes

6. THE EMOTIONAL LEGACY OF FATHER LOSS

The worst thing for me is abandonment. Any hint of abandonment, and it's like "Old Faithful." I just erupt.

—Paula, fatherless daughter

Certain fears, attitudes, and defenses will come into play sooner or later in the life of any woman who loses her father at an early age, inhibiting her and possibly altering the direction of her life.

The human psyche is a complicated entity. It is made up of a huge collection of behavior patterns that reflect character and temperament, which give each person her uniqueness and vitality. Many studies have been done to discern whether the human personality is the result of nature (that is, the genetic gifts that are present from birth) or nurture (the influences of family, society, and life experience). Despite much debate, most experts agree that an individual's personality is pretty much a blending of the two.

Many aspects of nurture will color how a daughter experiences her father's loss: whether the loss was the result of death or divorce, the girl's age at the time she lost her father, the quality of her relationship with her father before he disappeared from the home, the personality and capabilities of her mother, and whether another significant male figure entered her life during her formative years. Of course, each fatherless daughter's unique personality traits, many of which are present at birth, will come into play as she processes her loss in the short and long terms.

I have identified a cluster of emotional characteristics found in almost every woman who was raised in a home without her father. These traits form the emotional legacy of father loss:

- Fear of abandonment
- Anger
- Shame
- Low self-esteem/feelings of worthlessness
- Problems with trust
- A tendency to romanticize men/view men unrealistically
- Fear of intimacy
- Problems with sex
- Difficulties with assertiveness
- Issues with goals and personal boundaries
- Conflicting feelings of dependence and independence
- Resistance to commitment
- Fear of separation

Some of these factors, particularly fear of abandonment, anger, feelings of worthlessness, and the tendency to romanticize men, come into play almost immediately after a girl loses her father and certainly by late adolescence. Other traits—fear of intimacy and sex and difficulties with assertiveness, dependency, and commitment—may affect a person much later in life.

FEAR OF ABANDONMENT

The fatherless daughter's intense fear of abandonment is by far the most prevalent and inhibiting result of early father loss. Indeed, I believe that it is the hallmark of the fatherless daughter.

Ideally the presence of a supportive father in a girl's life provides her with a sense that she will be cared for and protected. That sense of security gives her a feeling of confidence in herself that sustains her throughout her love life and her work life. If her father dies or otherwise departs, he leaves his daughter with the message that no man can be counted on to support her. Her fear of abandonment, which to a large extent is often unconscious, permeates all her actions and relationships, particularly those with men.

Not surprisingly, the fatherless daughter's fear of abandonment is usually coupled with an inability to move on, whether from dead-end jobs, draining friendships, or abusive love affairs or marriages. As Victoria Secunda states in *Women and Their Fathers,* from the moment of a father's death or desertion "much of life [for the fatherless daughter] becomes a matter of avoiding another good-bye." The fatherless daughter clings tenaciously, even in hurtful situations. In its most extreme and existential form, the fatherless daughter has terrible problems accepting death.

Fear of abandonment colors virtually every aspect of a fatherless daughter's life, not just her love life. When combined with other personality characteristics, it is a powerful inhibitor.

ANGER

Coupled with the fatherless daughter's intense fear of abandonment is almost always a well of fierce anger. Indeed, her rage results from the abandonment. This anger can appear on the surface and be an obvious aspect of a woman's personality. Or, it can reside deep in her psyche and appear as sadness, depression, or addiction to alcohol, drugs, or food. In any case, the rage is deep and terrifying, and it comes into play in virtually all of her personal and professional relationships, often inappropriately.

Rage is one of the most common emotions fatherless daughters bring to their relationships, particularly their love relationships, and *most* particularly their relationship with their father, even if he has died. Anger is potently expressed in Sylvia Plath's famous poem, "Daddy."

Critic Elizabeth Hardwick beautifully describes the quality of Plath's rage in *Seduction & Betrayal:* "In Sylvia Plath's work and in her life the elements of pathology are so deeply rooted and so little resisted that one is disinclined to hope for general principles, sure origins, applications, or lessons . . . her work is brutal, like the smash of a fist." It seems obvious that Plath harbored tremendous anger toward her father, who died when she was nine. As Hardwick says:

"Always, behind every mood, there is rage. . . . In some poems the rage is directed blankly at her father, in others more obliquely, but with intensity, at her husband. . . . Is the poem 'Daddy' to be accepted as a kind of exorcism, a wild dramatic monologue of abuse screamed at a lost love?" Frankly, I think so. Although Plath's father died after a long illness, she shows no pity for him in her long poem. Instead, she portrays him as a murderer, while she, the daughter, is the victim. Although "Daddy" is an extreme, brutal, and possibly even pathological work of art, it is a powerful expression of the sort of rage experienced by many fatherless daughters.

Anger can also be associated with a number of psychological symptoms including projections, compulsions, and phobias, as well as depression (often the hidden side of anger) and even shame, especially for women. As one fatherless daughter put it: "Being angry was something that I was taught was really, really bad. I just wasn't taught how to handle it at all. The big signal from my mother was, 'You're making me angry.' That meant, 'Back off, go to your room,' whatever. When my mother got angry, she was not in control, so that's what I thought anger was—not being in control."

✌ PAULA ✌

"I hope you're planning to have a chapter on rage."

This was almost the first statement out of Paula's mouth as we began our interview. I laughed politely; I could relate to anger. But for me, it was a bit incongruous coming from Paula, who until our interview, I had seen only as a quiet, lovely young woman. Paula is extremely pretty in a gentle, feminine way, but as we talked, I was struck by how the hard edges of her anger belied the softness of her features and personality.

At the time of our meeting, Paula had just finished writing a book about her life as a nurse, and I had been her editor. Always gracious, good-natured albeit subdued, I knew little about her personal life, except that she had been married for about eighteen months and had recently given birth to a beautiful baby girl.

Paula was born in the late 1960s in a small town on the eastern Connecticut shore. Her mother, Jane, was in her late thirties at the time of Paula's birth. Her marriage to Paula's father, Ted, was her second, her first having ended in divorce, leaving her alone with two boys, ten and twelve years older than Paula.

After the breakup of her first marriage, Jane had brought her boys to live with her mother in a small apartment in Bridgeport, Connecticut. Jane and her mother had a volatile relationship, but Jane felt she had no choice but to take her children and move into her mother's home. She remained single for several years before she met Ted, a mechanic at the local gas station. They began dating seriously almost immediately.

Then, one day, Ted just disappeared. They'd had a date, and he had simply stood Jane up. She didn't hear from him for almost two years, until he called her out of the blue. According to Jane, he announced that he'd been a fool, that he had missed her terribly, and soon afterward they were married. Jane told her daughter, Paula, that Ted really wanted a child of his own, so they had Paula soon after the marriage.

In an attempt to make a home, Ted legally adopted Paula's half-brothers and bought a small house in a Connecticut beach town. Nevertheless, the marriage began to disintegrate almost from the start. Ted was brutish, verbally abused Jane, and even threw hot coffee at her. When Paula was nine months old, Jane sent the boys to live with their biological father and sent baby Paula to live with her sister in a small town in Florida. As Paula put it, with an edge to her voice, "She dropped me off when I was nine months old and picked me up again a year and a half later."

By the time Jane came back for Paula, she had separated from Ted and moved back to Bridgeport. Jane believed not only that Ted was bisexual, but she was also convinced that he had sexually abused her boys. As a result, she never allowed Paula to be alone with her father. He would occasionally come over to their apartment, but thanks to Jane's scare tactics, Paula was afraid of him and basically ignored him. They would sit together in front of the TV set, saying nothing.

The last time she saw her father, Paula was nine. He had promised to buy her a bicycle and took her to a toy store to pick it out. Meanwhile, he stood around talking to the salesman, apparently about business. She got the bicycle, but actually it wasn't something she particularly wanted. Paula was left feeling that her father didn't take any joy in buying her the bike.

Over the next few years, Paula and her mother moved frequently, and her mother jumped from job to job, until she finally ended up unable to get work. Although she had trained as a hairdresser, she often got drunk during the day and was depressed, so she had trouble holding down jobs. By the time Paula was twelve, they were living almost entirely on welfare.

Paula's oldest half-brother had moved to Los Angeles. When Paula was thirteen, her mother followed him out there, and she and Paula lived in Santa Monica. Jane sometimes worked as a secretary or clerk in a store, but often, because of her drinking and depression, she wasn't able to hold down these jobs for very long. Still, Paula stayed in school, miraculously got good grades, and ended up going to the University of California at Berkeley.

"Something told me that I had to survive," Paula says. "I'm a total overachiever. I was a really good student, and I loved to lose myself in my studies. It's what I did to help me feel good about myself."

Getting her degree, however, wasn't easy. After two years, her own depression got the better of her, and she dropped out of school for a year. She had been guided to psychologists and psychiatric counselors at Berkeley, so she spent about six months in intense therapy, and it helped. She went back to school and finished her B.S., then moved to New York City and got an M.S. degree in public health from City College.

For Paula, study, and later work, were her anchors, but they also became addictions. So did exercise. Although she did not become an alcoholic like her mother, she definitely inherited an addictive personality. As a teenager, she had suffered from various eating disorders, so she turned to exercise in a compulsive way in order to keep her eating problems under control. As Paula says, "I'm in the gym seven days a week. I will lose sleep, I will miss a meal in order to get in two or three hours of exercise. It's very compulsive, very neurotic."

Not surprisingly, Paula's other compulsion was sex.

"I've always channeled my emotional stuff through sex," she says. "I slept around a lot. I've always been very promiscuous. Actually, I don't like the word *promiscuous*. Let's just say 'easy,' very quick to get together with a man. I can't believe how quickly I have slept with a lot of guys.

"I did this because I was desperate for love. Desperate. I had an incredibly cold mother who really didn't want to be a parent, or certainly a parent to me. She was just so miserably unhappy that she couldn't love me the way I needed.

"Now I'm addicted to my husband, Andy. I had nothing but unsuccessful relationships until I met Andy. My relationship with him is the longest one I've ever had, which is just a little bit over three years. Before that, I had many sexual encounters—some went on for a couple of years—but no real long, healthy relationship."

Paula met Andy at a "right to die" meeting. Her mother was diagnosed with terminal cancer, and Andy's mom had recently passed away. "I was dubious about getting involved with him because I knew my mother was dying and I would be a bit crazy. But we met and we had an instant attraction. It was very passionate, lots of sex, but after a few months I just packed my bags and left him for a few days. But Andy was very patient with me and I felt somewhat safe with him, so we got married.

"Even now, even after having the baby, I fear that he will want a divorce, that he will leave me." Interestingly Andy appears to be a calm, kind man who seems completely devoted to Paula and absolutely over the moon for his baby daughter, Hannah, for whom he assumes at least half the parenting responsibilities. His devotion is not lost on Paula. "He's very committed to me. He's so committed to us," she readily admits.

Nevertheless, Paula still feels insecure, and her insecurity shows up strongly in their sexual life. "I get very clingy with Andy," she says. "If we don't make love for a few days, I get very upset. It's almost funny, in a way. It's almost like the reverse of most new parents. Andy will say, 'Paula, we have a baby. I'm tired. Don't take this as a sign that I don't love you!'

"I'm constantly looking for approval in the form of adoration and love. The worst thing for me is abandonment. And the rage that I feel is rage at my father for abandoning me and rage at my mother for emotionally abandoning me. Any hint of abandonment, and it's like 'Old Faithful.' I just erupt.

"All my daughter seems to want is for you to say, 'Hi, sweetheart. I love you.' No one did that for me. And I'm still furious."

SHAME

Shame may come up repeatedly in many different guises. For me, feelings of shame came up almost immediately after my father died. I was embarrassed if anyone mentioned my father's death, even to express sympathy. As late as my freshman year in college, I still had trouble explaining my father's death, and I asked a friend to tell others about my situation. Not surprisingly, girls whose fathers deserted the family have even greater issues with shame.

Shame may go underground and become a subconscious response associated with dependency or problems with love and commitment. Shame can be an insidious emotional response to father loss.

LOW SELF-ESTEEM

The fatherless daughter's abandonment fears often evolve into an emotion perhaps even more powerful than anger: intense feelings of worthlessness or low self-esteem. A child may say to herself, "If Daddy left our home, there must be something wrong with me." I found this feeling to be true at a very deep level, certainly among women whose fathers had deserted the family, but even, like me, among women whose fathers had died.

In their book, *The Father-Daughter Dance,* Barbara Goulter and Joan Minninger give these feelings of worthlessness a feminist foundation: "The small daughter of a patriarchal father soon learns that Daddy's gender is far more respected and admired than her own. It seems natural, therefore, for her to idealize him, to try to win his attention, and to value herself according to how much he seems to value her. Thus, it follows that if he leaves—even when his loss results from death—he is saying that he does not value her, or worse, that she has no value."

Goulter and Minninger devote an extended chapter to the lost father and the yearning daughter. They explain that the fatherless daughter "will usually lack confidence in herself as a person and a woman, and fail to get rewarded in proportion to her abilities." Moreover, the fatherless daughter "may have a far greater-than-average craving for male attention and affection. Because she loved her father and yearns for what he never gave her, she will tend to choose distancing men—that is, men who are less attentive and affectionate than she wants or needs—because, ironically, that is what she knows and believes she deserves. The result is a vicious circle in which she keeps craving more and more and getting less and less and having her confidence further undermined at every turn."

The fatherless daughter may go to great lengths not only to avoid consciously facing feelings of worthlessness or low self-esteem but to vindicate what she experienced emotionally as her father's rejection, even if he had actually adored her and had not deserted her by choice (that is, he died). Still, at a deep subconscious level, she experiences her father's death as abandonment and confirmation of her lack of worth. She needs to prove to herself over and over that her father loved her.

PROBLEMS WITH TRUST

Given their fear of abandonment, free-floating anger, and problems with low self-esteem, not surprisingly, many fatherless daughters have problems with trust. Issues regarding trust come up in virtually every aspect of life; physically, intellectually, and emotionally. A woman may not trust that she is attractive; she may not trust her opinions or her judgment; she may not trust her emotional responses. Fears and insecurities relating to trust come up frequently in all her human contacts, including with family members, friends, and professional colleagues. And, of course, problems with trust are most obvious in her love relationships, often causing potentially good relationships to stall and fizzle.

A TENDENCY TO ROMANTICIZE MEN

It may appear that fatherless daughters hate men. These women may seem coolly detached or have explosions of anger in relationships with the opposite sex. However, most fatherless women don't hate men; they overly romanticize them, particularly, of course, in sexual or love relationships. Because they fail to see men realistically, they believe that they need them desperately, and, as a result, are almost always terrified of them.

Basically the tendency to overromanticize men (and the resulting fear) is played out in one of two ways. If a woman has some confidence in herself, she will at least initially be able to easily cultivate superficial relationships with men. Since she has very little emotional information about men, she dives right into love affairs without the protection of knowledge and common sense. Because she does not see any potential problems or flaws in the men she pursues, she tends to go to the opposite extreme and conjure up an idealized picture of her man, an image of a man who probably does not exist.

Most men are flattered when they are seen as romantic gods and will respond positively. The success of their relationship depends on the relative maturity and emotional health of both the fatherless daughter and her man. But the prognosis is never good. Sooner or later (usually sooner), her fears come into play and she must find a reason to destroy the relationship. He then becomes confused and angered by her sudden change of heart, and the affair explodes. To complicate matters further, she has trouble ending the relationship because of her abandonment fears, so the breakup is made even muddier and more painful, and is often protracted.

In contrast, the fatherless woman's fears may be closer to the surface of her personality, and she may lack any form of self-confidence. Moreover, her romantic view of men only exacerbates her insecurity and shyness. To her, all men are handsomer, smarter, wittier, richer— whatever—than she, and therefore they only desire women who are more beautiful, intelligent, witty, or wealthy than she is. How could this God possibly be interested in me? she asks herself. And, in her mind, even if he became interested in her, he would eventually leave, and the idea of the end of a love affair is intolerable for her. As a result, she may be unable to cultivate any relationships with men at all.

If she does manage to form a relationship, it is often characterized by detachment or chaos. In either case, because she has an unrealistic view of her boyfriend, she fails to understand him, to empathize with him, and to work with him to reach a deeper intimacy. She is so busy protecting herself from loss and hurt that she simply cannot really love or love deeply. As a result, the affair explodes or quietly dies.

Not surprisingly, love affairs with older or married men are prevalent among fatherless daughters, and in many situations, they mark the love of a woman's life. In a certain way, these relationships are quintessentially romantic. Obviously, an older man symbolizes Daddy; and psychologically (or oedipally), a married man also represents Dad, since he is aligned with another woman who not so coincidentally is usually the mother of his children. He appears to be a father surrogate ("Daddy came back!"), and yet he cannot abandon her because by being married, he has, in effect, already left. In a perverse way, the fatherless daughter feels secure, in control, and as safe as she possibly can.

But these affairs, like her others, are doomed. Of course, most affairs with married men inevitably come to an end. In the rare cases when the married man does leave his wife for his lover, the affair follows the course of her other relationships with men. She has impossibly romanticized him, and the moment he is realistically available, her abandonment and intimacy fears become aroused, and she can't cope.

Many of these traits, particularly feelings of worthlessness, anger, and overly romanticizing boys, are common among teenage girls whether they have the benefit of a father's influence or not. Because these characteristics are ubiquitous among young girls, the fact that they are taking a deeper hold in the personality of a fatherless daughter can go unnoticed by her mother or others concerned with her welfare. By the time the fatherless daughter reaches her twenties, the fears and feelings are deeply entrenched, serving as fertile soil for the insidious problems ahead.

⌁ PENELOPE ⌁

Penelope is in her late sixties. Although she is a bit overweight and has stubbornly resisted dyeing her iron-gray hair, she remains a very attractive woman. She enters a room like a Broadway star, usually dressed in a low-cut dress or tight sweater and stretch pants, with a signature scarf flowing around her neck. She has a slightly Bohemian demeanor, although she comes from an old New England family, and her upper-class voice and subtle self-assurance betray her decidedly WASP background. According to an old male friend of hers, when she was an undergraduate, her beauty was so electrifying that men were stopped dead in their tracks.

Penelope is the eldest of three children, her two younger siblings being boys. As a child, her father clearly favored her, teaching her to ride horseback, ski, and sail. Best of all, she remembers that he spent hours simply talking with her, introducing her to books and ideas, cultivating her intellectual and creative life, and taking her obviously high intelligence quite seriously. In contrast, Penelope's mother was a remote, insecure woman who eventually succumbed to serious alcoholism.

When Penelope was eleven years old, her father died suddenly of heart failure. From the moment of his death, Penelope's life changed dramatically. But it was not the externals of her life that were altered; it was Penelope's inner self that was deeply wounded.

For Penelope's family, the loss of the primary breadwinner was not an acute financial disaster. Although her father did not come from a wealthy family himself, her mother had inherited a substantial amount of money from her own father, and the family was left with a comfortably large home in Greenwich, Connecticut, and a sizable income.

Within a year of her father's death, Penelope was sent off to a boarding school near Boston. Unlike many girls who lose their fathers, because of her family's affluence and her almost immediate departure for boarding school, Penelope was never pushed into a pseudo-mother role. What's more, Penelope had long looked forward to going away to school at age twelve, so she harbored no sense of being shunted aside because of the troubles at home.

Already confident about her intellectual capabilities, Penelope became pleasantly aware of her exceptional good looks during her early adolescence. She discovered that she had to exert little energy to secure the interest of boys, and since she had always been outgoing and fun-loving, her early forays into dating were easy and delightful. She breezed through boarding school, a success both academically and socially.

At seventeen, she entered Wellesley College with confidence and great expectations. Penelope performed well academically, and her social life continued to be happy and full. She started dating David, a senior English literature student at Harvard and the scion of a respected Philadelphia family. This was the 1950s, and Penelope was reluctant to begin a sexual relationship with David, not only because she wasn't sure she was in love with him, but because she feared becoming pregnant. Also, as the school year progressed, Penelope became more and more interested in David's roommate, Lou.

Although not conventionally handsome and a product of a working-class background, Lou possessed a rough attractiveness and tremendous self-confidence. Penelope was used to men responding to her good looks and vivacity, but Lou treated her coolly. In fact, he often rudely ignored her. For Penelope, a girl who found the attention of men easy to come by, Lou's cavalier behavior was an irresistible challenge, and Penelope flirted with him outrageously.

Ultimately, her overt behavior had its desired effect. During

the last weeks of her freshman year, Penelope began a secret—
and for her, very exciting—affair with Lou. Lou and his close
friends (although they were roommates, David was not one of
them) drank excessively. In order to party with the abandon they
wished, they rented an apartment in Boston's Back Bay and took
their dates there for good times.

"There was a lot of drinking," Penelope says. "One time,
Lou and I went over there alone, and we got very drunk, and
we started making out, and we had sex, and I lost my virginity
not knowing it. And I was crying and fighting him, and it was
all very confused."

Despite the angst and confusion, Penelope then believed
that she was deeply in love with Lou and promptly broke up
with David. Shortly thereafter, at the end of the spring semes-
ter, David and Lou graduated. David was spending the summer
with his family in Philadelphia and was scheduled to begin a
graduate program in literature at Columbia University in New
York City in the fall. Lou left for the University of Chicago,
where he was enrolled in medical school. Penelope returned
home to Connecticut.

Penelope blithely assumed Lou would call her right away and
make arrangements for them to see each other. She even entertained thoughts of transferring to the University of Chicago in
the fall in order to be close to him. But days went by, and Lou did
not even attempt to contact her. She tried to telephone him and
wrote him several letters, but somehow they never connected.

And then, disaster: Penelope missed her menstrual period.
She finally was able to reach Lou on the telephone and told him
that she suspected she was pregnant. His response shocked her.
He said that he couldn't possibly take responsibility for this baby.
He knew that she had been seeing David all along, and as far as
Lou was concerned, he believed the baby could just as easily be
David's. The subject of marriage didn't even come up. He sim-
ply insisted that she have an abortion.

Penelope was stunned by Lou's coldness. For reasons she
could not even explain to herself, Penelope decided that she

would tell David everything. She only dimly acknowledged to herself that her confession might hurt him deeply.

Her instincts were not wrong. When David heard about her plight, he responded with gentleness and empathy. He admitted that he could see why people found Lou charming—he had enjoyed Lou's company for four years, but he had never trusted him. He could also see how Penelope could have become sexually involved with Lou. David came to Connecticut to comfort her and to help her figure out what to do. Then, in a sort of anticlimax, Penelope's period arrived and the drama was suddenly over.

Penelope expected David to be done with her. However, instead of ending their relationship, David told her how much he still loved her and that he believed that they could create a rich life together. He suggested that she could transfer to Columbia and together they could lead an exciting literary life in New York. In fact, he wanted them to marry right away so that he could take care of her. Without thinking, Penelope accepted, and they were married quietly in Penelope's mother's living room over the Labor Day weekend.

For the first few years of their marriage, Penelope was content. She felt secure. As a married woman, she didn't have to cope with the vagaries of dating or the possibility of experiencing another rejection of the magnitude of the one she had endured with Lou. Her goal was clear and immediate: she needed to finish her college degree. She even managed to drag out her college experience, and her sense of security, by spending an extra year earning a master's degree in English literature, one of the few interests she shared with David.

After four years, David completed his doctorate degree and got a teaching job in a small college in Ohio. He also began talking about starting a family. Penelope's response wasn't strong, although deep down she was starting to feel that she didn't want children, at least not with David. What she did know was that she was bored with David, bored with her studies, and bored with her life.

During the summer before they intended to leave New York for Ohio, Penelope took a part-time job as an editorial assistant at a prestigious book publishing company. She loved the publishing business. Even more, she enjoyed the company and intellectual stimulation (without the snobbishness of academia) of her colleagues. For the first time in years, she felt that men were looking at her as a desirable woman, not just David's wife, and within weeks, she began an affair with one of the editors at her firm.

"His name was Jason, and he was divorced," Penelope explains. "He was much older than I, and I was closer in age to his son than to him! Anyway, this man and I just took to each other passionately. Thinking back, I guess he was also a raving alcoholic. But I was completely entranced by the fact that an older man was interested in me. He knew all sorts of interesting people—writers and artists. He knew Saul Bellow. He knew Robert Frank. He knew Claes Oldenburg. He went to all these people's apartments for cocktail parties and dinners. I don't know what I told David I was doing; working late, I guess."

As with Lou, Penelope believed that she was passionately in love with Jason. When the time arrived for Penelope and David to leave for Ohio, Penelope casually informed David that she didn't want to move and that she was going to stay at her job in New York, at least for the time being.

This time David was not calm. Although he did not know about Penelope's affair, he was fed up with her lack of commitment to their marriage. He told Penelope that if she did not come with him, he would consider their marriage to be over. Penelope, enchanted by her new love affair, simply let David go. David filed for divorce as soon as he got to Ohio, and within six months, Penelope and David's marriage was history.

At the time of her divorce from David, Penelope was twenty-four years old. She had no doubt that she would marry again and assumed that she would have children, although she couldn't see herself "pushing some baby carriage down Broadway," as she put it. Not surprisingly, Penelope's love affair with Jason ended almost the moment he discovered that her marriage was over. However, instead of being devastated, to her surprise, Penelope felt liberated, and for a few years, she enjoyed a string of angst-ridden, highly emotional relationships with various men. She told herself that since she had married so young, she needed time to explore.

When she was thirty, Penelope began an intense affair with Robert, a married man almost twenty years her senior. Robert was a very well-known and successful lawyer, but he had a complicated marriage, four children, a problematic financial life, and a serious drinking problem.

"I met Robert in the late sixties at a political dinner," Penelope says. "He was just dazzling. He was all about 'cause' stuff—the Vietnam War, protesters, race relations. He was all on the right side (meaning the left side), and I was completely dazzled, absolutely swept away, absolutely, absolutely, just—I can't tell you.

"Robert and I were like two magnets, just *pfft!* We started having an affair. And it became absolutely maniacal. I was completely turned on by this man and so sure that he was the only person that I ever wanted to be with. It was crazy.

"We met every day after work. He lived in Connecticut with his family, but we met in the city. Most of the time, we went drinking. But occasionally we'd run off to a hotel. It was the height of mania."

The mania part of Robert and Penelope's relationship actually went on for four or five years, but still Robert made no moves toward getting a divorce. Nevertheless, Penelope and Robert remained deeply involved with one another and were seen as an item by their mutual friends, even those who knew Robert's wife. Finally, after a decade, he left his wife and moved in with Penelope, although by this time he was virtually broke and in very poor health. Penelope attributes many of their problems to Robert's problems with money.

"I came to realize that he had no control over his financial life," Penelope says. "Getting divorced from his wife meant that he had to sign an agreement with her and dish out money to her every month. And he didn't have it to dish. Robert finally got divorced after ten years, but by that time, I had sort of gotten the picture. I realized that Robert was just never going to be the person that I first thought he was. In fact, he probably never was that person, but it took me a long time to figure that out."

Penelope and Robert lived together for another few years, but the relationship never evolved beyond the semicommitted level on which it had been during the years when Robert was still married. Only now the sexual mania—the romance—was gone. In fact, if anything, from the moment Robert moved in with Penelope, their relationship began to disintegrate. Penelope nagged him not only about his finances but also about his drinking, his health, his workaholism, and even his neglect of his children.

After five years, Penelope was at her wit's end. She simply couldn't cope with Robert's problems. Robert moved to San Francisco to live with his married daughter. He died there a few years later.

Penelope's professional life reached an arid plateau in much the same way that her personal life had stalled. Being intelligent, personable, creative, and attractive, she rose through the ranks of her publishing house quickly in the beginning. Within four years of being hired as an editorial assistant, she was promoted to senior editor, and for several years she enjoyed a number of successes with the authors she had brought to the publishing house. However, by the time she entered her forties, after more than fifteen years with the firm and during the years she was living with Robert, she became frustrated because she had not been promoted to a management position.

"I was doing great work for them," she says. "But I was miserable. I was sitting there frustrated with my work life and in this insane affair in my private life. I mean, I was playing with fire."

In an eerie echo of her romantic relationships, Penelope also found herself in constant conflict with senior executives at work, particularly, of course, her male bosses. Finally, after more than twenty years with her company, she left for an editorial director's position at a smaller, less prestigious publishing house. At first, this change seemed to be an intelligent career move; however, at the new company, she again developed problems with her superiors and had difficulties managing the younger employees who reported to her. After four years, she was fired.

At about the time that Penelope lost her job, her mother died, leaving her with a modest trust income. With that money, she bought a comfortable apartment, took a less exalted but secure job as a senior editor with another publishing firm, and tried to settle into a more contented life.

Today, Penelope works, sees friends, travels frequently, and pursues a number of interesting hobbies such as horseback riding, skiing, and painting. Still, when she describes her life to friends, her voice sounds hollow and strained. For Penelope, her work, her travels, her friends, and her activities all serve as exercises in filling time. She does not appear to be fully committed to any of them, in much the same way she could not completely commit to her husband or her deepest love, Robert. Life has not met her expectations. When she is asked what she wants, she talks only of finding a man to love.

Ironically, although she appears to be completely independent, Penelope has spent virtually all her energies searching for someone to lean on, someone to care for her, someone who will accept her unconditionally, someone with whom she could share a special communication and trust. Someone like her father.

FEAR OF INTIMACY

As they reach middle age, many fatherless daughters experience deeper problems rooted in the earlier fears of abandonment. Problems related to intimacy (including sexual intimacy), assertiveness, and dependency, which were probably always at work, tend to show up more overtly when fatherless daughters must commit to a career or a marriage and a family of their own. Not all fatherless daughters end up alone as Penelope did, but many find that their relationships are chaotic, detached, and brittle.

The fear of abandonment, the attendant rage, and low self-esteem leave the fatherless daughter with a fear of intimacy, both emotional and sexual. Because she is afraid of being rejected and lacks self-confidence, she does not, and cannot, reveal her deepest feelings easily. Her personality, especially in sexual and love relationships, often seems detached and artificial.

Kathleen, whose dad died when she was two, said, "I don't know from intimacy. I mean there's no way that I would reveal myself— would be vulnerable—to another human being, to just relax totally, and be playful and childish. That's what one's pets are for!"

Penelope's relationship with Robert is a classic reflection of a fatherless daughter's problems with intimacy. Her feelings for the love of her life, Robert, were mature and powerful, but ironically her relationship with him was not particularly intimate. Penelope never doubted that she loved Robert or that he was devoted to her, and in its early days, their affair was extremely exciting sexually. Of course, the telling factor about their relationship was that for the first decade of their involvement, Robert was married, a classic and compelling component for many fatherless daughters. When Robert finally divorced his wife, Penelope was unable to enter into a deeper relationship with him. Although they lived under the same roof, they fought constantly and were never able to create a stable, nurturing environment at home. More to the point, they never married.

By the time Robert moved in with Penelope, he was close to retirement age and clearly needed to lean on her for support, both financial and emotional. But this type of demand from a life partner triggered Penelope's deepest fears and resentments. By addressing his needs, by accepting his weaknesses and dependency, she would be forced to give up her romantic notions about Robert, ideas steeped in the hope that, like a father, he would be there to take care of her. Despite the fact that she loved Robert, Penelope simply could not make an abiding commitment to him.

PROBLEMS WITH SEX

A father helps a girl define her sexuality; his support and acceptance allow her to feel comfortable in her own skin. If a young girl has not been given love and reassurance from a man, particularly an accepting and loving father, she becomes uncomfortable with her deeper feelings, especially her sexual ones. As a result, she lacks to a great extent the ability to create a rich sexual life, at least one in which both partners are committed and engaged emotionally.

It is not surprising that fatherless daughters often have difficulties cultivating healthy and fulfilling sexual lives. Sexuality is the most intimate human expression, and if a woman fears abandonment and feels worthless, her ability to open up will naturally be inhibited. And, in fact, many fatherless daughters exhibit their sexual fears by being shy, withdrawn, and shut down.

However, a significant number of fatherless daughters express their fears of sexual intimacy by going to the opposite extreme, giving the impression of being sexually free and indeed often behaving so. In W. Hugh Missildine's landmark book, *Your Inner Child of the Past,* he explains that adults who failed to have their needs met as children often eroticize their terrors: "In most instances, persons who have suffered from neglect in childhood tend to overvalue sexual satisfaction. They have eroticized their dependent longings and emphasize these needs above all others. Not having had these dependent needs met in childhood, they cannot be satisfied, and cannot discriminate because their need is so great. However, this emphasis on the physical satisfactions of sex tends to exclude the emotional interchange which is necessary if sexual love is to be meaningful."

DIFFICULTIES WITH ASSERTIVENESS

Generally speaking, men are trained to value rationality, to form opinions, and when solving problems, to come to quick solutions. Women born before the feminist revolution (that is, the mothers of most middle-aged women) were trained to be soft and pretty, to catch a husband, and to create a beautiful home. They were often told to refrain not only from expressing opinions but even from forming them; they were not brought up to think in a clear, analytical way. Postfeminist women, those born during and after World War II and certainly those who are just now coming to adulthood, were certainly encouraged to be more aggressive, to pursue careers, to speak up, and to believe that they could have a rewarding life at home as well as an exciting life out in the world. However, many of these women discovered that having it all was not so simple and that to a great extent it was still the proverbial man's world.

Fatherless daughters, of course, received the same mixed messages from society about the attractiveness of hard-driving rationality and assertiveness. But for them, it was doubly problematic because they had no father to guide and support them. Elyce Wakerman says in her book *Father Loss:* "Deprived of the ongoing encouragement of father [the fatherless daughter] is also characteristically anxious about her femininity. Ambition and its cohort, aggressiveness, pose a threat to her already shaky sense of appropriate female behavior." This missing link of aggressiveness and ambition is clear both with regard to her work as well as her emotional life. In neither case does she assertively establish goals and try hard to achieve them.

Most fatherless daughters feel strongly that they should earn their own living. Usually, this powerful urge results from a woman's basic fear of abandonment; she has no reason to assume that anyone, particularly a man, will support her, and therefore she had better figure out a way to earn a living herself. In some instances, a strong need for attention and approval also drives fatherless daughters to strive toward conspicuous heights of success. A large number of successful actresses and entertainers, past and present, are fatherless daughters, including Lucille Ball, Myrna Loy, Angela Lansbury, Marilyn Monroe, Ellen Burstyn, Barbra Streisand, and Julia Roberts.

However, in most cases, fatherless daughters tend to choose noncompetitive, secure jobs (for example, public school teacher or librarian), as opposed to risky, high-paying careers. Elyce Wakerman explains: "Just as a fatherless daughter's penchant for employment may have begun as an antidote for childhood sorrow, so too may her preference for reliable employment be traced to her childhood loss. She is not as confident as other women, or as bold. Security—personal and professional—is a highly prized commodity, and she is loath to jeopardize however much of it she has attained. To be conspicuous or competitive in the workplace is to make herself vulnerable to rebuke, disappointment, rejection—experiences of which she has had quite enough."

Because of the lack of a father's firm guidance, combined with society's lingering expectations for females, fatherless daughters make most decisions with regard to their life's work based on their emotional needs rather than on rational thought. They act from weakness instead of from strength.

ISSUES WITH GOALS AND PERSONAL BOUNDARIES

One of the most important elements a good father provides a daughter is a clear sense of emotional boundaries. The most obvious place where these directives come into play is in a woman's relationships with men, not only, of course, in intimate or sexual relationships, but also with business associates and even friends. A good father shows his daughter what is acceptable and unacceptable to men. He tells her what men want from a woman, what they don't want from a woman, what she should be prepared to give, and what she should not be so ready to give.

Fatherless daughters tend to be unable to establish boundaries in their love affairs, often doing anything to preserve a relationship or marriage, even when they are unhappy in it. When it comes to making intelligent decisions about marriage, fatherless daughters are often clueless. They were denied the example of a good man (or even a not-so-good man!) while growing up, so they lack the criteria for choosing a husband who might realistically meet their needs.

Moreover, they cannot accept anything less than their romantic vision of a man. At a subconscious level, that romantic vision has much to do with a fatherless daughter wanting to be the special, perfect daughter to her benevolent and undemanding father. These women tend to romanticize the men in their lives just as they have romanticized their absent fathers. As a result, many of their relationships with men fizzle.

Many fatherless daughters never establish viable goals for their professional lives. They may manage to earn a living, but despite intellect and talent, they never pursue a career aggressively. Instead, they are always searching for a man to take care of them, sometimes unconsciously viewing their superiors at work as father figures. When they fail to find a father surrogate, rage and resentment come into play, often in the workplace, and often in relation to their male superiors. When a woman expects her boss to be like the father who was missing in her life, she has put herself smack in the middle of a no-win situation.

CONFLICTING FEELINGS OF DEPENDENCE AND INDEPENDENCE

To a great extent, the reason fatherless daughters have trouble asserting themselves and establishing boundaries and goals is because of their dependency needs. Ironically, the primary way many fatherless daughters deal with their dependency needs is to assume a stance of extreme independence. This deep conflict between dependence and independence dogs them all of their lives.

On the surface, they often appear to be remarkably independent. Most of them do earn their own living, and, in some cases, are obsessed with their jobs. Many live singly, either because they have never married or because they have divorced. If they are married, they give the impression of not really needing their husbands, financially or emotionally. In a sense, they seem to be constantly bucking the marriage. They often belittle their husbands, or express their independence more overtly by carrying on a string of extramarital affairs. When fatherless daughters have children, they sometimes seem to reject the maternal role. Even if they deeply love and adequately care for their children, they strive to give the impression that they are much more than simply wives and mothers.

However, despite this cavalier appearance of independence, just beneath the surface lies a yawning dependency. If anything, the facade of independence is a reaction to intense feelings of dependency. These needs, which are usually unconscious, wreak havoc in their lives: in their work, in their friendships, in their love relationships, and, of course, most noticeably in their relationships with their husbands.

Untying this dependency/independency knot is extremely difficult. The conflict is informed by all of the other factors that affect the fatherless daughter: the fears of abandonment and of intimacy, anger, the overromanticizing of men, and the inability to assert herself. To complicate the issue even further, much of a fatherless daughter's awareness of this conflict is unconscious; if and when she becomes aware of it, she panics.

RESISTANCE TO COMMITMENT

Despite their problems with dependency and their often obsessive need for a man, when push comes to shove, many fatherless daughters have severe problems with commitment, whether it's committing to a career, a new house, a vacation plan, or even a date for Saturday night. Of course, marriage is the biggest problem.

Many fatherless daughters marry when they are quite young, some even in their teens, but most by their early twenties. Most feel that they are deeply in love, and that may be true. However, at the point where the marriage shifts from being romantic and sexually exciting to a lifelong pledge to create a home, raise children, even mow the lawn, many fatherless daughters can't do it. These marriages frequently fail, and although these women may have several subsequent relationships, even marriages, there are still problems related to deep commitment.

When faced with making a lifelong commitment to a man, fatherless daughters have all those deep and abiding fears that were the result of their father's death or desertion: fear of abandonment, anger, lack of trust, fear of dependency, confusion about boundaries—the whole cluster of painful emotions.

When you choose to marry, you are saying to yourself that you are worthy of the love of another human being; that you are capable of sustaining a long-term exclusive relationship; and that you are mature enough, thoughtful enough, and confident enough to become intimate partners with another person through whatever storms you may face together. You are acknowledging that at least one other person (and more if you want children) will be able to count on you. You are opening up to the responsibility of creating a successful union.

But it is scary that there is little or no guarantee that this marriage will last. You have no assurances that the person you love will continue to love you, and you have no doubt that if it ends, the pain will be excruciating.

It takes bravery, self-esteem, trust in your own judgment, trust in your partner, optimism, and an indomitable spirit to commit to marriage. Not everyone is up to it. Among the women I interviewed, several were able to make deep, abiding, thoughtful commitments to marriage and family. Without exception, these women were the happiest and seemingly the most centered of the fatherless daughters I talked to. It would seem that they were able to come to terms with their powerful demons.

FEAR OF SEPARATION

Despite resistance to commitment, virtually all the women I interviewed expressed fears of and problems with separation. This involved not only parting from loved ones or graduating from high school or college but leaving unfulfilling jobs, giving up toxic friendships, and, of course, breaking up with a lover or divorcing a husband. Any separation brought up the dreaded fears of abandonment and all the painful emotions that come with it.

7. OUR BODIES, OUR DADS

Everything you see I owe to spaghetti.

—Sophia Loren, actress and fatherless daughter

I came to write this chapter with a number of preconceived notions. I certainly believed that our fathers played a major role in how we feel about our relative beauty. As I began researching and interviewing, I often thought of an old friend of mine who in the great scheme of things was average-looking. She was not homely, but neither was she considered a great beauty, except by one person: her dad. Her father adored her and made no secret of his affection, love, and regard in every way, including physically. As a result, I believe, she was extremely comfortable in her skin. I don't think she was deluded. I think she was simply self-confident, and as a result, was considered very attractive and sexy by most of the guys we knew. (Which, of course, was the main reason most of us wanted to be beautiful.)

My sense of my own attractiveness was affected by other factors besides my father's absence, which began just as I entered puberty. As a little girl, I did feel adored by my father; however, by the time of his last illness, I was very tall for my age and had developed early. As I hit adolescence, I felt gawky and hopelessly unattractive. The feminine ideal for a teenage girl where I lived was a petite blond cheerleader with a turned-up nose and a perky personality. I was tall, dark, and bookish, and I certainly didn't perceive myself as interesting. In addition, my mother was an acknowledged beauty and had been a beauty queen when she was in college. Frequently people who knew my parents would say to me: "Your mother is so beautiful! And you know, you look just like your father!" Both statements were true, and indeed my dad was a handsome man. But I added another line to that comment: my mother was beautiful and I was not.

Not every young fatherless daughter has these problems. Daphne, whose father died when she was eleven, had received much reinforcement for her beauty even by her early teens. "I'm afraid I relied on being better-than-average-looking in an unbalanced way. After my father died, my mother landed on me like a ton of bricks. She was very unhappy. She was very alcoholic. She was angry at me. Then I began to realize that I was attracted to men. I needed some approval in my life because my mother wasn't giving me any, and my father wasn't there. Maybe it was because my father had been very encouraging to me when I was a child, but I think it was just that I discovered that I could get affirmation from boys. I really relied on it for quite a long time."

Fathers do play a role in how their daughters view themselves physically. But how women perceive themselves and how others perceive them in terms of beauty is often dictated by all sorts of external societal factors, including regional preferences, nationality and race, age, their relationships with their mother and their peers.

Among the fathers I interviewed, most of them played down their daughters' physical beauty. Instead, they were interested in their intellectual development, their health, and, to some extent, their athletic abilities. Jon, who has two exceptionally pretty daughters, dismissed the whole notion of physical beauty in women, particularly as it pertained to his girls.

"I didn't want some girly girls who were totally concerned about clothes and makeup, who are chatting like nincompoops on the telephone. If I catch them doing that, I say 'You're acting like a girly girl.'

"I didn't want [my daughters] to be pretty, actually. Beauty has its own destiny. In a funny kind of way, it creates an aura around them that's wrong. People expect beautiful women to act in a certain way. Girls become their good looks, so they walk into a room and they expect people to look at them. Not because they are smart and because they have something to say, it's because they are good-looking animals. And that ain't right."

WEIGHT, BODY IMAGE, AND SEXUALITY

In a magazine interview, Rosie O'Donnell discussed the issue of weight with Sarah Ferguson, the Duchess of York. Rosie, whose mother died when she was nine and who has long suffered with being overweight, said, "It's really so interesting how many, many people with weight issues have suffered early loss. There's a definite correlation that people use food as comfort."

Sarah Ferguson, whose parents divorced when she was a child and who was the subject of fat jokes during her marriage to Prince Andrew, responded with a resounding, "Yes, definitely." (In the Duchess's case, the joke was ultimately on her detractors. The former "Duchess of Pork" has earned millions as a spokesperson for Weight Watchers.)

This observation held up for me; a significant number of the fatherless daughters I interviewed suffered with weight problems (including myself). Food was used for comfort, or, as one fatherless daughter said, as her "narcotic of choice." Moreover, overweight and other body image issues are directly related to fears regarding sexuality and are a way to hide not only from those fears, but from sexual relationships.

I observed this physical act of hiding played out in many ways. A number of the fatherless daughters were markedly overweight and seemed to have struggled with this problem all their lives, although few seemed open to discussing it. In part, their weight problems may have been genetic; however, padding yourself with an armor of fat is a perfect way to hide from sex and to protect vulnerable feelings. One woman spoke of being deeply hurt because a man she had been in love with and who seemed to enjoy having sex with her had constantly criticized her physical appearance. She believed that he ultimately rejected her because he didn't like her body.

Conversely, several of the women kept their bodies superslim and childlike. (Interestingly, most—but not all—of these very thin women had lost their fathers before age five, or the first oedipal challenge.) These women also cut their hair short, avoided wearing makeup, and chose clothing that was not feminine or alluring. They weren't trying to appear masculine; they simply appeared sexless.

Suzy, who professed to dislike intercourse, seemed to repress her sexuality through her physical appearance. Although also naturally quite pretty, she was extremely slim with small breasts and no hips. She seemed to go out of her way to hide her feminine side. Her clothes, while not exactly boyish, were not particularly feminine, either. She wore straight-legged pants and high-necked shirts, all seemingly designed to hide her sexuality.

The issues of body image and food are best expressed in the book *Father Hunger: Fathers, Daughters, and Food* by Margo Maine: "The emotional consequences of father hunger become apparent as daughters approach adolescence and their need for contact and love from their fathers intensifies. When girls don't know their dads or don't feel valued by them, moving out of the family and becoming part of the culture where men have most of the power is not very enticing. Left unsatisfied, father hunger becomes converted into problems with food, body-image, self-esteem, and relationships."

Several fatherless daughters did not have obvious weight issues, but they still subdued their sexuality through body language. Not long ago, a woman I knew slightly told me that her father had died when she was ten. I was especially curious about this woman because I had observed that although she was quite good-looking, people failed to notice her immediately because her entire demeanor was withdrawn and depressed. She was a quiet personality by nature (perhaps), but she walked with her head down, wore very conservative and nondescript clothing, and in general seemed to blend into the woodwork. I suspected this was her way of hiding from men and from sex.

DADDY AND SPORTS

When I was about seven years old, I was sitting in the backseat of our old green Chevrolet leaning up against the front seat. It was summer and my family was on their way to a vacation cottage on a lake in Indiana. Daddy was at the wheel.

I remember that we were driving up a rather steep hill. Partway up the hill, we passed a cyclist pedaling hard up the steep incline.

"He's a good biker," Daddy said casually, with obvious admiration in his voice.

I was fascinated and sort of taken aback by his comment. I had learned to ride a two-wheeler not long before, and I was still feeling rather proud of the fact that I could ride my bike (a beautiful red bicycle given to me by my dad for my seventh birthday) without the training wheels. The notion that there could be levels of expertise to riding a two-wheeler was a stunning revelation to me.

What's interesting about this comment is that it could only have come from my father. My mother would have had no interest in a biker, and, like me, would not have known that there were levels of biking expertise.

I grew up believing that I was a pretty good athlete. In high school, I was always picked for teams and played a fairly good game of volleyball, soccer, field hockey, and basketball. I also enjoyed ice skating, roller skating, swimming, and biking. However, it wasn't until I was well into adulthood that I realized that I am, at best, only a mediocre athlete. I'm not fast, I'm not supple, I'm not particularly strong, and my eye/hand contact isn't all that great. I'm fairly graceful, I have a strong level of endurance, and, as one good friend says about my late-in-life efforts at skiing, "Well, you're game."

Even though my father died when I was ten, he had an enormous influence on my view of my physical self, at least in terms of athletics. My mother is not remotely athletic; nor is she particularly interested in sports. And yet I have participated in sports all of my life, not in a competitive way (I guess I would have needed more of my father's influence for that!), but I've always enjoyed sports. I can only attribute that to my father's influence.

Certainly our fathers (or their loss) affected our views of ourselves vis-à-vis the issue of beauty. However, in my interviews with fatherless daughters, their recollections concerning their dads and physical issues much more frequently had to do with sports. Moreover, those recollections were among their most treasured memories of their dads.

Like me, many women remembered being taught how to ride a bicycle by their fathers. Others talked about going swimming, learning to sail or ride horses, or even playing ball with their dads, an activity usually associated with fathers and sons. Marilyn, whose father died when she was sixteen, remembers that her dad was concerned with teaching her things that involved "courage and daring."

"My father taught me how to swing, how to drive, and how to dive off the high diving board at Jones Beach," Marilyn says. "He liked physical mastery type stuff. He was always thrilled when I figured something out. I remember once when I was about eleven or twelve years old, I was doing a crossword puzzle with him, and I figured out a word he didn't know. He was thrilled! I even still remember the word. It was *flabbergasted*. That's an intellectual thing, but he felt the same way about athletics. He was always happy when I mastered something!"

SERIOUS PHYSICAL ISSUES

Sometimes men are at once braver and yet more "cut and dried" than women about serious issues, including physical ones. This can be particularly true when the issues involve children. Whereas mothers might tend to pamper a disabled child, fathers may be more inclined to push the child to work through the issues.

Jane Wilmot Crane is a marvelous example. Jane was born deaf, but her father, renowned British journalist Chester Wilmot (who was Britain's answer to Edward R. Murrow), refused to be daunted by her disability. Nor would he permit Jane to be. He insisted that she be treated—and educated—as much as possible like any other child. And she was.

Sadly, Chester Wilmot was killed in the crash of a risky Comet airliner, the Concorde of its time, over the Mediterranean on January 11, 1954. At the time he was returning to Britain after touring Asia as a military correspondent for *The Observer* and for the BBC. Jane believes that he was probably rushing home so as to not miss her eleventh birthday.

At the time of her father's death, Jane's family, including her two younger siblings, Caroline and Geoffrey, were living in Buckinghamshire on a small farm. Jane's mother was only thirty-six when she was widowed, and although she was born in Australia, she elected to stay in England, believing that it would be easier to raise children on her own in England. It was also a better place to care for a deaf child.

As her father had requested, Jane continued to be raised and educated as though she had no handicap whatsoever. She attended boarding school and then Leicester University. After graduation, she became a librarian and later a lawyer. She married another lawyer, David Crane, and they had two children, Elizabeth and Jonathan. For many years Jane has been very involved in disability politics.

Jane has endured more than her fair share of challenges and sadness in her life. But she has met every challenge and every heartache with tremendous courage and stoicism, two qualities her father would have admired. Perhaps that is his greatest legacy to her, and her great gift to him.

I came to this chapter with the assumption that fathers—or the lack thereof—play a huge role in how women perceive themselves physically, most particularly how they perceive their relative beauty. What I found, however, is that although fathers have some effect, a woman's perceptions of her body and her beauty are largely formed by other factors, including regional, ethnic, and peer preferences as well as the influences of models and actresses as they are portrayed in advertising, television, and the movies.

But even more interesting is that I found that a loving father adores his daughter no matter how she may rank in relative beauty. His primary concern, with regard to her physicality, is that she be healthy, strong, and fit—physically and morally. If he is absent from her life, she may well miss out on this strong, balanced influence, and it can affect her life forever.

8. LOVE AND SEX, SEX AND LOVE

A woman's capacity for a mutually loving and sexually fulfilling attachment is directly related to her relationship to her father.

—Victoria Secunda, *Women and Their Fathers*

In the process of creating the proposal for this book, I crashed head-on into the most powerful fatherless daughter demon: problems related to sexuality, sexual love, and marriage. Let me rephrase that. I didn't exactly crash head-on into it. I sort of tripped over it. I had actually written and revised this book's outline countless times before it dawned on me that I was missing a chapter on sex!

My lapse is rather bemusing. My bookshelves, which are the focal point of my office, are peppered with titles that indicate sex, love, and relationships with men are obviously highly important to me. With hardly a glance, I can see *The Joy of Sex, The Magic of Sex, What Every Woman Should Know About Men, What Men Won't Tell You but Women Need to Know,* and even a particularly hilarious book titled *The Kama Sutra Pop-Up Book.*

Also on my shelves is a paperback copy of *The Prisoner of Sex* by Norman Mailer. Although the pages of this book are crisp and browned, the spine is not broken, which tells me that I've had the book for a long time, but I've never read it. Perhaps the book annoyed me so much after its first three pages that in a feminist snit I threw it across the room and never opened it again. (It's copyrighted 1971, which means it has been sitting on my shelf for more than thirty-five years.) But I doubt it. Such a statement would indicate that I was in touch with my sexuality and could be appalled by the views of a guy like Mailer. That is simply not true. The fact is that I'm terrified of a force of nature—read "sexy guy"—like Norman Mailer.

Which brings me back to the real reason I "forgot" to include a chapter on sex in my original proposal for this book. Not only was this clearly a subject that I wanted to avoid; it was a topic that absolutely terrified me. And I came to find out as I did my interviews, it frightened many—if not most—other fatherless daughters as well.

SEX AND THE FATHERLESS DAUGHTER

A girl's relationship with her father serves as the model for all her relationships with the men in her life, romantic and otherwise, but the impact it has on her love life is usually the most dramatic. In *Women and Their Fathers,* Victoria Secunda explains: "The father-daughter relationship is the proving ground for a daughter's romantic attachments, her dress rehearsal for heterosexual love."

Interestingly, Secunda goes on to say: *"And women who have difficulties in this area almost always had fathers who could not be counted on, or who were emotionally or physically unavailable, when they were growing up."* The italics are Secunda's, but they could easily be mine.

Over the course of my life, I have had a number of unsatisfying romantic relationships with men, and I know for certain that many of my problems were caused by the absence of my dad's guidance. My romantic relationships seem to have fallen into two distinct categories: very sexual connections that did not develop into anything deeper and satisfying friendships that did not work out very well sexually. As much as I hate to admit it, I have reached middle age with little understanding of men, at least from a romantic perspective. I don't seem to perceive how I come across to men, what a man might expect of me as a woman, and what I might expect in return. I still have not learned to trust my instincts and my intelligence, to establish appropriate boundaries with men, to like myself. As a result, I am afraid of intimacy. Revealing my true self to a man has been close to impossible. My way of coping with this quagmire of feelings has been to retreat, to hide, and to focus primarily on my work.

In a way, I've been stuck in some sort of adolescent morass, or more particularly, trapped emotionally in the mind of a ten-year-old, the age I was when my father died. And, as I said, I believe deeply that my relationship problems with men, to a large degree, are a direct result of my dad's absence in my life. What's more, I believe my observations to be true not only for myself but also for many of the fatherless daughters I interviewed.

Daddy's Role

One of the most important functions of a father is to help his daughter shape her sexual identity and her ability to relate lovingly and effectively with the men in her life. A father's influence takes hold initially when his daughter is about four and then again when she enters puberty. I found among the women I interviewed that girls who had loving and attentive fathers, even if they had lost their father early in life (but after puberty), tended to have stronger and healthier romantic relationships with men than girls whose fathers had died or abandoned the family when they were children. Girls with loving, involved fathers learned how to interact with males (in all ways, not just romantically) by using their personal father-daughter relationship as a model. If they had a warm, interested male adult to talk to, they felt accepted and loved by at least one man.

In Claudette Wassil-Grimm's book, *Where's Daddy?* she says that "girls without fathers often became desperate for male attention." Wassil-Grimm also came to the same conclusion that I did regarding the difference between girls who lost their father through death and those whose dad left. In general, "The girls [whose fathers had died] often either shied away from males altogether or went after them like sirens, being sexually used in the bargain. . . . Daughters of divorce tended to be promiscuous, while bereaved daughters tended to be overly shy around males."

Although Jill, whose parents divorced when she was nine, had a continuing relationship with her father, she always felt her dad was simply doing his duty. Jill carried insecure, hopeless feelings that her father really didn't care about her into her relationships with men, starting in early adolescence.

"Anytime I would meet a guy, there was always that huge inse-curity factor," Jill says. "I figured he was not really going to be inter-ested in me. Why would anybody be interested in me? I'm not that attractive . . . I'm overweight . . . I'm this . . . I'm that. In high school, I wouldn't say I dated, but I went out with guys, and I probably had a lot more sex than I should have. I had to get male affection some-where, and that's where I got it. [My parents'] divorce led to my mis-trust of men and my feeling that the only way that I could be visible to men was in a sexual way."

Everybody has embarrassing or funny stories to tell about early dating experiences; however, these experiences tend to be extreme for fatherless daughters and often painful. Lisa, whose dad died when she was ten, tells of being fixed up on a blind date when she was a twenty-year-old college student. "My roommate had a dinner party at our apartment, and she invited this very attractive lawyer for me to meet. After dinner, she said to me: 'What happened to you? You excused yourself from the dinner table, and you went to the bathroom for thirty minutes.'

"'Really?' I said. 'I spent thirty minutes in the bathroom? Don't tell me that I did that. Only mad people do that!'

"'Yes,' she said. 'I think he was a little bit too eligible for you.'"

Her roommate was right. Most people are nervous on a blind date, but they manage to stay present. Lisa's anxiety was so overwhelming that she simply had to excuse herself and go hide for most of the eve-ning in the bathroom.

THE FEAR OF ABANDONMENT AND
OTHER EMOTIONAL DILEMMAS

In no other area of a fatherless daughter's life do the emotional legacies of father loss come into play more dramatically than in her romantic relationships with men. The fear of abandonment triggers the fear of intimacy and sex; an inability to trust men; problems with self-esteem; difficulties with assertiveness and establishing appropriate boundaries; conflicting feelings relating to dependency, separation, and commitment; and sometimes inappropriate shame.

In romantic relationships, these emotional dilemmas cause many fatherless daughters to act out in hurtful, frequently extreme, and sometimes downright dangerous ways. They tend to seek out intense emotional highs, become obsessed with inappropriate or disinterested men, hide from men physically and emotionally, behave like children, and fail to trust their instincts and their intelligence.

Extreme Emotional Highs

Because fatherless daughters usually have not experienced the attention and love (and that may include disagreement and criticism) from a devoted, trustworthy father, they frequently believe that a love relationship must be *electrifying* in order to qualify as true love. When a woman experiences these highs, she often loses all perspective and fails to accurately judge the man involved.

M.J., an actress whose dad deserted her family when she was six, expresses this feeling: "It's like you're the Rockefeller Center Christmas tree, and he's plugging you in. He fills you with five billion watts, and you are the most of everything! You're the most attractive, the most intelligent, the most—it's like Santa Claus came and gave you all these boxes and put them on the table. So you love him!"

But this sort of come-on is often just a ploy to get you into bed. As M.J. put it: " . . . until he gets you. And then, it's like Santa Claus takes all the presents away. 'There's another little girl who I have to give these presents to now,' he says, or sometimes doesn't even bother to say, and there you are, dumped, abandoned, alone again, and this time even more desperate than before. You have to protect yourself—but until you've learned how to do that, you could be in big trouble!"

Obsessions

As teenagers, many fatherless daughters become obsessed with boys, and in many cases, these sorts of adolescent obsessions continue well into adulthood.

Frequently, the object of a fatherless daughter's obsession is a particular man who, for whatever reason, is not providing the attention she wants, and at a very deep level, needs. Stalking is, of course, an extreme example, but normally these obsessions are far less dangerous, although still hurtful for both the fatherless daughter and the object of her intense feelings.

Carol, a fatherless daughter who had been married and divorced twice, had dated Scott, a successful architect, a few times; but as any casual observer could see, he clearly was not interested in pursuing the relationship further. He stopped asking her out and didn't return her numerous calls to him. At this juncture, Carol became obsessed with Scott. She went over to his house and insisted that he give her an explanation for his behavior. She attempted to analyze his actions and even suggested that they try psychotherapy together. Scott was in his mid-fifties, had never been married, and may well have had psychological issues of his own. However, it didn't matter, because Carol was deep into an obsession that really had nothing to do with Scott.

An obsession is frequently a defense against experiencing an unpleasant or frightening emotion. For a fatherless daughter, that unpleasant emotion is very likely reexperiencing the grief of her father's death or the humiliation of his departure. When a man in a woman's life fails to respond the way she wants, she can easily become obsessed with trying to secure his response. But she is at once avoiding her real feelings of loss and making every effort to vindicate them.

One woman I spoke with put it this way: "I had a girlfriend at summer camp who didn't have a dad, and she was simply crazed about boys and about the male camp counselors. She just wouldn't leave them alone. It was pretty embarrassing, actually. It's interesting that I never felt any of that neediness, even though my father died when I was in my late teens. Maybe it's because I had this very strong male figure in my life until I was seventeen. I think he gave me a lot of what I needed before he died. Now that I'm a teacher, I notice that the girls who have no fathers need to have some kind of male support somewhere or father figure in their life. They just seem desperate for it. I can understand that, but it makes me kind of sad, because they so often choose such inappropriate people to fill that role."

Hiding

Another way fatherless daughters cope with the troubling emotions surrounding their relationships with men is to hide. Hiding can be expressed physically. A woman may allow herself to become extremely overweight, or childlike in her skinniness. She may make other efforts to appear unattractive. Hiding may involve becoming overly concerned with a career or a hobby, like running or skiing, leaving no time for establishing a relationship. Finally, hiding can mean simply not participating wholeheartedly in the world at large, or withdrawing from the world of men and sex.

Most of the women I interviewed who seemed to be hiding in one way or another from relationships with men were daughters of fathers who had died. The act of hiding was an expression of shyness.

I also observed a form of hiding in women whose fathers left the family. Sunny, the daughter of a man who abandoned his daughters emotionally (although not physically), spoke about hiding from relationships by continually choosing guys who were not really available. In a funny way, the attraction, or what she called love, was his emotional absence, which of course was both comfortable and familiar. It was just like being with her father.

As Sunny puts it: "I think that in my own relationships, I always picked these guys who couldn't possibly be there, because they were addicted to something or they were married. I just would always pick somebody who couldn't be there—and was not there. For me, I think it was a fear of being close, and then of losing someone I was close to."

Behaving Like Children

Some of the women I interviewed behaved in a childlike manner in their romantic relationships with men. Many enjoyed dating older men (allowing the women to act the part of young daughters), while others, although in relationships with men who were more or less their own age, submerged their assertiveness by giving the men power over everything from ordering breakfast at a diner to telling them who to vote for.

Often this childlike quality showed up physically, in women whose bodies appeared preadolescent and asexual. These women might also dress in a sort of sexless way. Interestingly, many of these women had lost their fathers when they were very young, often infants.

Not surprisingly, this childlike asexuality usually accompanied a fear of sex. Some of these women were quite straightforward about fearing sex, or at least disliking it. For example, Suzy, whose father had died when she was twelve, bristled when I first asked her about sex. "To be honest, I don't like intercourse very much," she said a bit coldly. "I don't know why. Maybe I don't like the idea of something from the outside coming inside of me . . . invading my space." It was interesting because Suzy was a very pretty woman who, it seemed to me, would have no trouble attracting men. However, I was fascinated to learn that although she appeared to be in her twenties, she was in her early forties. Also, despite her lack of interest in physical sex, Suzy had a boyfriend, a student more than fifteen years her junior.

In other areas of their lives, including their professional and family lives (some were wives and mothers), these women were responsible and adult. It was in the romantic realm that the childlike qualities appeared.

Failing to Use Good Sense

Many fatherless daughters lack an understanding of personal and social boundaries, particularly with regard to men, and as a result they often fail to follow their intelligence or their instincts when it comes to male-female relationships.

Ideally, parents teach children about boundaries in most facets of life, from good manners to getting to school on time. Fathers are vitally important when it comes to teaching daughters about boundaries as they pertain to men, most particularly, of course, in romantic and sexual relationships. A loving father will instill a sense of self-esteem in his daughter. Moreover, if he is present and loving throughout the first fifteen years of his daughter's life, he will both overtly and covertly show her what is acceptable to men. As a little girl, he will find her adorable, perhaps unconditionally. During preadolescence and adolescence, he may begin to criticize her about how she dresses, the tone of her voice, how she should behave around boys, particularly sexually, and even the way she treats her boyfriend. If she rebels, she will at least learn his acceptable boundaries. Most of all, she knows that even if her father is furious with her, he still loves her.

If a girl has no father, she very likely has been denied unconditional male affection, at least from the point at which he left or died. She may have had no opportunity to learn about male boundaries and no chance to challenge them in a safe environment. If she is aware that she is out of her depth, she may try to compensate by repressing her sexuality, by projecting a childlike demeanor, by padding her body with fat in order to hide, or by forming relationships with men who somehow feel safe, such as older daddy figures or much younger men. Or, she may go into a sort of mystifying mode of denial.

For example, Patricia, a fatherless daughter in her late thirties whose dad died when she was nine, described being asked out for a drink by a glamorous film producer she had met through her work. She knew he was married, but she thought it might be exciting (extreme emotional high!) to have a fling with this man. When she arrived for the date, he was there with another (married) man and an attractive young woman in her early twenties. As soon as she saw the second man and the young woman, warning bells went off in her head, but just as quickly, she repressed them. In fact, she even remembered feeling sorry for the young girl because she could see that the girl was being used. Patricia ended up having a very brief affair with this man that ended badly. "I ended up feeling angry, hurt, and used," says Patricia. "And kind of shocked! I mean, how could he use me that way? However, in retrospect, I realize that I saw the whole deal right away, but instead of using good sense and respecting myself, I allowed myself to be hurt!"

One well-known fatherless daughter exhibited many of these qualities in a particularly striking way: Marilyn Monroe. It might seem odd to use Marilyn, a quintessential symbol of female sexuality, as an example of someone who had problems with sexual relationships. But I believe Marilyn was simply another manifestation—sort of the flip side of the coin—of the same issues that so many fatherless daughters face.

↙ MARILYN ↘

Sometime in the mid-1950s, a friend of mine who had worked as an actor in Hollywood was walking through Washington Square Park in New York's Greenwich Village. He met up with an actor pal of his from California who was taking in the sights with a pretty, albeit rather nondescript-looking, young woman who he introduced simply as Marilyn. The three chatted for a couple of minutes, laughed a bit, and then parted. My friend walked a good two or three blocks before, suddenly stunned, he realized that the young woman he had just been blithely joking with was Marilyn Monroe.

In February 1954, Marilyn Monroe appeared several times over a period of days before more than one hundred thousand servicemen at camps in Korea. At one famous performance, she wiggled (as only Marilyn could wiggle) onto an outdoor stage wearing only a little black tight-fitting cocktail dress, although the temperature was frigid. She sang a breathy rendition of "Diamonds Are a Girl's Best Friend." Needless to say, the GIs were thrilled. And so was Marilyn.

At this time, Marilyn was on her honeymoon following her marriage to baseball player Joe DiMaggio. Afterward, she supposedly told Joe, "You never heard such cheering!" But Joe, no stranger to throngs of excited men shouting their approval, replied calmly, "Oh, yes I have!"

Marilyn knew she was famous and had already experienced the crush of overly zealous fans. But she had never known anything like the outpouring of adulation she received from the GIs. As she said, "I felt for the first time in my life no fear of anything. I felt only happy." This from a woman who could become literally paralyzed when asked to perform before a tiny audience of friends.

Marilyn Monroe was many things: an incredibly beautiful woman, an incandescent movie star, the sexiest woman of her time, a world-famous celebrity, a legend. Like scores of actresses, she was also a fatherless daughter. And, to me, Marilyn Monroe was the quintessential fatherless daughter. I believe she suffered from many of the same sexual insecurities that all fatherless daughters fear.

Born on June 1, 1926, in Los Angeles, Marilyn Monroe came into this world named either Norma Jean Baker or Norma Jean Mortensen. Neither Mr. Baker nor Mr. Mortensen was Marilyn's biological father. At the time of Marilyn's birth, Norma Jean's mother, Gladys Monroe Baker Mortensen, was married to but separated from Martin Edward Mortensen, probably for good reason, since the new baby was the offspring of yet another man, the result, apparently, of a brief fling.

Baker, the name by which Norma Jean was most commonly known throughout her childhood, was the surname of Gladys's first husband, John Newton Baker, from whom she was divorced. Since she had had two children with Baker, Jack and Berniece, perhaps Gladys decided it was simply more convenient to give Norma Jean the surname shared by her two half-siblings. However, by the time Marilyn was born, Baker had taken his children and moved to Kentucky.

The identity of Norma Jean's true biological father was never proven. Marilyn believed him to be a debonair Clark Gable look-alike named Charles Stanley Gifford. Her mother kept a photograph of Gifford in her bedroom and may well have told Marilyn that he was her father. At least twice in her adult life, once after reaching the height of her fame, Marilyn attempted to contact Gifford, but he always refused to see her in the cruelest, most rejecting way.

Despite her astonishing success as a movie star, Marilyn's life, especially her private life, was significantly influenced by her fatherlessness. First, her fatherlessness was pitifully absolute: Marilyn's father didn't die or abandon her after divorce from her mother. He simply did not exist! Second, her mother was very unstable (perhaps schizophrenic), and for most of Marilyn's life, her mother was absent, too.

Marilyn's mother came from a rootless background herself.

Gladys's own father had died when she was four, supposedly of a form of dementia or insanity. Gladys's mother, Della, was an attractive, exuberant, but equally unstable character. Gladys was married off at age fourteen to John Newton Baker, had two children within the next twenty months, and separated from him before her eighteenth birthday. Between her separation from Baker in 1921 and Marilyn's birth five years later, Gladys led a good-time sort of life, often while sharing a house or apartment with her mother, Della, who was equally wild. Oddly enough, despite her lifestyle, Gladys was described as something of a plain Jane, a petite, dainty, retiring young woman who used sex as a way to please men and to be liked.

Still, despite her instability, Gladys held down a job as a splicer, or cutter of film at Consolidated Film Industries in Hollywood for a number of years. It was at Consolidated that she met Gifford, who was foreman of the day shift. It was also at Consolidated that Gladys met Grace McKee, a person who would become a pivotal force not only in Gladys's life but also in Marilyn's.

Grace was a few years older than Gladys, also divorced, and a much stronger personality. Grace encouraged Gladys to marry Martin Edward Mortensen in 1924, but the marriage lasted for only a few months. By late 1925, Gladys was back on the party scene with Grace and was soon pregnant with Norma Jean.

Within two weeks of Norma Jean's birth, Gladys placed her in foster care with a highly religious couple named Bolender, where she remained for several years. In 1932, when Norma Jeane was six, her mother took the child from the Bolenders to live with her. But by early 1934, Gladys succumbed to severe depression and was hospitalized, and Norma Jean was put in the care and supervision of Grace McKee, where she would remain for the rest of her childhood. Between the ages of eight and sixteen, when she married, Norma Jean had lived in at least a half-dozen different households as well as enduring a two-year stay, between the ages of nine and eleven, at an orphanage within walking distance of the RKO Studios.

According to Marilyn, by the time she was twelve, she had been sexually assaulted in at least two of these homes, and possibly others. Time and again, Grace had to find another family to take her in, often because even the very young Norma Jean was found to be sexually provocative. This experience gave Marilyn a confounding collection of mixed messages. On the one hand, although in fact she was the victim of sexual abuse by several despicable men, she was made to believe that it was all her fault. On the other hand, especially as she moved into adolescence, she realized that she was very attractive to men and that her sexual allure could be very powerful.

Under Grace's tutelage, she also became completely absorbed by the fantasy of the movies, a world of glamour and beauty that bore no relation to her own existence. This fantasy seemed attainable, if only because she had spent her entire life within a few miles of Hollywood. Norma Jean believed that one day she would be a great movie star and then no one would dare mistreat her again.

At age sixteen, apparently thanks to Grace's maneuvers, Norma Jean married an affable neighborhood boy named Jim Dougherty. It was 1942 and World War II had just begun. Still, for two years Norma Jean and Jim were happy, possibly because, as Dougherty said, "I was her lover, husband, and father, the whole tamale." In fact, throughout their marriage, Marilyn called her young husband Daddy.

When Jim shipped out in 1944, Norma Jean got a job at an airplane factory and was discovered by a photographer who was looking for pretty girls for an article on the war effort. She soon began modeling professionally, and within a few months, she began appearing on scores of magazine covers. Her success with modeling quickly triggered her latent acting ambitions, a few nibbles from some movie studios, and the end of her marriage to Dougherty.

Shortly after divorcing Jim Dougherty in 1946 and at the

insistence of 20th Century–Fox studios, Norma Jean changed her name. She chose her mother's maiden name, Monroe, and coupled it with the alliterative Marilyn. The year 1946 marked the beginning of her difficult climb to stardom. It took her seven years, which must have seemed like forever to a young woman with no money, no friends, no family, no education, and little experience with the world, in fact, little more than her physical beauty. But she worked hard, taking acting classes, dancing classes, voice classes, all the work of a serious student.

Marilyn was often broke, and by many accounts, secured work with her sexuality. Perhaps the most famous example was the infamous nude calendar photograph, which she posed for in order to get her car repaired and for which she was paid $50. Still, part of what makes the photograph so incredible is Marilyn's obvious delight in her body and in the pleasure she knew she could give with that body.

In the early 1950s, Marilyn was often a guest in the home of famed theatrical agent Charles Feldman. In this setting, she was thrown into the company of well-known movie and theater executives and artists, like director Elia Kazan, and even her future husband, Arthur Miller; men who could be useful to her career. However, the implicit price for being included at these parties was sex.

On a very deep level, Marilyn's sexuality was the single quality that she was absolutely sure of, and had been since puberty. According to Gloria Steinem and George Barris: "By exciting and arousing, she could turn herself from the invisible, unworthy Norma Jean into the visible, worthwhile Marilyn." In fact, she seemed so hungry for the love and approval she had been denied in childhood, particularly from a father, that she "offered sex in return for male support and affection."

By 1953, after appearing in minor roles in nearly twenty films, Marilyn was on the verge of stardom. With the release of *Niagara, Gentlemen Prefer Blondes,* and *How to Marry a Millionaire,* in 1953, Marilyn emerged as a superstar, surpassing even the fame of her childhood idol, Jean Harlow. From mid-1953 until her death on August 5, 1962, she was on a roller-coaster ride, and ultimately not a very happy one.

In January 1954, she married Joe DiMaggio, who she apparently loved and who, by all accounts, loved her. But love ended up not being enough, and the marriage was over before the end of the year. By then, Marilyn had formed a business partnership with a photographer named Milton Greene. With Greene's support, Marilyn moved to New York City, where she began studying under Lee Strasberg at the Actors Studio, and she began a romantic relationship with Arthur Miller, one of America's most distinguished playwrights. Over the next two years, Marilyn made two well-received films, *The Seven Year Itch* and *Bus Stop,* which not only solidified her fame but also revealed that Marilyn was more than just the proverbial dumb blonde. By 1956, Marilyn was at the pinnacle of both her professional fame and her quest for personal happiness.

In June 1956, Marilyn married Arthur Miller, and with this marriage, she thought she had found everything she wanted in life. Her marriage to Miller would be her last and longest. He filled more of the requirements of an idealized father than either DiMaggio or Dougherty had done.

Her relationship with Arthur Miller was probably the most mature of Marilyn's life, but because of her emotional instability, she could not cope with the problems inherent in the marriage from the start. Miller felt guilty about leaving his children, was experiencing severe financial problems, and was being pursued by the House Un-American Activities Committee. Marilyn's awesome fame was also a problem for the couple. Marilyn tried hard to be supportive, but she lost faith in Miller, partly because she was looking for unconditional love from a father figure, not a mature relationship with a husband.

They were married for only four years, and although she made three more movies during the next four years, including *The Misfits,* written especially for her by Miller, the marriage was

in shambles almost from the beginning. Marilyn had two mis-
carriages, thus failing to produce a child, which she desperately
wanted. She also lived through two or three suicide attempts,
with Miller coming to the rescue at the last minute every time.
Finally, Miller apparently gave up.

Perhaps the simplest explanation of the end of their marriage
came from Dr. Ralph Greenson, who interviewed Arthur Miller
when he first took Marilyn on as a patient. Dr. Greenson found
in him "the attitude of a father who had done more than most
fathers would do, and is rapidly coming to the end of his rope."

It's fair to say that the last years of Marilyn Monroe's life
were hell. Marilyn allegedly indulged in a number of affairs,
including with Frank Sinatra, President John F. Kennedy, and
his brother, Robert. She seemed to return to her old routine,
believing that sex would get her what she wanted, a childlike
sense of warmth and nurturing.

Gloria Steinem says: "What Marilyn wanted from men
was . . . almost as magical as what they expected from her. She
hoped to learn, not to teach; to trust completely but not to be
completely trustworthy; to be the child, not the parent. In short
she looked to men for the fathering—and perhaps the mothering—that she never had."

Marilyn Monroe died of an overdose of barbiturates on
August 5, 1962. Although her death was steeped in gossip and
innuendo, the official word was that it was suicide. It could be
said that Marilyn Monroe's sexuality was so overt that it was
almost artificial. She had learned early in life that the things
people valued about her were her looks, her body, her sexuality.
Without a father or a stable mother to help her learn to believe
in herself, she decided that sex was all she had to offer. Ironically for Marilyn, her aggressive sexuality became the flip side
of hiding out. Instead of hiding from sex, she used sex to hide
from herself.

LOVERS AND OTHER STRANGERS

Certain clichéd notions seem to surround fatherless daughters with regard to their sexual relationships. These include the fact that fatherless daughters prefer older men (Daddy), married men (Daddy in an oedipal triangle), and even women (lesbian lovers). Like most clichés, I found some truth in all of these notions. As Maggie Scarf said in her insightful book *Intimate Partners:* "How often, in the dawn of life, are we presented with certain kinds of problems which we attempt to recreate and to work upon, subsequently, with our partners. We seem to be uncannily *efficient* [Scarf's italics] when it comes to choosing partners who will help us get into situations that recapitulate earlier dilemmas that have never been successfully mastered. It is as if we were guided by a dizzyingly complex and yet remarkably precise internalized radar."

Older Men

In *Father Loss,* Elyce Wakerman states that she found only women who had lost their fathers in adolescence to be obsessed with older men. Among the women I talked to, I also found similar evidence, with some variation. Most of these women were daughters of fathers who had either died or deserted the family shortly before the girl had entered puberty or was at puberty. Also, the men they found attractive were usually ten to fifteen years older, not literally the age of their fathers (or a father substitute), but old enough so that the men often treated the women like adored children.

I also discovered that often these relationships were relatively fleeting. The fatherless daughter seemed to be working out some sort of emotional knot in relation to this particular man, and when she had resolved her feelings, she let the relationship go.

Sheila, whose father died when she was seventeen, describes a typical relationship with an older man: "I never dated in high school and dated very little in college. After I left college when I was living in DC, I had my first serious relationship with a man who was sixteen years older than I was. He was a very, very sweet man, . . . but I can't really say he was a father figure. He was older, but I don't know if that attracted me to him. I guess, in a way, he was a safe harbor for me. I broke it off very suddenly. Something woke up in me and I said, 'Nope, this isn't it. This isn't right.' And I just broke it off. I guess it was time for a serious commitment, and I suddenly realized the age difference was too huge. I think it was his fortieth birthday and I was only twenty-four, and somehow that just scared the heck out of me."

Married Men

The idea of the fatherless daughter in a passionate relationship with a married man is a cliché. In theory, it makes sense; a woman with unresolved oedipal issues seeks out a man who is in a similar situation as her dad; that is, he's married to "Mom." Depending on the level of psychological development of the daughter, she is probably stuck at either the earliest oepidal level (around age four) or at puberty.

Several of the women I interviewed had had highly sexual, important relationships with married men at some point in their lives. Most of these women had lost their fathers between the ages of nine and thirteen, and were equally divided between women whose dads had died and those whose dads had consciously abandoned them. Finally, although sometimes the married lovers were also older men, these women were frequently involved with married men who were more or less their own age. Not only were these men often the loves of their lives, but the relationships allowed them to work through unresolved oedipal issues, which accounted for the addictive craziness many of these affairs promoted.

For example, as Penelope, who had had a long relationship with Robert, an older, married man, said: "There was definitely an addictive thing for Robert and me. His wife was blond and blue-eyed, and my mother was blond and blue-eyed, and they were both named Elizabeth, and this apparently worked me into a frenzy. I was determined to get this man away from Elizabeth. Elizabeth's father had died young, too, so she basically fitted into the same pattern as I did. I was ruthless, in a way. I was ruthless because I was sure that if I had Robert, I would be happy forever."

Affairs with married men provide a number of useful illusions for the fatherless daughter—the illusion that she is involved in a relationship, the illusion that she is loved, the illusion that she has some control—when, indeed, her lover is not at liberty to either be involved with her or to truly love her, and she, most certainly, is not in control of herself or the relationship. Still, these illusions seem to provide fatherless daughters with both excitement and comfort.

Interestingly, affairs with married men also give fatherless daughters a place to hide. Sometimes it can be a sort of starter affair, which oddly enough can offer a form of safety. As Wendy, whose dad died when she was three, described: "With this married guy, it was great, because I knew from the start I really didn't want to marry him . . . and it was just my first grown-up affair. He was a little older, he was married, and he was a teacher at the school where I taught." As with many such relationships, Wendy found out that her lover was also seeing at least one other woman at the same time as he was seeing her, *and* while he was married. Although this revelation would have devastated Wendy at a later point in her development, it really didn't bother her all that much at that point in her life.

Another fatherless daughter, Nina, who herself is a therapist, doesn't quite buy the married man/Daddy cliché. She said: "I had a long affair with a married man. He was fourteen years older, but I don't think it was a Daddy thing. . . . Everybody says older man– married man–daddy thing. I think the most important reason that I was with this man was because he could ask nothing of me. A daddy—a parent—launches you. A married man keeps you from being launched as long as you stay in the relationship."

✌ ERIN ✌

Erin and I met on an afternoon in midsummer at her apartment in Gramercy Park in New York, where she had lived for many years. Her apartment was small but comfortable and welcoming with lots of books and a few pieces of nice furniture, carpets, and art. Erin herself was much like her apartment, attractive and comfortable. At the time of our meeting, she was in her late fifties, which surprised me because she looks and acts much younger. She is rather short and blond, but with a kind of regal bearing. Erin has a low voice, a warm, ready laugh, and was generous and thoughtful about telling me her story.

Erin came from a small, exclusive suburb of Chicago. She was the oldest of three children; her brother James was a year younger, and her brother Bob, three years younger. Erin's father, James O'Donnell, was a second-generation Irishman, born in 1922 into a working-class background in Chicago. Her mother, Hope, was an upper-middle-class girl, whom James married while they were both still attending Northwestern, where he had gone on the GI bill after fighting in Europe during World War II. After college, the couple settled in the same Chicago suburb where Hope had grown up, James landed a job at a large Chicago-based corporation, and they started a family. Within a few years, James was well established on a fast-track executive job, and they were enjoying the epitome of 1950s American life with three beautiful children, a lovely home, an enjoyable social life, and every expectation that this life would continue. Then James was killed in an automobile accident on a rainy night during the summer before Erin entered sixth grade.

"My dad's death was so shocking," said Erin. "Even at the time, we thought it was strange. That evening, my mom and dad had been fighting about something—my mom doesn't even remember what—and Daddy had to go out for some reason. The rest of us—my mom, my brothers, and I—were sitting in the den watching television. He did something he had never done before. He walked out the door, still obviously angry at my mom. We heard him start the car and then turn off the motor. He came back into the house and apologized to my mom for whatever it was that they had been fighting about and kissed her good-bye. Then he left, and within about half an hour, the police were at the door telling us that Daddy was dead. A guy driving a truck had just blindsided him.

"I think my dad died at a really pivotal time for me," Erin explained. It was obvious that she had given this subject considerable thought, and she later told me that she had had several years of psychotherapy. "I was ten when he died. That summer,

I had just started taking tennis lessons, and Daddy was eager for me to learn to play well. He loved to play tennis, and we even played together a couple of times. I think we were just beginning to have a more grown-up relationship, and then he was gone! . . . Also, after my dad died, I had a lot of issues with my mother."

At the time of her husband's death, Erin's mother, Hope, although a graduate of a prestigious university, had never worked a day in her life. But it soon became evident that Hope was going to have to get a job to support herself and her children. With the help of her father, who was well connected in the community, Hope got a job teaching first grade in a nearby elementary school, a job she would keep for the next ten years.

Hope had always been quite a beauty, the proverbial apple of her own father's eye. However, although exceptionally attractive and charming, Hope was also quite spoiled and self-centered.

Erin was, even at ten, a different sort of girl. She was always a popular child with lots of friends, but she wasn't considered beautiful; her claim to fame was her intelligence, her humor, and her friendly personality. In this regard, she was much more like her father, and her mother seemed to encourage this perception. As Erin would realize as she passed from childhood to puberty to adulthood, her mother had no interest in relinquishing her own role as the beauty.

As Erin began to be interested in boys and dating, her mother seemed to discourage her. She was cool and critical of the boys who appeared at the door or called the house, wanting to take Erin to the movies or a school dance. When Erin was fourteen or fifteen, she was devastated because a boy she liked, and who seemed to be interested in her, suddenly began taking out another girl. She returned from a party in tears, and her mother essentially ignored the entire episode. Before Erin reached the age of sixteen, she had learned to keep her personal problems to herself.

Jim and Hope's best friends, Carol and Dick Stevens, lived in the same town. During the first weeks after Jim's death, Carol and Dick were at the O'Donnell home frequently, and during the first summer after James's death, the family spent two weeks at Carol and Dick's beach house on Lake Michigan.

As the months passed, Dick began visiting the O'Donnell household frequently. He was in the construction business, so he would drop by during the day or early evening and have a couple of cocktails with Hope. One day, Erin happened to walk in on Dick and her mother kissing passionately. Hope laughed it off, but Erin was upset. From then on, Erin watched as her mother behaved in a decidedly flirtatious, sexual way with Dick, and it upset her even more.

On a couple of other occasions, Erin observed her mother flirting with the husbands of other family friends. These incidents, and Hope's ongoing relationship with Dick, angered and troubled Erin. She would occasionally have screaming fits, then go to her room and cry. Later, after she learned to drive, she would storm out of the house and drive around for hours. She tried talking about her feelings with her brothers, but their mother's behavior didn't appear to bother them. And as for Dick—well, they liked him a lot. Although she could not have articulated it at the time, her mother's behavior confused her. Her mother's affairs, whether brief or long term, were with men who were married to women who were supposedly her mother's friends. Erin didn't understand this.

By the time Erin was fifteen or sixteen, she was completely bewildered and inhibited with regard to boys and sex. At home, she seemed to be living in a sexual hothouse, with her mother acting out inappropriately with inappropriate men. With regard to understanding herself physically, emotionally, and morally, Erin was at sea. Although she had always been friendly and outgoing, she now became more subdued. When it came to dealing with the sexual attention of boys, Erin was clueless and finally gave up trying.

Beginning in junior high school, Erin developed secret crushes on certain teachers, usually men in their early thirties: men not quite old enough to be obvious father figures, yet considerably older than Erin. Fortunately, these crushes were played out only in Erin's mind. The only consequence was that Erin would work very hard in her classes to please her teachers, often getting A's in subjects like chemistry, which would not have interested her if she had not found her teacher so appealing.

Although Hope wanted Erin to go to Northwestern, Erin was determined to get as far away from home as possible and was accepted at Wellesley near Boston. Her secret teacher crushes continued as she began college, and as in high school, it helped her get better grades. During her sophomore year, however, Erin's roommate and good friend, Anne, began having a torrid affair with one of their professors, a much older married man. Erin was shocked and upsct; although she had continued to have crushes on various professors, it had never occurred to her to pursue a real relationship with any of them. Also, at some level, she knew she couldn't have handled it. Throughout her first two years of college, Erin dated casually but never had a significant boyfriend.

Two things happened after Erin's sophomore year in college. First, after eight years, Hope remarried. Her new husband, Dave, was a widower from a neighboring town with three children, all of whom were about the same ages as Erin and her brothers. Although initially Erin had trouble accepting her stepfather, she very soon realized that not only was he an exceedingly nice man, he was also giving her mother a stable, happy life. This helped Erin's relationship with her mother become easier, too.

The second pivotal event was that Erin decided to spend her junior year at Oxford University in England. She was not aware of it at the time, but her mother's remarriage had liberated her, and being far away from home freed her even more. She was relaxed, excited, and eager for adventure, and for the first time, she found herself easily attracting the attention of boys and men.

Everywhere she went, it seemed, she met a guy who asked her to go out, and she had a marvelous time.

Before too long, Erin started steadily dating another American student, John, and they soon started sleeping together. John was her first serious boyfriend and first lover, and the relationship initially threw her into an emotional tizzy. By Erin's own admission, her behavior toward John was a little heartless and insensitive.

"I liked John, but I wasn't in love with him," Erin says. "Yet sleeping with him seemed okay. Maybe it was because I felt sure that he cared about me. Also, this was the beginning of the 1960s sexual revolution, and my friends were involved in similar relationships. And what's more, it was pleasurable. Still, I had no idea what my moral values were, what my emotional and physical boundaries were, or even what I was looking for in a boyfriend. It was all free-floating emotion. Also, to my surprise, although I had been yearning for a steady boyfriend since high school, I now was not so sure I wanted to be tied down to one boy. I wanted to explore! After several months, I broke up with John. I wasn't very nice to him, I'm afraid."

For the remainder of her junior year in England, Erin enjoyed a free and fun social life. She also traveled extensively with friends.

Then, disaster: she got pregnant. To make matters worse, she got pregnant by a boy she had met casually one weekend while traveling in Italy. She did not realize that she was pregnant until she had returned from her trip, and, of course, the notion of contacting this boy and expecting him to accept responsibility was absurd. She found herself in a particularly ironic situation for a fatherless daughter: she was having a baby, but there was no father.

It was the mid-1960s, and abortion was not yet legal in either the United States or Britain, but the boyfriend of a close friend helped her arrange for an abortion in London.

"It was performed by a Hungarian GP in his office," says Erin, "with just the doctor and a male nurse present. The doctor was kind, but he warned me that he was not at liberty to give me any anesthetic. In the end, I didn't even take off my skirt. When the procedure was finished, the doctor, apologizing, insisted that I stand up and walk out the door right away, and I did.

"I walked a block or two to a wide boulevard, where I thought I could get a cab. As I turned, I saw the male nurse who had been with me just a few minutes before following me down the street. I started to wave to him, but he looked away and passed me by without acknowledging me. I've always wondered if he had been sent to follow me to make sure I got a cab safely. It all felt very strange and more than a little frightening."

Within a week, Erin was back home in Chicago, acting as if nothing had happened. "On the surface, I sailed through this ordeal with seeming aplomb. But inside, I was torn apart. But I didn't discuss it—I couldn't discuss it—with my family at all."

During Erin's senior year, she began dating a boy named Dan, whom she had dated casually before going to England. A junior at Yale, Dan was an intelligent young man with an easygoing disposition and a terrific sense of humor. At first, Erin wasn't serious about him, but as her senior year progressed, she began to feel that she was very much in love.

Dan made few sexual demands on her, and on the surface, this upset Erin a lot. "I was falling in love with him," Erin says, "but he didn't seem to feel the same way about me. I blamed myself—I thought I wasn't pretty enough or sexy enough or personable enough. You name it." However, at a deeper level, Erin came to realize that his sexual passivity suited her, given the trauma that she had just gone through in London. He was safe. And at this time in her life, she needed safety.

"Years later, I would seriously question why I clung to that relationship," Erin says now. "But at the time, I just couldn't let go."

After graduation, Erin and a girlfriend took the train to New York, and quickly got an apartment and jobs as assistant publicists at a book publishing house. Although she knew a few people casually, her first year in New York was the loneliest she had ever spent, and as a result, she clung even more to her relationship with Dan.

"In retrospect, I think he was at loose ends himself," says Erin. "He didn't know what he wanted to do professionally, and it was the height of the Vietnam era, and he was facing the draft. Like me, I suspect he saw that many of our friends were beginning married lives, and somehow marriage seemed like the right road." Dan ended up skirting the draft and going to graduate school at Columbia. And in the spring of 1970, he and Erin were married.

Within months of the marriage, Erin began to suspect that the marriage was wrong, probably for both of them. "I loved Dan," Erin said. "But I never felt that I excited him, particularly sexually. I tried everything—sexy nightgowns, losing weight, even counseling—but our sex life never got any better." Still, it took almost seven years for Erin and Dan to divorce. "I just couldn't seem to let him go," says Erin.

By the time the marriage dissolved, Erin was in her early thirties and had established herself as a respected publicist with a major publishing company. She was soon made a vice president and publicity director. Over the next several years, Erin dated frequently. By now, it was the early eighties, and people were open and free about sex. Erin believed that she was, too. She had her share of short, highly sexualized relationships. However, none of these relationships developed into something deeper. Either the men failed to pursue Erin, or Erin ended the relationship the moment the man indicated that he was interested in something more than sex.

But most tellingly, during the years following the breakup of her marriage, Erin had a number of troubling relationships with married men. One was with Mort, who had been a friend for some time and whose own marriage was breaking down. They actually had a very good relationship on many levels, and for the first time, Erin felt she was able to integrate friendship with a delightful sexual relationship. But when Mort's marriage finally ended, their relationship fell apart as well. After Mort,

Erin had a long romantic friendship with Alan, a much older married man, yet when his wife died and he appeared interested in finally marrying Erin, she demurred.

More than any of her women friends, Erin was the recipient of inappropriate passes by a number of men. On several occasions, husbands of good friends came on to her very aggressively. Erin was always caught off guard and did not respond well. "This happened at least three times that I can remember," Erin says. "These were all men I really liked. I enjoyed their company; I found them smart, funny, and fun. Perhaps they thought I was flirting with them. If I came across that way, it was unintentional. In one case, I had gone to the country house of my friend and her husband for the weekend, and he was so aggressive with me, I had to take the bus home a day early. My friendships with all these couples went up in smoke, as you might expect."

When Erin was about forty, she fell madly in love with a very powerful, well known politician, a man about fifteen years older than she was. They met when he was writing a book for her firm. The relationship was exciting and sexy, and both of them were very indiscreet. However, the affair lasted only a short time before he tearfully ended it because his wife had found out. He told Erin that his wife was about to leave him because of his unceasing affairs. Erin had thought he was in love with her as she was with him, and was dumbfounded to learn that not only did he care deeply about his wife, but Erin was not the only other woman in his life.

Erin was devastated by this relationship, but out of her embarrassment and hurt, something finally clicked for her. She came to understand that not only was she behaving in an adolescent way with men, her perceptions of men were extremely immature. Moreover, with regard to her relationships with married men, she empathized with the wife for the first time. Many times in the past, she had said, "I have no interest in hurting his wife," but this time she saw that regardless of whether her lover's wife found out about the affair or not, she was intruding in someone else's relationship.

And, of course, she finally connected the dots between her own behavior and her mother's long-ago affairs with Dick and others. "Somehow it had eluded me that having affairs with married men was wrong—that it was hurtful," Erin said. "I know that sounds sort of crazy. And maybe I was trying to vindicate my mother's behavior. I don't know. But finally I got it."

Erin is now in her early sixties. She has a comfortable life filled with work, friends, and travel. But she feels that at some levels, she has failed at two of life's most important facets. She regrets not having children, but more, she is sorry she has not been able to form a loving, committed relationship with a man.

"I suppose it's not over until it's over," Erin says. "I'd love to find someone and share our sunset years together. Maybe even be somebody's step-grandmother! It's just taken me a very long time to get here."

Erin believes that had her father been present during her adolescence, she would not have arrived at middle age with quite so many regrets.

"I think Daddy would have shown me how to relate to boys more easily," Erin says, "and he might even have helped me feel better about my own awkwardness. I would have felt protected. I think I would have been smarter about men."

Younger Men

Some of the fatherless daughters I interviewed were involved with much younger men, at least during certain periods of their development. Often relationships between older women and younger men are about sex. For the older woman, the young man is more lusty and potent; for the younger man, the older woman is more experienced. However, for fatherless daughters, I believe that relationships with younger men are a way to deal with sexual fear.

Suzy, who appeared much younger than her age and had indicated that she found sex invasive, also questioned the relatively young age of her boyfriends. "I don't know if it's something related to growing up without a father," Suzy said, "but my boyfriends have been younger than myself. I'm kind of afraid to go out with someone my age or older."

For Suzy, and I suspect most other fatherless daughters, dating younger guys was simply a way to keep her boyfriend at arm's length and under control.

Lesbian Lovers

Six of the women I interviewed (about 6 percent, or about the same percentage as the lesbian population nationwide) were in committed relationships with another woman. None of these women could say with absolute certainty that father loss had contributed to their sexual preference and to their desire to pursue a lesbian lifestyle. Ellen, who had been married and had two children, stated: "I have no idea if father loss had anything to do with my lesbianism. I mean, I know lesbians whose fathers have been important people in their lives. Choosing a lesbian lifestyle seemed very natural to me. It seemed natural in a way that being with men never felt. Never. Whenever I was with men, I always felt like I was acting, but I also realized that the sexual abuse in my family began before I knew who I was as a sexual being. I was programmed from the start."

Ellen had been sexually abused by her stepfather when she was about five or six. Actually, a few of the other lesbian fatherless daughters also hinted at sexual abuse from brothers or stepfathers, or, at least, fear of abuse, and I had the feeling that their deep fears led them to find more comfort and safety in relationships with women.

Still others talked of deep hurt not only from their fathers but from subsequent lovers. (Eleanor Roosevelt comes to mind. She apparently had at least one lesbian affair after learning of her husband's infidelity.)

Many lesbian women I interviewed said they had deep problems trusting men. Some admitted to preferring sex with a man but having an intimate relationship with a woman. "I have infinite trust in women," said Marsha. "I could never have that completely in men. Sexually I'm still attracted to men, but emotionally it's the trust component that is missing, because all the men in my life, in one way or another, let me down. They weren't there for long. They either left me like my father or they were drunks like my brothers. I couldn't count on them, whereas I could count on my mother. I knew no matter what problems I may have had with her, no matter what trouble I was in, whether she understood it or not, she would always be there and I could talk to her."

Others felt completely the opposite. Laura, a physician who had been married for several years before forming a long-term relationship with a female partner, spoke fondly about her ex-husband: "We had real intimacy, but it wasn't very sexy. We had sex, but it wasn't good sex. Since then, I have had infinitely better sex with women, but I don't know that I ever had more intimacy than I did with him."

Real Men

Obviously many fatherless daughters have trouble relating to real men. For these women, real men, with real problems, real personalities, and real feelings, just aren't that thrilling. Often in the course of a love affair, as soon as she glimpses the real man, the fatherless daughter is out the door and back on her search for the next emotional high.

However, for many fatherless daughters, once they are able to establish a mature relationship with someone who loves them in return, they have gone a long way toward getting over their feelings of low self-esteem and becoming loving, committed adults. For Terry, it was her boyfriend, Mike, whom she met during her junior year in college. "He changed my life," she says. "Our relationship began when I approached him at a Halloween party and I said to him, 'Before this night is over you have to dance with me.'" Terry and Mike went together for several years. For various reasons, they eventually broke up, but he remains one of her best friends. "He turned my life around. He was the first man who loved me unconditionally."

LOVE, MARRIAGE, AND DEEP COMMITMENT

One of my favorite philosophical discussions about the emotion we call love is found the in classic book *The Art of Loving* by psychologist Erich Fromm. What I like about Fromm's thesis is that he views love as an activity. No matter what sort of love he is discussing—brotherly love, motherly love, fatherly love, erotic love—the emotion involves choice, commitment, and activity with regard to the object of love. In particular, Fromm focuses on four qualities essential for mature love. As Fromm puts it:

> Care, responsibility, respect, and knowledge are mutually interdependent. They are a syndrome of attitudes which are to be found in the mature person; that is, in the person who develops his [or her] own powers productively, who only wants to have that which he has worked for, who has given up narcissistic dreams of omniscience and omnipotence, who has acquired humility based on the inner strength which only genuine productive activity can give.

Many fatherless daughters get stuck emotionally at the age they were when their father died or abandoned them. Most of them develop other aspects of their personalities—their intellectual lives, their professional lives, their friendships, other family relationships. But their sexual relationships with men are often inhibited in some way. A woman whose father died when she was an infant seemed very childlike in her romantic relationships. A woman whose dad died during her puberty behaved like a young teen. A woman whose dad died when she was two acted very withdrawn around men. A woman whose dad abandoned the family when she was seven or eight seemed to have less sexualized, more friendlike relationships. In general, fatherless daughters often have trouble integrating sex and love in a mature way.

Of course, a fatherless daughter's romantic experiences can be mitigated by any number of other factors. A woman whose father died when she was two may have had a loving and accepting stepfather, who, in effect, virtually negated her father loss. An eight-year-old whose father left may be lucky enough to fall in love with a particularly mature man when she is in her early twenties, and together they can work through her demons.

But most fatherless daughters have real difficulties when they fall in love. Annie, who at the time of our interview was finally in a secure marriage, said: "I often found myself drawn to men who weren't available in a way. They all showed a little bit of emotional aloofness. I always went after someone who wasn't quite there. Looking back on it now, I realize that it was probably me. I just hadn't been ready for a real relationship."

The Shock of Breaking Up

Everybody has problems negotiating the waves of romantic relationships, but for fatherless daughters, serious romantic relationships are often excessively fraught. The act of breaking up a love affair, a troublesome decision for most people, is often virtually impossible for a fatherless daughter. She may be crystal clear intellectually that a man is not right for her (or worse, is abusing her), but she cannot break up with him because the separation would force her to revisit the pain of her father's loss. She may not be conscious of the reason for her feelings, but she is well aware that the feelings are overwhelming.

Anita, a young woman whose dad died when she was twelve, felt the breakup of one of her first romances actually forced her into mourning for her father: "One of my first boyfriends in high school wasn't sure what he wanted to do with his life, so he broke up with me. It was horrible. I just couldn't believe that this had happened to me. It was such a sad, dark time for me, and then it hit me: Here I was at eighteen and it had taken me six years to experience my father's death! I hadn't really let myself feel much when he died. Not until I was eighteen and I lost this boyfriend did it hit me that the people I love, leave. The important men in your life don't always stick around. I was depressed for weeks, but then he wanted me back again, and by that time I didn't want him. It had been a fickle high school thing, and I was done with it. I had gone through my mourning."

⤳ LISA ⤶

For Lisa, a thirty-eight-year-old magazine editor, the ending wasn't quite so happy. She'd been in a pleasant though sexless marriage to an attractive lawyer a couple of years her senior. They lived in Manhattan with their two children, ages seven and nine, and everything was fine, or so she thought, until she met Peter, also married, one evening at a dinner party. "I don't know what came over me," she said. "There he was, this nothing-special guy, but on some level, way down deep, he reminded me of my father, and I just had to have him." For the next year, they began to talk on the phone a lot and have lunch together whenever they could. Then the seduction.

"I was never sure who seduced whom, but it was amazing, absolutely wild and loving and warm and crazy, and I was just lost. Since my own father had abandoned us for another woman and never looked back, the last thing in the world I wanted to do was to put my children into a similar situation, but I was obsessed. So my husband moved out, we divorced, and for the next three years I was caught up in the thrall of what ended up being a pretty destructive relationship.

"When Peter finally left me, as I was always terrified he would, I thought I was going to die. The kids were relieved, I think, because they would hear us fighting. Toward the end of the time we lived together, he had started becoming violent, and that scared them. It scared me, too, of course, but I was so insecure and so caught up in reliving the drama of losing my father, only trying to make it come out differently this time, that I had completely lost sight of the impact this was having not only on me but also on the people I cared most about. And worst of all, I kept thinking that it was my fault. If only I had been prettier, or richer, or cooler so that his constant flirting with other women wouldn't have bothered me so much—if only I had been more of what he needed, maybe he wouldn't have left.

"When I look back on it now and see what a nasty, narcissistic, womanizing man he was (just like Dad, actually, so I got that part right), I'm simply horrified. I think it all happened because I was so desperate to find someone like my father, get him to care about me and *not* to leave me. But I realize now that my father and Peter are both the kind of men who *always* leave women. The only answer for me was to finally get to the place in my life where I truly realized that I was okay, it wasn't my fault that my father left, I couldn't have done anything about it no matter what, and even though there may be a lot wrong with me, I really don't deserve to be treated that way by my dad, or Peter, or anybody.

"The other thing that happened is that after I finally got some distance on my relationship with Peter, I realized that he wasn't really such a good person, to put it mildly. He was funny, zany, and gifted in the charm department, but his lying was pathological, his womanizing obsessive, and his physical violence with me was the most telling of all.

"Then I started thinking about my dad. I was twelve when he left us and my brother was only nine. We were living in Illinois and he went to California, ostensibly to look for a new job. This seemed normal enough, as he was always changing jobs. But this time was different. He never came back. Not only that, he never called, he never wrote, he never even sent my brother or me a birthday card. It was as if we had not existed for him, and in fact, he lived the rest of his life as if we hadn't.

"My mom decided to deal with this by pretending that it hadn't happened, too, so as you can imagine, things at home were pretty surreal when I was a teenager. We all pretended, sort of, that Dad was just away, and the funny thing was that I still idealized him, mostly because I just couldn't cope with what had happened.

"But when I got older and realized what a creep he'd been, the anger really kicked in for a while. Ultimately, though, I began to realize that both of these men were pretty weak and unhappy and that there was nothing I could do about it. I just had to let it go. Of course, it's one thing to say this and quite another to feel it. It took me years, but I finally got it."

The Paradox of Commitment

Fatherless daughters long for love, are obsessed with love, are sometimes almost merciless in their pursuit of love, like Lisa. Often, though, when love is finally given to them, they have a serious problem committing to the relationship. Penelope, who had an intense decade-long relationship with a married man, was ruthless in her quest of him and ultimately failed to form a secure, committed relationship with him. When he finally left his wife and moved in with her, the relationship quickly stalled and began to disintegrate.

I regret to say my own marriage was much the same. I began dating my ex-husband, Tom, when I was a senior in college. I fell in love with him, and, to this day, don't doubt that I loved him deeply. However, at several junctures in our relationship it was clear that we were not ready to marry. Our marriage lasted for seven years, but almost from the beginning, my commitment to it was shallow and immature, although this was not clear to me at the time.

I came to realize that many of the troubles we had in our marriage were related to issues surrounding the loss of my dad, particularly problems about money and financial support and children.

The years of our marriage were characterized by a constant state of turmoil. We were married in 1970, and several times during the first four years of our marriage (graduate school, army reserves, searching for a job, changing jobs), I ended up having no doubt that my paycheck was essential to our livelihood. To my astonishment, I resented it deeply. I loved my career, accepted that I needed to earn money, but I was stunned by my strong wish to feel supported by a man financially.

This is not to say that Tom was a deadbeat; far from it! He was ambitious and hardworking. Within a couple of years of our divorce, he became the president of a major educational publisher. However, during the years we were together, we were still young people getting settled and struggling. What I couldn't see was that eventually this situation would change. I also could not express any of these feelings to Tom. I'm not even certain I understood what was going on myself.

At the moment our marriage began shifting to a more intimate level, most particularly when we began to discuss having children, I simply could not move forward. I was desperately afraid of being left alone and abandoned, particularly with children, as my mother had been. Again, I was not consciously aware of these feelings until long after our divorce. But they were real and very frightening.

Tom and I separated after four years. I attributed the break-down of our marriage to any number of difficulties, but they were just superficial symptoms of much deeper problems, not the least of which was that I had much growing up to do. Still, like many father-less daughters, I continued to cling to Tom, and it took another three years for us to finally divorce.

The Secret to Happiness

Very early in my research for this book, I began to conclude that the fatherless daughters who performed the best in life, who managed to heal their pain, who seemed the most productive and happy, were those who for whatever reason were able to establish and maintain a successful marriage. (I include lesbian partnerships in this state-ment.) Also, at a certain point, I came across a statement made by the esteemed sociologist Judith S. Wallerstein in her book *Second Chances,* a landmark study about the effects of divorce on children. This state-ment was part of Wallerstein's explanation of her famous concept of the "sleeper effect," the debilitating anxiety experienced by daughters of divorce years after the event.

As Wallerstein says, fear of commitment and obsessive jealousy "rise to prominence as young women [who are daughters of divorce] move into later adolescence and young adulthood, when the devel-opmental task is to establish an intimate, loving relationship." I was riveted by the concept of the sleeper effect, but for me, the most star-tling words here were *developmental task*. I understood that com-mitment was a problem for fatherless daughters, but somehow, I had failed to comprehend the importance of creating an intimate relationship.

Still, despite all the evidence of problems with love and commit-ment, many fatherless daughters marry happily. Despite fears (like my own of ending up as a single parent), they have children. How some of my interviewees were able to put together satisfying mar-riages and raise children successfully was sometimes confusing even to them. Very often, they had gotten married young, had children young, and just stuck it out. Or, by a stroke of luck, they had married a man who was able to help them face their father-loss demons. Many of the women had pursued psychoanalysis and were fortunate enough to have found an intelligent and empathetic therapist.

For whatever reason, these women were able to push through their fears, inhibitions, and conflicts. Perhaps it was simply that they had had to learn to care about someone other than themselves. As Erich Fromm might express it, they were able to show care, responsibility, respect, and knowledge not only for their husbands but for their children and themselves.

9. THE DILEMMAS OF WORK

One of my failings as a human being, in my own estimation, is that I never learned to do anything except work.

—Angela Lansbury, actress and fatherless daughter

It has never occurred to me that I would *not* work. The idea that I would always work, that I would have a career, was hardly even a conscious decision on my part. What's more, I don't know when the notion entered my unconscious, although I suspect it was very shortly after my father died. I remember when I was in seventh grade, two years after my dad's death, I wrote an essay about how much I wanted to be a journalist, so not only was the concept of a career already firmly in place for me, but I was fairly clear about the direction I wanted that career to take.

I'm also certain the notion of a career had something to do with my mother's influence. She went to work shortly after my father's death, although previously she had been a traditional 1950s stay-at-home mom. She had graduated from college and taught school for a couple of years before she married, but from the moment of my oldest brother's birth in 1942, she stayed at home. (Until well into the 1950s, married women were not allowed to teach in the public schools in the town where I grew up.)

After my father's death, money was scarce and my mother needed a job quickly. For a few years, she worked as a secretary in a nearby junior high school, a job she kept until my youngest brother finished grade school. Then she renewed her teaching license, and taught

English and sewing in a junior high school in the city of Cleveland until we children were launched. By then, she had remarried, but she felt she should pay for her own children's education.

I suppose at some point I entertained the thought of teaching English, like my mother had done. I was an English major in college, adored literature, and was urged by my college advisor to get a teaching certificate, but the idea of teaching *Hamlet* to a classroom full of bored tenth graders was anathema to me. I wanted something much more exciting—I wanted to be in the publishing business in New York City! The realities that publishing didn't pay well and that actually finding a job could be a risky venture for a girl from the Midwest didn't enter my mind. I wanted to escape, and no one could convince me otherwise.

In the end, it turns out that work for me was always much more than just a job. In fact, it has even been much more than just a career. As a woman whose financial provider was swept away in a heartbeat while I was still a child and whose mother was required to assume sole financial responsibility for her family, the issues surrounding work and career took on a deeper meaning than they do for most women. As a fatherless daughter, my career is a large part of my identity. But I have found that many paradoxes surround that strong identification with work.

The Paradoxes of Work

Like many women of my age and background, I was influenced by the last vestiges of middle-class mores of the 1950s ("Find a husband at college or else find a fun job, but get married by the time you're thirty!"). At the same time, I was also strongly affected by the feminist movement of the 1960s and 1970s. ("You can do it all; you can have it all!" Incidentally, it is interesting to note that several well-known women associated with the feminist movement are fatherless daughters, including Germaine Greer, Gloria Steinem, Bella Abzug, Geraldine Ferraro, and Susan Sontag.) Most of all, my attitudes toward my adult work life reflect the emotional effects of father loss. On one hand, without being fully conscious of it when I first started working, I was adamant about providing for my own security. I knew in the deepest part of my being that no man was ever going to take care of me financially. I had to work; I had to earn my own money.

On the other hand, despite this powerful need to provide for myself, I did not choose a safe, practical route. Instead, after college, I moved to New York City (one of the most expensive places to live on the planet) and promptly got a job at *Time* magazine. Glamorous, yes. High paying? No way! I was unbelievably naive about money. During the early years I lived in New York, I constantly chastised myself because I simply could never make ends meet. Only years later did I discover that many girls were subsidized by their parents: Their rent was paid by Dad; their bills from Saks or Bloomingdale's were sent to their parents' home; they were receiving a nice check every month from Grandfather's trust fund. This certainly was not the case for me.

Nor was I practical. I could have taken a hard look at my prospects and chosen a more lucrative career, like banking. I could have moved to a less expensive city. I might even have set my sights on a wealthy husband. But I chose none of these options; indeed, I never even considered them.

Instead, I exhibited a number of paradoxical attitudes that I saw exhibited again and again in my talks with other fatherless daughters. Because I had had no father, I was intent on providing for myself. However, for the same reason, I had no voice of authority telling me that I should be doing something more practical or advising me to make more financially appropriate decisions, given the reality of my situation. But the truth is, although I needed advice, I probably wouldn't have listened to it. I wasn't used to having a man tell me what to do, and I wouldn't have welcomed it or appreciated it. Also, although I had a strong wish to have a career in book or magazine publishing, I was timid about competing or asserting myself, particularly around men.

The ultimate paradox emerged after I married when I was twenty-four. During the first years of our marriage, we were in a constant state of flux. My husband, Tom, was in graduate school, then in the army reserves for six months, then looking for a job in New York, then changing his own career. During the times when he was unemployed, I supported us, or, at least, it was expected (by both of us, by the way) that I contribute financially. To my amazement, that expectation made me furious, although I was unable to articulate it at the time. I wanted to be supported financially! (And probably every other way, too.) And I was bewildered by my anger.

It turns out that my paradoxical outlook with regard to work is remarkably common among fatherless daughters. I observed a number of issues regarding work and career among the fatherless daughters I interviewed, quandaries that I believe are the direct result of father loss. These include:

- A wish for a career coupled with resentment about having to work
- A need to earn your own income coupled with childlike notions about money and financial responsibility
- A desire for financial security coupled with a propensity for choosing risky professions
- A quest for glamorous, attention-grabbing careers coupled with a strong need to hide
- A strong drive to succeed professionally coupled with confusion regarding how to compete effectively in the workplace
- An overly adoring attitude toward authority figures—particularly men—coupled with resentment about being told what to do
- A desire for a balanced life coupled with difficulties integrating work with marriage, family, and private life

I NEED TO WORK, BUT I WANT MY HUSBAND TO SUPPORT ME

Margaret, whose dad died when she was eleven, describes her attitude toward work: "When my father died, what his loss said to me was, 'You better start looking out for yourself because you can't depend on a man.' So, I had a tremendous work ethic."

Margaret also remembers being influenced by her mother: "It's very funny, since I've felt a lot of negative stuff about my mother. But she did give me some great advice. When I was about seven, I remember standing by the pantry door in our house in New Jersey, and she said, 'There are three things that I'm going to tell you: You've got to learn to type; you have to learn to drive a car; and don't ever share a bank account with anyone.' And did I remember that? Yes indeedy! I learned to type, I learned to drive a car, and I always had my own money. That's why I can take care of myself."

Margaret's statement that she knew she would have to support herself is remarkably typical among fatherless daughters. However, equally typical is the sometimes subconscious but equally strong wish to be supported by a man. In some cases, this wish kicks in almost from the moment a father dies or leaves. In Margaret's case, although she was accepted at a top-level university and did well, she chose to marry after her freshman year. Still, she managed to finish college while often holding a part-time job; established a career in banking and worked long past normal retirement age; and married two more times, although she always chose men who either had low-paying jobs or serious financial problems.

"I have never felt that I could rely on a man to support me," Margaret explains. "Since the age of eleven, when my dad died, I have never been supported by a man. Even when I was married, I was earning half our income and sometimes supporting us. I think I believed that no one could love me enough to want to support me. This made me furious!"

When Joan was twelve, her father literally went out for a quart of milk and never returned. Although Joan's manner is more reserved than Margaret's, she clearly feels much the same: "I could never believe that anyone would want to support me financially because my father did not support me. I've always been afraid to allow a man to support me because he might leave, and not only will I have to endure that loss all over again, I'll be left destitute. This is my definition of love: Taking care of me financially. Period. But, you know, when I think back on the way my father just walked out one day and never looked back, it's pretty clear that he didn't love me much. As a result, I've never felt I could allow a man to support me."

CHILDLIKE ATTITUDES TOWARD MONEY

A childlike attitude toward money is sometimes closely related to the paradox of wanting to support yourself while craving support from a man (father). I saw this more frequently among fatherless daughters whose father died or deserted the family before his daughter turned ten.

Sandy tells of her own expectations that came into play during her dad's last illness when she was six: "One day, the aide who was taking care of my dad [during his last illness] took a napkin and made me this little nurse's cap, and he said that I could be the nurse. I swear, from the time I was six until the time I was applying to college, I always said I want to be a nurse. I never thought about how I was going to support myself, because my idea was that I was going to marry someone who had limitless resources, *limitless* resources. I was going to live in a palace and I was going to work for free. I was never going to have to charge any money for my services because I was going to have somebody else support me. Oh, absolutely!"

This magical attitude toward money and financial support frequently came up among fatherless daughters who actually were married to affluent men, who, in fact, were supporting them very well. Several of these women lived stunningly affluent lifestyles, yet considered themselves to be primary contributors to the family income, although they actually held relatively low-paying jobs, such as substitute teachers, photographers, or other artisans. They somehow didn't see that the income they were generating couldn't possibly support three houses, a couple of luxury automobiles, their children's college education, and two or three nice vacations every year. Because they might pay for their own clothing or never have to ask their husband for spending money, they somehow deduced that they supported the family.

Other fatherless daughters were just plain irresponsible about money, in a remarkably determined way. Although they had jobs— and sometimes very well-paying jobs—they were chronically late paying their basic bills, refused to save for retirement, and spent uncontrollably on vacations, expensive clothes, and other luxuries. These childlike attitudes toward money signal many of the emotional problems that plague many fatherless daughters: fears regarding dependency, problems with trust, and, in some cases, an obdurate kind of anger.

SECURE JOBS VERSUS RISKY PROFESSIONS

In her book *Father Loss,* Elyce Wakerman found that most fatherless daughters looked for secure professions. As Wakerman says, "Fatherless women are a hardworking group, leaning toward salaried, steady employment that involves interaction with and assistance to others." Many of the women I interviewed also showed a similar inclination and sought careers as teachers, nurses, lawyers, and psychotherapists.

At the same time, paradoxically, I was struck by the number of fatherless daughters who were writers, artists, musicians, and most particularly, actresses. Here, for example, is a short list of actresses who are fatherless daughters: Myrna Loy, Bette Davis, Joan Crawford, Jean Harlow, Lucille Ball, Angela Lansbury, Kim Hunter, Marilyn Monroe, Sophia Loren, Rene Russo, Barbra Streisand, Ellen Burstyn, Jodie Foster, and Julia Roberts. Many of these women were required to work to support their families from a very young age and continued to do so throughout their lives.

What could be more risky than a writer's, a painter's, or an actor's life? What's interesting, too, is that many of the fatherless daughters who become artists are convinced that had their fathers been around, they would not have been able to pursue their artistic endeavors.

"I remember my father didn't always approve of what I wanted to do," says Sheila, whose dad died when she was seventeen. "He didn't approve of my pursuing a musical career. It wasn't safe, and he wanted me to pursue something very secure. He said that if I wanted to be a musician, I would have to learn to type, which is funny, because I did work my way through college by being a secretary. But had he lived, I don't know whether I would have been able to major in music or not."

◃ MARTHA ◃

Martha is a painter and art professor who grew up in central Canada, but now lives in a wonderful apartment on the Bowery in New York City with her husband, Carl, who is also an artist. She was thirteen when her father died, changing her overnight from a well-brought-up daughter of English parents to a tough, troubled teen, and finally to a respected artist and teacher.

"My dad was a doctor," she explained when I sat down in the living room of her sunny loft. "He went to his office one night, and suddenly he died. There is some vagueness attached to what actually happened. Different people in the family seem to have different ideas about what happened, but I think that he just shot an air bubble into his vein. Basically [he] gave himself an aneurysm. My father had been abusing drugs and alcohol for a long time, and on the afternoon of the night he died, my mom and older brother had finally confronted him about this. From what I understand, they said, 'You've got to do something about this. We just can't live this way anymore.' So things had obviously reached some kind of critical state. And he left the house that evening and we never saw him again. He went to the office and killed himself. He was only forty-seven.

"My father's relationship with his children was not great. There were four of us, my older brother David and my younger sister and brother Fiona and Andrew. I actually had a tortured relationship with him and was stunned by his death, but my sister remembers feeling like a weight had been lifted off her shoulders, and my next oldest brother remembers feeling relieved as well. You know, he just didn't feel bereft. And my older brother, the one who knew our father the best, never talks about it. I think my dad's death was the hardest on him, definitely.

"Everything really started to fall apart between my father and me when I hit puberty. It probably dovetailed with his drinking getting heavier, and he would be very cruel to me at times. He was remote and weird and very detached.

"I guess he felt he should explain to me about sex, so he asked me to come to his office. He was very stern as usual. He told me to pull down my pants, and I was only twelve and pretty scared about what he was going to do. He put on a plastic glove and stuck his finger up my vagina, and said, 'That's where your vagina is.' And then he drew a little drawing on a pad of paper and said, 'This is what happens.' It was all very clinical and distant. I came out of there and thought, What was that all about?

"Right after his death, I knew my childhood was over. I was only thirteen, but any feeling that adults were in charge, or knew more than I did, or had control over me, was gone. I was furious! I thought to myself: Nobody's ever going to tell me what to do ever again. Over the years, of course, I've calmed down, but at that age, my rage gave me the guts to go my own way completely and suffer the consequences.

"For my mom, the pain of my father's death was just indescribable. I had never seen her lose control like that. She was like a ghost. All the life just went out of her, and not long afterward, we moved from Edmonton to Vancouver. Looking back on it, I think this was probably a mistake, because we didn't know anybody in Vancouver except Dad's parents. She did finally manage to get a job, though, as an activity therapist in a local hospital, and she worked there until she was seventy-two. It was a good career for her because it brought her out of herself and helped her realize that the craziness we were all going through as teenagers was no different from other people's craziness."

Martha managed to put herself through college and art school, and after a series of rocky romances, she finally met and married Carl, and she gives him all the credit for helping her finally to heal and to resolve the anguish associated with her father's death.

"I would have had a very different life if my father hadn't killed himself," she says. "A very different life. There were plans for my brothers. It's not that I think there were no plans for me, but I think the idea was that I should get some sort of education and get married and have children. And probably be an occupational therapist, or something like that. I think they wanted a very conventional life for me, and the irony of it was that there were times when I was a teen that my mother was simply happy that I wasn't in jail. The fact that I was so rebellious and independent and that I became an artist would have undone my dad.

In fact, I don't think I could have become an artist if my dad hadn't died."

When I asked Martha if she felt that the death of her father affected her paintings, her reply was, "Oh, yes, very definitely. There was my personal story, and then there was also this idea that the beginning of the twentieth century, there was a lot of industrial architecture that took place on the edges of most cities.

"I'm fascinated by the relationship between machines and human beings. It continues to be very, very complicated. But the way that they were painted was sort of allegorical in a way. And there was a feeling of absence, like the feeling I have about my father. And that's the only way I can describe it. I know it. I know where it comes from, but I don't think that anyone else would, just by looking at the paintings.

"There is a kind of sadness about these places. I would tramp around them, climb over the No Trespassing signs, and do drawings and paintings. I think there's a feeling of an absence or a void that was so powerful in my life for a long time. Sometimes they are blackly humorous. The humor was never there in the earlier paintings, and now the humor is there. That started to be possible about ten years ago. I just began to see the humor in all this.

"Sometimes I still feel sad about my father, though. I thought about him every day until a few years into my relationship with Carl. I went back to the city where I grew up for the first time recently. It was a kind of surreal experience. I don't know how it helped, but it did sort of weirdly help in some odd way. It was as if I was finally able to tie things up. I went to all the pit stops: I went to our old neighborhood; I went to my father's office building; I went to our church.

"There were a couple of times when I was really overwhelmed with sadness. But I was there with Carl, which was great, and I felt like I'd overcome a lot of what had happened. I think if I'd gone back at any other time in my life, it might have been really shattering in a way, but this time it felt like I wasn't interested in it anymore. It was done. I'm in my late forties. I don't want to think about this anymore. So that was a good feeling. I was there with someone I love, and I felt like I just want to go on with my life now, I've paid my dues, or I've done my time, and now I can just let it go."

STUNNING ACCLAIM VERSUS THE DESIRE TO HIDE

Many fatherless daughters have a strong desire to be highly successful at their chosen career. They don't just want to land a job as a teacher at a local high school or win an internship at a nonprofit organization; they want to bring down the house on Broadway in their first show like Barbra Streisand or be nominated for an Academy Award after their first film like Angela Lansbury. In a way, this desire for great public acclaim is a quest for the unconditional love and adoration they were denied by the loss of their fathers. Needless to say, this kind of success doesn't happen to most people, but many fatherless daughters overachieve to compensate for their emotional demons. At the same time, they may run up against major problems with self-esteem if they fail in their quest, which in turn can force them to retreat from ambitious pursuits or to hide.

Problems with low self-esteem plague many of us, but lack of self-confidence can be uniquely inhibiting for fatherless daughters. Since no father was there to guide them (or catch them if they fell) as they were growing up, many believe they have no tools with which to succeed as adults. They may start out in their careers with apparent confidence, but the moment they hit a bump in the road, they lose all hope and leave the track entirely.

Amy, whose dad died when she was a baby, is a fascinating example. A strikingly beautiful woman and gifted actress, she started out in her late teens getting lots of ingenue roles in plays in both Chicago and New York. In her mid-twenties, she hit an inevitable dry patch. The months she spent without work aroused deep feelings of dependency and loss. At that juncture, she married her current boyfriend, had two children in quick succession, and gave up not only acting but pursuing any profession at all.

"I haven't committed to a career," Amy says. "My interests are all within the artistic arena, unfortunately, but I also think that I could have gone into a more practical area, if I had been committed enough. I think I'm bright and I could have done practically anything, but I didn't, I guess because I was afraid to go out there and do it."

In contrast, father loss sometimes works to a woman's advantage. She knows that since she had to fight to survive after the loss of her father, she can do it again. (I found this to be more prevalent among women who had lost their fathers after puberty.) Sheila, for example, felt the restraints of low self-esteem with regard to her wish to be a violinist, but she fought her demons ferociously.

"I struggled with low self-esteem," she confesses. "But I always fought it whenever it reared its head. I just said, 'No, no, no, I'm not going to throw my life away.' I could have become a secretary; I could have taken that road, especially when times were tough at school and I might have left. But I remember making the conscious choice that I just wanted something better."

Sheila was also mature and realistic about her talent. "It was hard to accept that I wasn't the major talent that I wanted to be," she says. "I got into U-Mass. as a probationary student. That was really humiliating, but I squeaked by. Raw talent is one thing, and some people have loads of it, but I also think that talent has to be tempered with a lot of other things, like a willingness to work hard. I've seen people with enormous talent but no discipline. It's about talent, but it's also about strength of will and character. I'm talented enough, but I really put everything I had into school, and that's why I ended up doing okay. Because I had such low self-esteem, I think I was driven to prove myself."

Despite problems with low self-esteem, a surprising number of fatherless daughters do seek glamorous careers that offer public acclaim, particularly, as I said earlier, in the world of acting. In certain ways, success as an actor is a perfect art form for a fatherless daughter because along with the potential for public acclamation, acting, by the nature of the work, allows her to hide.

W. Hugh Missildine, M.D., in his groundbreaking book *Your Inner Child of the Past,* describes this paradox, which he calls the "security of neglect."

The childhood of persons who suffered from neglect usually reveals a father who somehow wasn't a father and a mother who somehow wasn't a mother. Thus, in adult life, *the neglected "child of the past" maintains the security of this familiar emptiness.* [The italics are mine.] The relationships of persons who suffered from neglect in childhood resemble those of an actor to his audience. In childhood such a person may have discovered that he could win . . . momentary attention and love, through his achievement. In such circumstances a child learns to expect nothing but applause. More than momentary warmth and love do not exist. . . .

Closeness threatens the security of neglect on which his "child of the past" has been nourished. To such a person, closeness is frightening, binding, and entrapping. Many such people, particularly women, are drawn into theatrical and movie work because, in this work and atmosphere, they can create a fantasy identity. Their inner feelings about themselves are so despairing that they do not feel they can pay attention to these feelings. As one such woman once put it: "When you're a nobody, the only way to be a somebody is to be somebody else."

DEALING WITH COMPETITION

Fatherless daughters very often do not know how to compete effectively in the workplace. Although they are often highly competitive (often without realizing it), paradoxically when they become aware that they must make a straightforward drive toward success, they are sent into a tailspin. Competition with a woman can arouse unresolved oedipal feelings surrounding Mom; competition with a man is so terrifying and unthinkable that it is not even considered or made conscious.

Marilyn Monroe is a striking example of a woman who was actually a fierce (and successful!) competitor, but she could be thrown for a loop if forced to realize that she was in a serious horse race for a role with another actor. If a hint of competition became apparent, such as with another equally beautiful and famous actress such as Jane Russell or Lauren Bacall, Marilyn reverted to a vulnerable, childlike personality.

Marilyn romanticized men often to the point of not seeing them as real people. This happened in her love life as well as in her professional relationships. It was not a calculated form of flattery (as it would be for a woman who was aware that she needed to compete using every asset she had), although the objects of Marilyn Monroe's adoration were no doubt flattered. Instead, it was honest, albeit usually unrealistic, hero worship on Marilyn's part. The problems emerged when Marilyn got a glimpse of the real person who existed under her cloud of godliness, or more specifically, unconditional fatherly love. Then she would become enraged and devastated, and act out in highly neurotic ways. This became strikingly clear in her professional relationship with Laurence Olivier during the production of the only film they made together, *The Prince and the Showgirl.*

Shortly after her marriage to Arthur Miller, Marilyn and Miller went to London to work with Olivier, who was both starring in and directing the film. Initially Marilyn was thrilled and flattered to be working with such a theatrical icon as Olivier. During their first few meetings, she cast him in the romantic and fatherly role that she always placed on the men she admired. As Miller said in his biography *Timebends,* "She had idealized Olivier as a grand artist without egoistic envy of her, a kind of 'father' who would think only of safeguarding her."

But Olivier turned out to be patronizing and critical of Marilyn, and Marilyn ultimately suspected that he was trying to sabotage her performance. Marilyn responded to this competition as she had done in her other films like *Bus Stop* and *Seven Year Itch.* She was constantly ill, compulsively late or absent on the set, and sent the whole production into chaos. At home, she could not sleep at night and kept Arthur up as well. It was torture for everyone.

As Miller put it, "What gradually began to dawn on me through all this friction [with Olivier during the filming of *The Prince and the Showgirl*] was her expectation of abandonment all over again . . . if she was so opposed, she could not be loved."

PROBLEMS WITH THE BOSS

Everybody is nervous around the boss. The boss holds your professional fate in his or her hands, so understandably everybody is a little frightened of this person. However, fatherless daughters bring an extra element into play with regard to authority figures in the workplace. A male boss is clearly a father figure, and fatherless daughters know that fathers can't be counted on, often don't care about them, and worst of all, can leave them high and dry. As a result, dealing with authority figures in the workplace arouses all the emotional issues that also emerge in their personal relationships with men, particularly fear of abandonment, anger, overly romantic hero worship, problems with dependency and trust, and a lack of clarity about boundaries.

As with love relationships, these emotional legacies of father loss are played out slightly differently for women who have lost their fathers to death than for women whose fathers abandoned them. The woman whose father died tends to be timid and awkward around male bosses. This is certainly true of me. I have long been envious of women—usually women who were adored by their fathers—who know how to be flirtatious in fun-loving, nonsexual ways with male authority figures. I'm not talking about the sleeping-your-way-to-the-top situation; I'm merely pointing out that some women know how to be very natural with their bosses, which in turn takes the heat off.

For the woman whose father abandoned her, if she doesn't like or respect her boss, confrontation and rage is more likely to rear up, which obviously can lead to job loss. But if she likes her boss, her respect can lead to unrealistic adoration, which can skew her professional opinion of him and may even lead to a romantic relationship, which professionally would probably not be good for her.

For many fatherless daughters, another paradox that emerges around authority figures is a strong feeling of wanting a boss (father) to help them coupled with an intense resistance to having anyone (particularly a man) tell them what to do. Since they didn't have a father during their developmental years, they are clueless about men, particularly how men behave in authority. When a boss says, "Get me a cup of coffee" or "Have that report on my desk by five," they bristle.

Deep down they resent the assumption that this man may have some kind of power over them.

The biggest problem in the professional lives of fatherless daughters is to learn how to accept and respect men in authority, not see them as either romantic possibilities or domineering ogres. These women must learn to compete effectively.

When the boss is a woman, most of those who work for her see her as a mother figure to some extent. But for fatherless daughters, a mother figure/female boss can have a special correlation. A fatherless daughter's real mother may have had too much power. She may have been overly intrusive or negligent, supercritical or completely absent, tyrannically strong or drainingly weak. In any case, a female boss is a woman with absolute control over her, however it is manifested, and there's no father to mitigate the situation.

THE QUEST FOR A BALANCED LIFE

Then there's the need to have a balanced life. Freud said, "Work and love . . . love and work, that's all there is," and that the goal of successful psychoanalysis was to allow people to create a balanced life. For fatherless daughters, it is sometimes not so easy to put work, love, and the pleasures of life together in a balanced way.

Actress Angela Lansbury, who had to work from the time she was a teenager in order to support her family, has said: "One of my failings as a human being, in my own estimation, is that I never learned to do anything except work. Really. Keep house and work, that's what I know how to do. Play? I don't know how to play. Never have. Just don't know how to do it. It's a failing, as far as I'm concerned. I feel as if I've missed a hell of a lot. It all goes back, I suppose, to early years of having responsibilities foisted upon me by certain events. My mother's widowhood. I just always had to be a responsible person."

Lansbury has also observed that "Having that rock [her talent, her work] at the center has been my salvation, because even though to outward appearances mine has been a life filled with success and happiness and joy and laughter and attainment, what was going on behind the apparent joys and happiness was in fact a war of turmoil;

in some instances the terrible tragedy of good intentions and having to deal with that in my own private life—our private life. The only way I could deal with it was by having this rock [work] which represented stability."

Work can serve as a stabilizing factor in life, as well as provide a sense of accomplishment. However, because of a fatherless daughter's strong need to provide for herself, work can become a substitute for life and love. The balancing act of work, family, friends, and fun often can feel out of reach. Since she has had to rely on herself for much of her life, self-reliance, often to the exclusion of intimate relationships, is what makes her comfortable.

All of the emotional problems particular to fatherless daughters follow them into the workplace. They often bring their fear of abandonment, anger, feelings of low self-esteem, and problems with dependency and appropriate boundaries right along with them. Some have a tendency to overachieve (since they feel that their worth is measured only by their accomplishments), whereas others underachieve (because they are so frightened, they need to hide). The workplace can be the best place of all to begin to deal with these problems, as long as a career does not replace other aspects of life. Often, though, it takes years for women to feel comfortable in their career, to let go of the old, self-defeating behaviors, and to appreciate themselves for who they really are.

PART IV

COMING TO TERMS

———◆———

10. MOURNING

Forever [is] a difficult concept for anyone to grasp. The fact that we will never see that person again is the core of the grief and pain.

—William Kroen, *Helping Children Cope with the Loss of a Loved One*

Mourning is a tricky business for a young girl who has lost her father. In some cases, she is too young to fully understand the meaning of his death or departure. In other cases, while she may be old enough to understand the concept, she may not comprehend the ramifications of her father's loss as it relates to her and her family. Also, for a multitude of reasons, she may be prevented from expressing her feelings and working through her grief, and as a result, she may not come to terms with her father's loss until she is well into adulthood, if ever.

In the late 1960s, Elisabeth Kübler-Ross, the famed medical doctor and psychiatrist, wrote a remarkable book that was to become a classic in the field of understanding death. *On Death and Dying* describes her work with terminally ill patients over a three-year period. Through her discussions with dying patients, Kübler-Ross was able to define five stages of dying, or the emotional aspect of the dying process:

1. Denial
2. Anger
3. Bargaining
4. Depression
5. Acceptance

While Kübler-Ross's study focused on the emotional experience of dying patients, her stages of dying also aptly described the emotional experiences of family members and friends who experience the death of a loved one; that is, the mourners. In fact, Kübler-Ross came to believe that the stages of dying characterized the emotional experience not only of those who were in the process of experiencing a death but who were mourning virtually any sort of loss.

"We only call it the 'stages of dying' for lack of a better phrase," Kübler-Ross said. "If you lose a boyfriend or girlfriend, if you lose your job or you are forced to move from your home where you have lived for fifty years, some people if they lose a parakeet, some if they lose their contact lenses, [all] go through the same 'stages of dying.' This is, I think, the true meaning of suffering." Clearly, daughters who have suffered the loss of their dads through death, and even through abandonment, experience these same stages of dying or stages of mourning, which virtually always begin with simple denial.

DENIAL

On the morning after my father died, my mother came into my bedroom, sat down on the edge of my bed, and told me calmly, without tears, that my father had died. Being almost eleven years old, I understood the concept of death. What's more, I was not altogether surprised, since for months I could see clearly that my dad was very ill, and I had overheard my mother on several occasions talking with friends, family members, and the doctor about my dad's condition. In fact, my mother had flat-out told me a couple of days before that my father was not going to get well. Still, of course, when she told me that he had died during the night, I began to cry.

It's funny. I say "of course," but actually the act of crying was not something that was done very often in my WASP-y, stiff-upper-lip family. I wept for only a minute or two, when my mother said: "Don't cry. Everything will be okay."

I've never forgotten that "Don't cry" admonition. I knew even then that she did not mean it to be cruel; in fact, I believe she meant to comfort and reassure me. But I did stop crying, and, as the years passed, I never wept again over my father's death, at least not consciously or overtly.

Years later, I was watching a television newscast about an earthquake in southern Italy. It showed a group of women, shrouded in black, kneeling down, pounding the earth, and wailing over the death of their loved ones. This is how losing a loved one to death feels, I thought to myself. But in my family, as in many others, expression of grief in such an open, dramatic way was simply not permitted. Our emotional pain was to be suppressed and denied. Indeed, in my family, hiding emotional pain was considered dignified, and we took pride in it.

The Importance of Denial

Denial is a very common human response to any surprising, usually disturbing, information. It means that the mind and the emotions refuse to accept the reality of the situation; denial protects the psyche until we are able to take in the information and process it, intellectually and emotionally. Denial can manifest itself as a momentary expression of surprise ("I can't believe this is happening!") even to a happy event, like winning the lottery. Or, more seriously, denial can function as a long-term state of mind, such as when an abandoned wife refuses to believe her husband will never return.

However, most of the time, denial is not a bad thing. It is nature's way of preparing our minds, bodies, and spirits for coping with psychic shock. Moreover, it is usually just a temporary defense until a person is more ready to deal with the situation.

Denial and Father Loss

Denial is, of course, almost always the first stage of the mourning process for a fatherless daughter. When her father has died or simply just moved out of the house as a result of her parents' separation or divorce, the emotional pain is excruciating. The first response is to deny the reality of the situation and the extent of the pain.

Denial can take on a vast range of guises, depending on the girl's age and situation. A very young child, when told that her daddy has died, may pretend she hasn't heard, or say something like, "I'm going to forget that you told me that." A fourteen-year-old may act out in ways like refusing to attend her father's funeral or staying out for days on end with her friends. In the case of divorce, she may just flippantly indicate that the situation has nothing to do with her, then go up to her bedroom, slam the door, and turn her favorite CD on loud.

Almost all of the women I interviewed discussed how their father's loss was characterized by denial in their home.

⌣ NINA ⌣

Nina is an old friend of an old friend of mine. Today, she is a professor of psychology with a specialty in family relationships, so when our mutual friend suggested that I interview her, I was particularly curious. When I arrived at her office, I was impressed by its understated elegance, and when Nina appeared, I was equally taken not only with her prettiness, but with the fact that she exuded a sense of centeredness; a cool, calm, and collected demeanor. However, I quickly learned that her looks were deceiving. Her emotional personality—strong feelings expressed with great wit and humor—ran counter to her conservative appearance.

Nina grew up in an upper-middle-class Jewish family in an affluent New York City suburb. Her father was a successful businessman, they lived in a beautiful house, and by all appearances they had what Americans consider a perfect life. However, when Nina was five years old, her father was diagnosed with cancer, and he was in and out of the hospital for a year. He was unable to walk, let alone continue to work. The situation was, of course, disturbing for the family, but Nina's mother's main defense—as it would remain for years to come—was denial.

"My mother did not tell anyone that my father had terminal cancer," Nina says. "No one; not even my father. My father also seemed to participate in this charade, because he, too, needed to pretend that he wasn't dying and that he was going to get back to work. In other words, they both needed to believe that life would soon return to normal."

Although it is not unusual for a spouse, and certainly not a child, to be unable to acknowledge the seriousness of a life-threatening illness right away, Nina's mother's denial went beyond that. It ended up isolating her. She believed she needed to keep her husband's illness a secret not only from her own family members but from her husband's mother. During his long stays in the hospital, Nina's mother would tell her mother-in-law that he was away on a business trip. Nina's father would go along with this ruse as well, pretending that he was out of town on business when he called his mother from the hospital. In the end, his mother died six months before her son, not knowing that he was so ill.

In the 1950s when Nina's father became ill, many people responded to cancer the way some people today respond to AIDS, with a sense of shame. Some even thought cancer was contagious. "It was mysterious," Nina says. "Maybe you got it if you did something bad. There was so much magical thinking [about cancer], and it was terribly embarrassing. [I felt like] something was wrong with me; something was wrong with us."

When Nina's dad died, the family denial simply continued; indeed, it escalated. The children were as embarrassed to come from a fatherless home as they had been about their dad's illness. "When my father died," Nina says, "I supposedly said to my brother, 'Are you going to tell anybody? Let's not tell anybody!' And I wouldn't tell anybody!"

Nina was six years old when her father died, and almost from the moment of his death, her family (which consisted of her mother, her brother, Michael, who was three years older, and herself) conspired to create a lifesaving family myth. On one hand, they all viewed the history of their family as "before Daddy died" and "after Daddy died." On the other hand, they didn't really acknowledge the huge rupture and acted as though everything could be the same even though a core member of their family had died. At least that is what they hoped.

After their father's death, Nina's brother, Michael, quickly became the focal point of the family. Nina's mother adored him, and so did Nina. Although for a while Michael had problems at school and was sent away to boarding school, he remained the center of Nina and her mother's world. A web of deep and complex relationships developed among the three of them, creating a strong barrier against the outside world. Although Nina's mother remarried several years after Nina's father's death, her second husband was never able to penetrate the family's emotional core and certainly did not become a surrogate father for either Nina or her brother. In one way though, Nina remembers loving that when they went out to dinner, they looked like everyone else. He died suddenly when Nina was in college, leaving Nina's mother a widow once again.

Without realizing it, it was Michael who became Nina's substitute father and protector. It was almost as though Nina worked out her oedipal issues with her brother instead of with her father, while Michael, in turn, developed a father/protector connection with Nina, a connection that interfered with the lives of both Nina and her brother.

Michael married in his mid-twenties. On the surface, it appeared that he was getting his life together. But as Nina now says, "He was never *really* married to my sister-in-law. In some ways (but certainly not all) he was more attached to my mother and me than to his wife."

At first, Nina dismissed (or denied) the notion of her brother marrying. (Nina now realizes that she felt abandoned when Michael decided to marry.) In the end, however, Nina, who was now in her early twenties, began to fashion her entire life around her brother and his family, and became very close to Michael's wife and the couple's two children. After Michael and his family moved to Long Island, Nina spent many of her weekends with them. Even when she shared a summer house with friends at the beach on the eastern end of Long Island, she would often not make it there on the weekends. Somehow, as Nina says, her car would leave the highway at her brother's exit, as if by magic. Nevertheless, at the time, Nina felt she was being a good aunt, and she enjoyed it. She failed to see that her life was out of balance.

Still, Nina appeared to be maturing. She had graduated from college, found a career she liked in New York City, and dated regularly. But like her brother, her life was not quite as stable as it appeared, and not the least of her problems were troubled relationships with men. She had several boyfriends throughout her twenties and thirties, but many were flagrantly inappropriate, including a man ten years her junior whom she dated when she was thirty-five and he was just out of college. She also had a complicated relationship with a married man who lingered in her life for years. She did not yet see that she picked men who could never challenge her role in the family.

"I'm the poster child for analysis." That's how Nina explains the reasons behind her ultimate healing. By the time she hit her late thirties, Nina had decided to study for her Ph.D. in psychology. Toward that end, she also entered analysis, which proved to be not only helpful but life-altering. Through analysis and deciding to take control of her life, Nina was able to rework her closest relationships, which in turn allowed her to form a new one.

However, the changes in Nina's life did not sit well with her mother or with her brother. "Ever since you went to school, you've gotten so mean," was how Nina's mother responded to her studies in psychology. Michael was even nastier, particularly with regard to Nina's developing relationship with Steven.

"Over the course of time, I started to say no to my brother," Nina says, "and he couldn't stand it. At one point, he called me and said, 'You know what? You're like a sister-in-law. You're not even like a sister.'" First Nina had to learn to tolerate what it meant to change and the effect it had on others. Only then could she meet someone and focus on making that relationship central.

This was an important lesson for Nina. "I guess one of the things I had to resolve was that I had to finally transfer my loyalties," Nina says. "That's what you do when you get married: You transfer your loyalty to the family that you're creating. Even if your husband acts unreasonably, you don't run home and tell your mother." Or your brother!

When Nina and Steven married, Michael walked Nina down the aisle. But then he cut off their relationship completely. He stopped responding to her calls. They had no contact for years. Nina only heard about him from his children and her mother. His behavior was a mystery, although Nina suspects he might have felt abandoned. One year, Nina's brother was having Thanksgiving with their mother and his children at his house, while Nina was celebrating Thanksgiving with her mother-in-law, who lived only a few miles away.

"Somebody said to me, 'Why don't you go over to your brother's house and ask why you don't talk to each other?'" Nina explained. "But then somebody else said: 'I suggest if you feel like getting run over by a train, go over to your brother's house! How many times does he have to run over you before you get it? Were you invited? You were not invited! You cannot go.'"

It was a painful period, but ultimately, Nina and her brother did find a way back together. Ironically, their reunion was facilitated by Steven, Nina's husband.

Although not all of the emotional issues in Nina's family were a function of her father's death, the complicated relationship between Nina and her brother—and their mother—was surely colored by the loss of their father. His death had been extremely painful for all of them, so the memory of that pain had to be denied. The subsequent painful feelings of separation that are a natural part of life (like transferring love from a parent or a sibling to a spouse or even to children) were almost impossible for this family to endure. But Nina, with the help of intensive therapy, was able to break through and create a happy life of her own.

Denial and Shame

For fatherless daughters, denial of their situation often results from, or is at least colored by, feelings of embarrassment or shame. As Nina said, "My father's death was embarrassing, terribly embarrassing. I felt as though something was wrong with me; something was wrong with us. I don't think I'd say, 'How come we drove him away,' but that was sort of how I felt."

Anne, who was twelve at the time of her dad's death, remembers feeling embarrassed about his death as early as the day of his funeral:

"I remember awkward moments when someone would call [on the telephone] and ask for my father, and I didn't know what to say. Daddy had died the day before, and for some reason my great aunt hadn't gotten the message. She called long distance from Wisconsin and asked, 'Is your dad there?' and I just said, 'No.' I mean, what could I say? 'He's dead'? It was weird."

Anne found it impossible to utter the truth that her father had died. She experienced this feeling as embarrassment or shame, but it was also a form of denial. For Anne to actually say "Daddy died" would simply make it too real, too painful.

I experienced similar feelings over my dad's death, and these emotions endured for years. Shortly after he died, a friend came over to play one Saturday afternoon. For some reason, she asked where my father was, and I told her that he had died. She didn't believe me, or at least that's what she said. I saw immediately that she was upset, and I felt embarrassed that I had such an odd family and was ashamed that I had upset her. Like Nina, I experienced our fatherless home as problematic. Clearly something was very wrong with our family, and it had to be hidden.

From then on, I stopped telling friends that my dad had died. Even years later, when I first arrived at college, several of the girls in my dorm were talking about their dads. I didn't participate in the conversation, and later I asked a friend to tell my other new acquaintances that I didn't have a father. I simply could not bear to do it myself. When my mother remarried during my sophomore year in college, several of my hometown friends were shocked, because they had no idea my mother had been widowed. Recently one of my oldest and dearest childhood friends, a friend who actually remembered being told by our Sunday school teacher that my dad had died, told me that she never talked to me about it because discussion of my dad was somehow out of bounds.

Denial and Divorce

Girls who lose their fathers through abandonment or divorce may mourn in more problematic ways than girls whose fathers have died. As families go through the breakdown of a marriage, the parents, and even less so, the children, often fail to see that the divorce is the death of both the marriage and the family unit as it once was. Still, if a father is then absent for most of the rest of the girl's life, his loss may feel almost like death to his daughter. But he may well live close by and be present in his daughter's life, although emotionally removed. Usually, however, it never occurs to anyone to mourn this loss, especially if the marriage, and the divorce, were especially acrimonious.

◡∴ STAR ∾

Star grew up in a hippie (albeit very affluent) community in Vermont in the 1970s. Her parents divorced when she was three, and Star, her sister, and her brother continued to live with their mother. Although her father, Bill, lived only a few miles away and saw the children frequently, he was a determined "nonfather." This was the mid-1970s, and Star's father was a child of the sixties, hell-bent on breaking away from conventional values, most particularly those of a patriarchal, coddling father.

Because Star visited her father frequently, she did not experience a sense of literal abandonment. Nevertheless, she felt emotionally deserted by him, but these feelings were suppressed. She was too young to understand them; therefore, she could not experience them consciously, let alone articulate them for many years. The feelings of father loss were denied not only by Star but also by her parents. However, when she was in her midteens, she had an experience that put her in touch with these feelings of loss.

"When I was probably fifteen," Star says, "my mom had a friend come from Norway. His name was David. My mom bred horses at that time, and he had come from Europe to judge horses at an international horse show. He stayed at our house during the visit.

"David was grandfather-aged, but he was the exact kind of father that I wanted. He was stern and committed to his ideas and his work, but he was very loving and very kind. He stayed with us for about three weeks, and he and I became great friends. Basically, I fell in love with him. That's how I think of it! But I fell in love with him in the sense that I wished he were my dad, because he put off all the energy of being a daddy, a dad. Not a father, not a stepfather, but a dad. When he left, I felt all of the mourning and loss and sadness come out of me that I'd been holding onto for years about my own father. I remember when he left, I just cried and cried and cried, and I remember just weeping to my mother that I wanted a daddy."

Denial May Last Forever

For many women, vestiges of denial regarding their father's death can last a lifetime. Several of the women I interviewed admitted that they found it impossible to talk with their mothers about their fathers, even decades after their father's death or departure. Particularly in cases of contentious divorces, often mothers simply did not want to dredge up all the bad feelings. As a result, the nature of their parents' marriage and their father's personality remained a mystery.

Denial can linger in certain families to avoid hurting the feelings of beloved stepfathers. To her surprise, Wendy ran smack into her family denial when she called her mother about being interviewed for this book.

Wendy's natural father had died when she was five years old, more than forty years before. Her mother had remarried when she was eight. Wendy wanted to clarify some facts, so she telephoned her mother a few days before our interview.

"I told her that I was going to be interviewed," Wendy explained, "and my mother interjected: 'And you want to know if it would be all right with me?' Actually, that particular notion had never crossed my mind, but I said, 'Well, yeah.' And she said, 'I don't have a problem with it, but I think you ought to talk to your father,' meaning my stepfather.

"So my stepfather got on the phone. To be diplomatic, I said, 'I just want to know if it would be okay with you.' And he said, 'It's all right,' but it didn't sound like he really meant it, so I decided to confront him straightforwardly: 'You say it's all right, but it doesn't sound like it's all right.' Then he blurted out, with hurt and anger in his voice, 'I always thought that I was your father!'

"'You are my father,' I said. 'But this is about that time of my life when I didn't have a father.' And then he said, 'All right.' I could tell that he felt a little better, but there was that little injured voice.

"This is all by way of saying that there was no real discussion of my [natural] father in my life; no information. Occasionally my mother and I would talk about him when we were alone. Sometimes I looked at old family pictures privately. The fact that I had had a father who died was never a topic that I felt was to be discussed, except secretly with my mother. I just felt it was a little odd growing up, knowing that I had had another father—a father I could remember—but was never able to talk about him."

ANGER

Sooner or later, a father's death or departure can be denied no longer, and at that juncture, anger leaps into play. The anger can be expressed in all sorts of ways, again depending on the age of the girl, her relative maturity, and how strong emotions are normally dealt with and expressed within the family. Her rage can range from quiet, simmering resentment, to intrusive sulking, to screaming fits on a daily basis. It may even exhibit itself as envy, such as a young girl who begrudges a friend her doting dad. In any case, the anger is experienced not only by the daughter but by all those around her. As Kübler-Ross says, "In contrast to the stage of denial, this stage of anger is very difficult to cope with. . . . The reason is the fact that this anger is displaced in all directions and projected onto the environment at times almost at random."

Anger is one of the most ubiquitous emotional legacies of father loss. Virtually every woman I interviewed for this book agreed on two emotional aspects that resulted from the loss of her father: fear of abandonment and anger. Although other personality issues showed up frequently among the fatherless daughters, only fear of abandonment and anger (with anger often being the result of the fear) were experienced by all of them.

Even seemingly mild-mannered, cheerful women would admit to a well of rage, a facet of their personality that continued to express itself into adulthood, and sometimes never disappeared. By the time she has grown up, a fatherless daughter may no longer have screaming matches with her mother or lose her temper unpredictably at work or with her husband or friends, but her anger may be expressed in less obvious ways. She may overeat, smoke, drink, take drugs, or exhibit other compulsive behaviors such as workaholism or sexual addiction. She may have a long history of broken relationships, particularly love relations that went up in flames. Indeed, Beverley Raphael says in *The Anatomy of Bereavement,* "Anger is prominent [among grieving children] and may lead to neurotic reactions in projection and phobias, compulsive behavior and depression."

Not only is anger omnipresent among adult fatherless daughters, but I believe that many fatherless daughters get stuck in the anger stage of the mourning process. (I also think many women become frozen in the subsequent depression stage, but depression is often a product of suppressed anger.) Thus, many fatherless daughters fail to work their way through the mourning process until they are well into adulthood, if ever.

BARGAINING

Bargaining is usually a rather brief stage between the stages of anger and depression. The fatherless daughter seeks to strike a deal with God or whatever other force she perceives can save her father and rescue her from her fear, sadness, and loss. In Kübler-Ross's experience with dying patients, bargaining was the stage where the dying patient sought to buy time, to satisfy the wish for an extension of life. The emotional bargain almost always involves a contract between the patient and God, is usually a secret, and is often a request to live long enough to reach a certain self-imposed deadline, such as a child's graduation or wedding. Also implicit in the bargaining stage is a wish for a reward for good behavior.

The bargaining phase for mourners—specifically fatherless daughters—is played out in much the same way. For example, a child who is aware that a parent is dying may pray that he lives long enough to see her achieve some goal, such as graduate from high school or college, get married, or even something as banal as return home from camp. The element of promising to behave better is also frequently part of the fatherless daughter's deal with God, especially younger girls.

I have a distinct memory of praying to God the night my father died, asking Him to spare my dad. However, although I was only ten years old, I somehow sensed that I was too late, that God wasn't making any deals with me with regard to my dad's life. I grew up believing that this prayer was a quintessential example of the concept of *futile*, a word I didn't even know at the time.

One of the women I interviewed recalls allowing herself to acknowledge that her dad was now alive, but he was soon going to be gone, and she wanted to make a little bargain with herself. "I had this bench in my backyard," she explained. "I remember standing on the top of it and saying out loud, 'My father is alive!' because I knew that eventually I was not going to be able to say that. I just wanted to say it and feel normal, because I knew that after that, that I'd feel sort of abnormal somehow. I didn't know how, but I knew that things were going to be different."

The concept of bargaining can be very obvious during the mourning of the breakdown of a marriage. For example, younger children will become very helpful, believing that if they are good the departed father will return, and the parents will reunite.

Bargaining and the Paranormal

Many fatherless daughters report having had paranormal experiences with their father who has died. Whether these spiritual experiences are real, they can be soothing and serve as a way of dealing with feelings of guilt and loss. These experiences strike me as a way of bargaining for one more moment with the loved one.

Margaret, a sophisticated New York City public relations executive, lost her dad when she was seven. A few months after he died, he visited her spiritually. The experience was absolutely real to her, and it has given her solace to this day.

"One morning, I was lying in my bed, and my father called my name: 'Margaret! Margaret!' I opened my eyes, and he was sitting on my bed. I remember it perfectly. He was sitting on the edge of my bed like he would always do, and I said, 'Daddy, is it really you?' and he said, 'Yes.'

"I started to sit up to put my arms around him to hug him. And he said, 'No, no, no, you cannot touch me or I have to leave.' Then he motioned for me to lie down again. 'I just came back to see you and your mother and Beth [Margaret's sister]; I just wanted to see you. I miss you all. I just came back for a little while.'

"'Daddy, I just want to hug you,' I said, and with that, I reached out to him and he disappeared. But I'm telling you, my eyes were open, it was bright daylight, it was morning. I was lying in my bed, and he was sitting there talking to me. I knew nothing about ESP, ghosts, or anything. He was there talking to me. And then, like this [she snapped her fingers], he disappeared.

"I've had no other visit from him, no other feeling of him. I never feel that he's around, although I always feel that I have a guardian angel. I've told my sister that I just know that someone is out there watching out for us."

DEPRESSION

I'm not enthusiastic about late fall, the Thanksgiving/Christmas holiday season, and the long, cold, gray winters that follow. I often experience depression during this time of year, yet in late February, this heavy malaise always lifts. I was well into middle age before I realized that the melancholy I experience more or less frames the period between the time my father entered his last illness in mid-November and his death on February 24. Of course, many people respond with sadness and depression over the cold, gloomy winter months, but my spirits always rise on February 25, even if the temperature remains frigid and the sky gray.

One fatherless daughter said, "I tend to get depressed in the spring, which coincides with my birthday at the end of April. But what little kid gets depressed over her birthday? Then I attributed it to, Oh, in the spring, everybody goes daffy, and it's because I'm missing something—like being in love. Then I found out that my father died in the beginning of May. I was startled by that!"

Depression is perhaps the most painful stage of the mourning process. The preceding stages are characterized by emotions that are unreal or externalized: the denial stage is defined by numbness, the anger stage features red-hot rage, and the bargaining stage is colored by a sort of perverse hope. With the depression stage, the mourner finally reaches the point where she experiences the reality of her loss head-on, and she feels despondent.

Two Types of Depression

Kübler-Ross broke down depression into two types for terminally ill patients: reactive depression and preparatory depression. Reactive depression is a response to the concrete realities of sickness and death, and might result from physical weakness and pain or the patient's inability to care for his family.

For a fatherless daughter, reactive depression might surround the realities of the loss of her father's paycheck and family's subsequent fears about money. Or it might involve her mother's need to work and her resulting inability to provide as much love and attention as she had previously. If the fatherless daughter is a bit older, she may become depressed over having to take on greater responsibility in the home, including caring for younger siblings or doing housework. In the case of divorce, reactive depression may result because the fatherless daughter has experienced fighting and possible abuse between her parents before her father departs, as well as feelings of abandonment after he leaves. As painful as these issues are, they are relatively concrete and can be dealt with.

Anita remembers experiencing tinges of depression and melancholy surrounding major events years after her father's death, particularly her wedding and the birth of her first child: "I got married in the parish where I grew up. I got married on my parents' anniversary. On the day of my wedding, I was ready and made up, and excited, but there was a little tinge of melancholy. I wished that my father had been there.

"Going through the birth [of my son] was also an extremely melancholy experience for me. My brother David came into the [hospital] room after the baby was born. David is a *very* emotional person. He came up and said, 'You did it.' And I said, 'Yeah, I did it, David.' And he said, 'I went and saw Dad, and I brought you this.' And he had brought me a flower from [our dad's] grave. 'He would have been very proud of you.' We cried together and he held me."

Preparatory depression is a deeper, lonelier, more painful state. For terminally ill patients, Kübler-Ross saw it as the depression that results when the patient finally faces all of his impending losses, including ultimately his life. She believed that when a dying patient begins to experience preparatory depression, he "should not be encouraged to look at the sunny side of things, as this would mean he should not contemplate his impending death. . . . The patient is in the process of losing everything and everybody he loves. . . . If he is allowed to express his sorrow, he will find a final acceptance much easier."

Preparatory depression is also experienced by mourners and involves preparing for the loss of the loved one and the subsequent life without him with all that it entails. However, for a girl whose father dies when she is very young, experiencing this type of depression and understanding its emotional meaning is almost impossible; very young girls don't have the intellectual sophistication let alone the emotional maturity to experience it. Even a girl in her late teens would find such an experience problematic at best. In all cases, it is just too painful.

For a girl whose father abandons the family, the grief over his loss and the death of the family are not only as excruciatingly painful as a father's loss through death, but the pain, in some cases, may even be deeper and greater. With abandonment, a whole cluster of emotions comes into play that is not present when a father dies. The father is choosing to leave, a fact that is appalling when finally viewed by his daughter. When a father dies, the family receives a certain amount of emotional support for their loss from other family members and the community. When a father leaves his family, even though divorce is more common these days, a family will probably not receive as much sympathy and may even be shunned. A girl's father is mourned when he dies; he is loathed and castigated if he abandons his family. The fact that these feelings are part of a complex mourning process is rarely taken into account, if it is even perceived. Certainly it wouldn't occur to many people to mourn the dissolution of a hideous marriage!

Getting Stuck in Depression

I don't think that many fatherless daughters make it through the depression phase, at least not during their childhood and teen years.

As with the anger stage, they very often get stuck; indeed, depression is often repressed anger.

Many fatherless daughters may make an attempt to deal with the depression, but in order to avoid experiencing the pain of the feelings they unearth, they bounce back to feelings of anger or even denial. And the mourning process begins all over again. Many women spend years working through these emotions, and many never finish mourning their father's loss.

These are the same emotions that are triggered by the loss or departure in the first place: fear of abandonment, an inability to trust, and problems with dependency, commitment, intimacy, separation, and loss. Mix into this painful pot any issues regarding low self-esteem, and the depression becomes even more pronounced. These emotions can come into play in any number of ways: with family members, with friends, with work-related colleagues, but most particularly with men in love relationships.

Coping with Depression

For terminally ill patients, Kübler-Ross believed that each type of depression required its own coping mechanisms, and the same is true for mourners. For reactive depression, action is required on the part of everyone involved. As she said, in "the first type [reactive depression], the patient has much to share and requires many verbal interactions and often active interventions on the part of people in many disciplines." To get through this level of depression, problems need to be discussed and action needs to be taken.

However, for the deeper depression, patients and mourners alike must simply *be* with their grief. "In the preparatory grief, there is no or little need for words. It is often done better with a touch of a hand, a stroking of the hair or just a silent sitting together. This is a time when the patient may just ask for prayer." Kübler-Ross further states, "I am convinced that we do more harm by avoiding the issue [of death] than by using time and timing to sit, listen, and share."

Any number of factors can set off a lingering preparatory depression. Obviously, it can come into play during sad or troubled times, such as the breakup of a relationship or marriage, the loss of a job, a serious illness, or the death of a loved one. It may even come up at a happy moment, such as a wedding or the birth of a child—those moments when a woman yearns to have her dad present.

Ann discovered her unfinished mourning when her father-in-law died. Ann's own father had died when she was in her early teens. She had been sad but had gone on with her life, finished high school and college, and married when she was in her mid-twenties. When her father-in-law died a few years after her marriage, Ann realized she had arrived at a place in her life where she could begin to accept the loss of her dad: "I just went to pieces [when my father-in-law died]. I loved my father-in-law, but my response to his death was too much. I realized that I had not really mourned my own father's death, and somehow, through my father-in-law's death, I could begin to experience those feelings."

ACCEPTANCE

Contrary to what we might expect, acceptance, the final stage of mourning, is not characterized by feelings of joy. Not by a long shot. As Kübler-Ross said with reference to terminally ill patients: "Acceptance should not be mistaken for a happy stage. It's almost void of feelings. It is as if the pain has gone, the struggle is over, and there comes a time for 'the final rest before the long journey.'"

"If a patient has had enough time and has been given some help in working through the previously described stages," Kübler-Ross says, "he will reach a stage during which he is neither depressed nor angry about his 'fate.' He will have been able to express his feelings, his envy for the living and the healthy, his anger. He will have mourned the impending loss of so many meaningful people and places and he will contemplate his coming end with a degree of quiet expectation." Kübler-Ross believed that acceptance is "a natural process, a sign perhaps that a dying person has found his peace."

For a fatherless daughter in the process of mourning the loss of her father, acceptance is also characterized by a sense of peace. Acceptance means she has finally not only faced but also felt the pain of her father's loss. Because so many women get stuck in earlier stages of mourning, especially anger and depression, acceptance may not occur until they are well into adulthood. Like Ann, another death may trigger extreme emotions, feelings that a woman realizes are somehow inappropriate for the particular situation or loss at hand. But she realizes she can endure. She can begin to experience the pain of her dad's loss.

Security and Acceptance

Not surprisingly, often a woman needs to achieve some level of emotional maturity before she is able to fully experience the painful feelings of her father's loss and thus arrive at acceptance. Usually this involves simply having lived life! Most of the women I interviewed who were over age fifty seemed to have come to terms with the loss of their father. Among the younger women who seemed to have reached that stage, without exception, these women had been able to create a secure and happy marriage. Many had also had children and had succeeded in other facets of life, particularly in their career.

∾ MARY ∾

I arrived at the door to Mary Simpson's house in Newport, Rhode Island, on a sunny morning in June. She lives on a quiet block a short walking distance from Newport's Colonial town square. Mary is a tiny woman, bursting with energy. She is beautifully dressed in a stylish white silk shirt, chartreuse silk Capri pants, and shocking pink flats. Her hair is cut in a short, fashionable bob.

After greeting me warmly, she led me into her lovely, understated living room decorated with a tasteful collection of antiques, comfortable sofas and chairs, and a few pieces that I suspect she collected while living abroad with her late husband, who had been an officer in the U.S. Air Force.

Mary is ninety-four years old. Her father died when she was only five.

"He was drowned," Mary explained. "He was on a cruise with some men friends—a stag cruise—and they were sailing on Lake Ontario. There was a bad storm in the middle of the night—all hands on deck! And a gust of wind came along, hit the boom, and knocked him overboard. And he was lost."

Mary grew up in Newark, New York, a small town about twenty miles east of Rochester. Her father had been married once before he wed Mary's mother, and she had a stepsister who was about eighteen years older. In addition, she had four full siblings: one older sister, two older brothers, and a younger sister who was born four months after her father died.

Although Mary was so young when her dad died, she has many lovely memories of him, memories that she treasures: "He was imaginative and ahead of his time. He listened to his children and appreciated them, and I remember him that way. I remember him taking me to Rochester one day to buy a teddy bear, and we spent practically the whole day shopping because I couldn't find the right one. He was very patient and understood that I had to have the one that really suited me. It was a regular brown teddy bear, and I kept it for years.

"Also, we had little signet rings, those little bands with initials on them. He smoked a pipe, and if you'd been especially good or thoughtful for a week, he'd put your ring on his pipe. I was always mad at my sister Charlotte because she was always having her ring on his pipe."

Her father had been a lawyer and had a small practice in Newark, but he also managed a successful lumber mill that had been started by Mary's great-grandfather in the mid-nineteenth century. After her husband's death, her mother decided to continue working the mill in order to support her family. However, Mary's mother had been raised in an affluent family and knew nothing of business. She hired a manager for the mill, who ended up running the business into the ground. From then on, things were financially tight for the family, and her mother took in odd jobs, like sewing, to keep the family afloat.

"Whenever she got to a point where she was really hurting or suffering, she did something for someone else. I remember her taking flowers to someone or making a cake. She was always relieving her pain by doing something for someone else. But I didn't realize it. You don't see that when you're young.

"I knew that my mother was having trouble, but with all this family, with all these kids around all the time, there was always something going on, and I just didn't realize the seriousness of it. When I got to be in my early teens, I noticed a difference in our household from our friends' households. It was due to the lack of my father, but I didn't realize it then. Everything seemed so quiet and so ordered and so proper and so stiff in everybody else's house, while our house was always busy. Friends coming in and out. We always sat down for meals together, but I can remember going to my friend's house for meals and it being so quiet with everything just so. But I never attributed that difference in our life to not having a father, but now I think [that was the reason]."

Although finances were strained, Mary's mother wanted the children to feel secure and happy. "My grandfather had a place on Lake Ontario. We'd sail, even after my father was drowned. There was no fear of the water, no shutdown of swimming or using boats. Our mother would go in swimming with us; she didn't want us to be instilled with fear. I sailed, and I used to crew for races, but there always was a little tiny fear."

Mary's mother also sewed for the children, making lots of their clothes, even winter coats. Mary remembers her mother taking her to the local milliner to make a hat to match the coat she'd made. She was creative.

"I don't know whether that's because my mother was so busy that I couldn't lean on her, really, but I have the feeling [that] perhaps it gave me the feeling of being unsure of myself, somehow. Of not having confidence in myself, confidence with people.

"Her bringing me up was always a very stiff kind of deal. I can remember if I went out on a date or to a party, the last thing she always said was, 'Don't forget to be a lady.' But this wasn't ever a heart-to-heart talk with her about anything. She was always raising me and directing me and schooling me in the way you should behave, but nothing very personal or deep, you know."

Mary went to Mount Holyoke College when she was eighteen. During her freshman year, she started smoking. When she went home, her mother picked her up at the station in the car. As they were driving home, her mother said, 'Well, I suppose you're smoking now.' And I said, 'Yeah, I've started smoking.' And she said, 'Well, all I ask is please don't do it in public. You can smoke at home, but please don't do it in public.'"

After college, Mary moved to New York City, where she joined her older half-sister, Margaret, and worked for an interior decorator. Margaret then decided to open a business in Rochester, and Mary went into business with her. After a few years, she married Bob Simpson, a friend of her brother's. Bob was a professional military man, and they moved to many places around the world, from several American posts, to Germany, to Mary's special favorite, Morocco. Mary believes she has had an incredibly full life: a warm childhood, a wonderful career, a happy marriage, two marvelous children, and five terrific grandchildren. Mary lost her husband in 1982 while they were living near Boston, and simply because she loved Newport, she pulled up stakes alone, found a house, and moved to a brand-new town where she knew no one. Today she has scores of friends and a full and active life with her clubs, activities, and visits from her children and grandchildren.

Mary explains that the loss of her father when she was only five was incredibly sad, but it was not an event that left her deeply scarred. After having spent just a few hours talking to this vibrant lady, I could see that she had absorbed life's blows, including the death of her father, and accepted them graciously. Nevertheless, as I got up to leave at the end of the interview, she said, "I have to tell you something: I think about him every day. I miss him still." She said this with a wistful sadness in her voice almost ninety years after her father's death.

Experiencing Acceptance

The feelings of acceptance, like the other stages of mourning, are fluid, and the emotions may come and go depending on other factors. Sometimes feelings of depression are reexperienced; other times, painful memories are denied. Maria, a young wife and mother whose father died when she was thirteen, talks about this with great feeling:

"My mother called me yesterday and said, 'Do you know what today is?' I said, 'Yes, of course.' Actually, I hadn't really thought about it, but I knew that it was my father's birthday. It's just one of those things that you never forget. I think that I could go back in time to that very moment [of his death] and to the feelings that we had. I could feel it all, recreate it in my mind because it was such a poignant memory for me. It's like a regular mourning period you go through.

"For many years, on his birthday I would feel something on the date and not know why I was feeling a certain way and we would all call one another. 'Oh, today is Dad's birthday,' that kind of thing. It's very . . . it's surreal almost."

Still, Maria believes she has accepted her dad's death: "I think that I did achieve a sense of acceptance five or six years after his death. That's when I first had the opportunity to really feel that loss. Do I think that I have fully done it? I think I've been through several cleansing times—different stages of my life, the birth of my son, the wedding, and my marriage. I think that those were poignant points in my life where I had wanted him there, and so in a sense I went through the mourning process again. I'd say [to my dad], 'Why aren't you here? I wish you were here. How could you leave me? This was a time for us. This was a time for you.' I think I continue to do that."

Mourning a lost father is an ongoing process. Perhaps it never ends. Maria explains: "My mother and I look back on it, and we talk about it and we're like, 'What?' I can remember that very day that it happened. And I can remember the look on someone's face and the feelings that I felt and the stress and ache and all of that. And I don't know if it will ever be over. I really don't."

11. GETTING TO KNOW YOUR DAD

Even if Dad never sets eyes on the child, he has a profound and long-lasting effect.

—Claudette Wassil-Grimm, *Where's Daddy?*

During the summer after my freshman year in college, about eight years after my father's death, my mother got a telephone call from my father's uncle, Ben Porter. Ben was a tall, thin man, at the time of this event probably in his mid-eighties, the brother of my father's mother. My main memory of Ben, whom I saw only a few times in my life, was that although I never saw him laugh (or even smile, for that matter), I have the distinct impression that he was very funny. Maybe I was told he was comical, or maybe I just have some subconscious memory of him telling jokes with my dad. In any case, I believe he saw the world as a most amusing place.

Ben's wife, Aunt Mary, was a small, plump woman who somehow managed to be both incredibly gentle and incredibly energetic. Unfortunately, by the time of this summertime call, Mary had had a stroke and was unable to get around very easily. My mother had maintained a relationship with Ben and Mary, and would visit them and help them out, especially now that Mary was incapacitated.

The purpose of this call was to inform my mother that one of my father's three brothers, Harry, had died. At the time of this call, I don't believe I had ever heard of Harry, and I know for certain I had never met him. But Mother seemed to know about Harry, and since Ben wanted to go to the wake, Mother offered to take him. I was already curious about these unknown Thomases, so I agreed to go along.

On the evening of Harry's wake, we started out to pick up Ben in our banana-yellow Chevy Impala convertible, Mom at the wheel, as I recall, although I also loved driving that car. It was a warm summer evening, and Mother and I put the top down, thinking that a ride in a convertible to a wake would be fun for Ben.

Ben lived on the south side of Cleveland, not far from where my dad had grown up, and when we pulled up in front of his house, he was already waiting for us. He whistled when he saw the car, then slid into the front seat next to my mother, very nimbly, I thought, for an eighty-five-year-old man.

"Great car," Ben said. "But listen, Roberta. Don't park it in front of the funeral home. Ada will think you've got money."

Ada was my father's sister. Apparently she had made all the arrangements for Harry's funeral, but Ben was afraid Ada might be having trouble paying for it. Seeing my mother drive up in a brand-new yellow convertible might give her ideas.

So we parked several blocks away from the funeral home, on a street where we could drive away without being seen. As it turned out, it didn't matter if Ada saw the car or not.

The funeral home was, like many funeral homes in our city, a converted Victorian house in what had once been an elegant neighborhood. I had met Aunt Ada a few times in my life, and I suspect she had once been quite a beauty. She was a tall, buxom blonde, although at this time, she, too, may well have been in her seventies. She was also very effusive and perhaps a little loud.

Not many people attended the wake, which made me feel a bit sorry for Harry. Another sister of my father's, Mildred, another relative I had never met (and would never meet again), was also there. We barely spoke, but I tried to sneak looks at her and saw that she was also interested in me. She resembled my father strongly, although she was very small and quiet. My mother hinted that Mildred had been a wild young woman, and Daddy had had to go out late at night to "rescue" her on several occasions, but Mother would never give me the real details. Many years later, my cousin Gerrie told me how incredibly sweet Mildred had been to her when Gerrie was a little girl. I'm sure both observations are true.

And then there was Harry. His coffin was open, so I was able to "meet him" in a rather straightforward way. As with Mildred, I was taken with his physical resemblance to my dad: the high cheekbones, the hawklike Celtic nose, the thick, dark hair. But, of course, that's the sum total of my relationship with Harry, and sadly, nobody else knew too much about him, either.

We didn't stay at the wake too long, and although we'd gone to great pains to avoid giving Aunt Ada the impression we had money (and, God knows, we didn't), she still asked my mother to help pay for the funeral. I think my mom gave her some money—maybe $20—but it was money my mom could ill afford at that time. Even today, more than forty years later, Mother says, "I don't think Roy would have wanted me paying for that funeral," although I suspect she's wrong. I think my father would have paid for the whole thing.

We left the funeral home rather abruptly, as I recall. Both Mom and Ben were angry. I was just nonplussed. I didn't know what to make of these people, and I had no clue what my dad had thought of them, either. I had a vivid memory of my dad speaking of yet another brother, Mose, and saying with great enthusiasm, "Mose is my favorite brother!" The fact is, Uncle Mose showed up at our house on the day my dad died, and we never saw him again. Needless to say, Mose didn't show up to say his good-byes to Uncle Harry on this particular evening, either.

I have so few memories and connections with my father's family. Perhaps because of that, all the memories I do have are very precious to me, even this rather odd exchange. I'm very happy I had a brief glimpse at Uncle Harry. I wish I'd known him. I also wish I'd had a chance to talk to Ada and Mildred, and even to Ben. But most of all, of course, I wish I'd known my dad.

THE IMPORTANCE OF KNOWING THE MAN

One of the most effective ways of working your way through the mourning process is to make an effort to get to know your dad. At first glance, this may seem like an odd notion. If your dad has died, getting to know him must surely seem utterly impossible, perhaps even a little nutty. Even if he is still alive but long out of touch, the possibility may seem equally out of the question. But not only is making an effort to reconnect with your dad possible, it is imperative. The upshot may not be what you hope for, but in the end the knowledge you glean from your search will open the door for you to the rest of your life.

So, why is it so important for a woman to try to get to know her father? I see three compelling reasons:

1. A child—especially an adult child—needs to know where she came from.
2. A child—especially an adult child—needs to know the truth about her father.
3. Only by knowing her father can a daughter proceed in a healthy way through the mourning process.

Knowing Where You Came From

In *Where's Daddy?* Claudette Wassil-Grimm says, "Even if Dad never sets eyes on the child, he has a profound and long-lasting effect because so many traits and talents are hereditary." Knowing about her father helps a child to integrate her personality and her perceptions. She not only needs to know the most superficial traits, like why she is blue-eyed and blond, enjoys music, or has the ability to run fast, but she also needs to be clear about traits that may have problematic repercussions, such as hereditary health issues.

Knowing as much as possible about her father also helps a daughter separate from her mother. As Wassil-Grimm says, "Children need to have an unbiased well-rounded picture of who Dad was so that they can sort out their own identities in relation to each of their parents." Many fatherless daughters become overattached and over-identified with their mother. They need to know as much as possible about their father in order to comprehend where Dad's influence ends and Mom's begins.

Learning the Truth

Children, including, and perhaps especially, adult children, need to know the truth about their dad. Regardless of how the father is presented to his children, it is imperative that children confirm or uncover the real story. Often, fathers who have died, especially those who have died in a war or through some other extraordinary occurrence, are turned into heroes. They become mythologized and sometimes even sanctified. In contrast, fathers who disappear after an acrimonious divorce are often painted as monsters; hateful creatures who never loved their children. However, it may well also be true that the deified man who was lost in the war was, in fact, a bewildered kid who was running away from his responsibilities, and the man who left, never to see his child again, may have been cut off from contact by his wife.

Beginning to Mourn

I came to believe that many of the women I interviewed for this book had not yet begun to mourn the loss of their fathers. They were caught in the anger or depression stages of mourning, and some were still in a state of denial. By uncovering the truth about your dad, you move from denial into the active process of mourning. In the end, not only will you have achieved a sense of peace with regard to your dad, but you'll also have learned much about yourself.

WHAT IF YOUR DAD HAS DIED?

Even if your father has died, getting to know him may not be as difficult as it might seem. In some cases, the task may be quite easy, or perhaps has been accomplished already.

Interviewing Your Mother

Talking to your mother about your father is the easiest and most direct avenue for getting to know him. In my family, my father was referred to quite naturally and openly, relatively often, but not obsessively. A lovely, smiling photograph of him, taken a year or so before his death, hung on our dining room wall for years (until my mother remarried, actually). We would refer to his possessions—"Daddy's dresser," "Daddy's closet"—not as though he were still alive, but simply as a descriptive statement of fact.

Even after my mother remarried, we never hesitated to mention him if it was appropriate, and, indeed, the same held true for my stepfather's first wife, who had also died. In our family, death was faced with stoicism and a sense of reality. Death was a part of life, and those who had died were still a part of us.

However, for many widows, discussion of their dead husband can be extremely painful. A widow may convey her feelings to her children, who in turn refrain from asking her much about their father. This is unfortunate. Not only do the mother's emotional blocks deny her children knowledge of their father, but often the mother's reticence leads the children to believe she is hiding awful secrets.

If this is your situation, or if your mother has also died, you can turn to other family members for information. Sometimes their views are more objective.

Talking to Other Family Members

Many widows make a point of remaining in touch with their deceased husband's relations, if only for the sake of their children. Thus, asking a father's siblings or parents about him can happen easily and naturally. However, in some families, access to the deceased father's family has been cut off.

In my family, even when my father was alive, we were not terribly close to members of his family, and this situation became somewhat exacerbated after his death. To my mother's credit, she did remain in touch with some of his relations, visiting my dad's elderly aunt and uncle occasionally during their last years, and exchanging Christmas cards with my cousins. Through these relations, I learned that my father, although he was not close to many members of his family, deeply loved his family.

Later in my life, I learned a few things about my Thomas grandparents from my cousins, Clifford and Gerrie—information I would otherwise never have known. Through them, I saw other traits that

I remembered in my dad, including loyalty, a strong sense of family, and a delightful sense of humor. By reconnecting with members of my dad's family, I reconfirmed many memories and conceptions about him, giving me a profound sense of comfort and security. Also, I felt that my father would have been happy that we stayed in touch with these relatives.

When Father Is Never Mentioned

Open communication about the father who has died may not be encouraged. In some families, in fact, a father who has died is never discussed openly. Many of the daughters I interviewed confessed to knowing little about their fathers, usually because their mothers have made it clear that talk of him was simply too upsetting for her. Sometimes this emotional barrier lasts for years after his death, and sometimes for a lifetime, at least the mother's lifetime.

Talk of the natural or biological father is often discouraged in situations where the mother has remarried and/or the daughter is adopted. Again, the daughter infers that not only would mention of her "real" father be painful for the mother, it would also be disloyal to her stepfather.

When Father Is "God"

In other families, the lost father may be virtually deified. Photographs of him may be scattered throughout the house long after he has died, he is always referred to in hushed tones, and nothing negative is ever said about him.

This situation is often the case when fathers are killed in dramatic situations, especially in war. Fathers who are lost in a war often pose extraordinary issues for their children. Almost always, men killed in battle are considered heroes. Although children of these men are proud of their fathers, they also are unintentionally inhibited from mourning the loss of their fathers. Many of these children were infants when their fathers died, and have no memory of him, and by the time these children become aware of the fact that their father has died, the notion of mourning his loss doesn't really occur to anyone who might help the child.

Many—perhaps most—children of war heroes grow up feeling separate and alone. Like most fatherless children, they experience embarrassment and even shame about not having a father.

American War Orphans Network

Several organizations exist that help families of those who fought and died in the U.S. Armed Services find out more about their loved ones. One of the best known of these organizations is the American War Orphans Network (AWON).

AWON is an organization of daughters and sons of Americans killed and declared missing during World War II. According to AWON statistics, more than 400,000 men died during World War II, leaving more than 183,000 children fatherless. Today these children are in their late fifties and sixties.

Ann Bennett Mix, the founder of AWON, was one of these fatherless children. Her dad, Sydney Bennett, was killed in Italy on April 19, 1945, leaving behind a young wife and three children under the age of six in Bakersfield, California. Ann was the middle child and was four-and-a-half when her dad died. For a host of reasons, Ann and her brothers were discouraged not only from talking about their father (except when her mother got drunk and woke Ann up in the middle of the night for long tirades about him) but from socializing with their father's family.

All her life, Ann longed to get to know her dad. Finally, in 1990 when she was fifty and her mother had died, Ann began her quest. She wrote for her dad's war records and began attending reunions of his battalion with the hope of meeting other men who might have known him. Through her research, she quickly became aware that many other war orphans felt exactly as she did.

Fortunately, she met Susan Johnson Hadler, herself a war orphan, and together the two women began putting together a collection of short biographies of World War II orphans, *Lost in the Victory: Reflections of American War Orphans of World War II*. It took several years for the book to develop, and in the interim, Ann started the AWON organization. Today, AWON has hundreds of members, many of whom have visited their fathers' graves in Europe, have attended not only large AWON meetings but reunions of their own fathers' battalions, and have found a place where they can mourn with others who know exactly what they have faced.

◡⁖ MAGGIE ⁖◞

For Maggie, the word *father* evoked a stack of letters handwritten on tissuey blue stationery and tucked in the bottom of a cedar chest in the back bedroom of her family home in Faulkton, South Dakota. She was three years old when her father, Richard Malone, was killed in Germany on March 24, 1945, and has no memory of him. For Maggie, her dad lived in these letters, and, not surprisingly, she was very curious about them.

Maggie's parents, Richard and Elizabeth Rodney Malone, were both from old established farm families in eastern South Dakota, very near the Minnesota border. Maggie's mother's mother had died when she was a child, and she had been raised in town by an aunt.

Maggie's dad, who was born on Leap Year Day, February 29, 1908, grew up on a farm. Like his wife, he, too, hoped to avoid farm life and to better himself. After high school, he began working at a bank. By the time Maggie was born, he was heading the Farm Security Administration office in Faulkton, a very responsible government job. By the early 1940s, the Malone family consisted of three girls: Kathleen, born in 1938; Mary, born in 1939; and the baby, Maggie, born in 1941.

Married men with children began to be drafted into the military in October 1943. When Maggie's dad was drafted, he was almost too old to go to war. In fact, because of his age (thirty-three at the war's onset), his three children, and his government job, he probably could have avoided the service altogether. However, as Maggie later learned from her sisters, he felt strongly about the state of the world and worshipped President Franklin Roosevelt.

"I suspect that my dad struggled about going to war," Maggie says. "But he was a voracious reader and kept up with the war news. He was very aware. Also, on the homefront, the war was very glamorous, but at the same time it was very serious. He really thought he'd be given a desk job because of his age and training, but he also had become a good marksman, and in the big churning war machine, he was ultimately assigned to an infantry unit."

Maggie's dad left home for basic training in February 1944 and returned briefly on leave in September of that year. Years later, Maggie's mother told her that Maggie just didn't want anything to do with him. "She said that he really worked hard to win me. He carried me everywhere and made a huge effort. But I was two years old, and I know I was totally attached to Mom. However, I eventually came around and really fell for him, all in a very short period of time."

Dick was sent to the European theater in November 1944. Like thousands of other servicemen, he was following the troops who had landed in France on D-Day, June 6, 1944, and would eventually be pivotal players in the Battle of the Bulge, the last surge to victory over the Germans. When that battle started, he was caught in the thick of it, but he survived, only to be killed later in western Germany on March 24, 1945.

News of Dick's death reached the family in early April 1945. Maggie has fleeting images of the day her mother received the news. Children are always disturbed when they see a parent cry, and Maggie was no exception.

"I was sitting on the floor and people were consoling my mother, and she was crying. I remember one of my sisters was crying, too. And I started in, too, and one of the women said, 'Oh, look, she doesn't even know what she's crying about.' Which was kind of true."

The weeks that followed were tumultuous. On May 8, 1945, just six weeks after Maggie's dad's death, the war in Europe was over. In Faulkton, as in every other city and town around the world, church bells rang, people cheered, and couples literally danced in the streets.

"My sister remembers VE-Day vividly," Maggie recalls.

"Mother was ironing, and around town, bells started to ring and people started to celebrate. Mary remembers that she and Kathy asked, 'Mom, what is that? People are having such a good time!'

"Apparently, my mother said, 'They're happy because the war is over.' Then she burst into tears and went to bed for a week, if not longer. We had no access to her, which is very scary for kids, and it made for a pretty shaky time. We were taken care of by relatives and friends, but we didn't know what was wrong. I remember thinking: Was it something I did? I can remember feeling like a bad person."

Not surprisingly, Maggie's mother descended into an acute depression that lasted for weeks. The war's end brought no joy for her. Instead, grief-stricken over the loss of her husband and worried over how she could support her three young daughters, she was left with nothing but pain.

While the town considered Dick Malone a hero, by summer 1945, people were tired of war and wanted to move on with their lives. Friends and neighbors were sorry for the Malone family, but the last thing anybody wanted to think about was a needy widow with three young children.

"Mother was an attractive woman, and we were beautiful children. Can you imagine in that little town, a pretty widow with three little girls?" Maggie remembers with some bitterness: "People would go, 'Hi . . . Oh, you're lookin' cute . . . Bye.' They didn't really want to know about us."

Still, every Memorial Day, Independence Day, and Veterans Day for years to come, the Malone girls were acknowledged and their father was praised for his sacrifice. But by the time Maggie was a teenager, those moments began to feel both hollow and extremely painful. "I remember feeling unable to say anything and just being filled up with 'my Daddy.'"

Life for the Malone family was typical of many once-middle-class, fatherless homes of that time. (Many middle-class families became poor after the father died and remained that way unless the mother remarried.) According to Maggie, "My mother certainly wasn't prepared in any way to support herself. Actually, our home was pretty chaotic."

Maggie explained: "Mother was depressed, I would say, for at least five years after my father died. She would do the basics—cooking, cleaning—but things were very disorganized with baskets full of clothes and stuff strewn everywhere. I'd go to my friends' houses and their houses would seem pristine, while we were like Bohemians. We had a piano, so we played and sang all the time. Mother got us books from the library, and we were always reading or drawing and painting pictures."

At the same time, Maggie's mother was in some ways very strict, probably stricter than she might have been had her husband been alive. "She was very religious and she didn't want any taint on her reputation or ours. We were very strictly brought up. And she paid enormous attention to our grammar and pronunciation."

The years passed. Maggie's mother worked as a secretary at the local high school, but she never dated, much less remarried. Maggie and her sisters all attended the College of St. Catherine, a Catholic girls' school in St. Paul, Minnesota, on their father's GI bill. When Maggie graduated, she immediately traveled to Europe to see her father's grave in a military cemetery in the Netherlands. Eventually she moved to New York, got a master's degree in library science from Columbia, and found work in magazine research and editing.

The dynamic among the three sisters also affected how Maggie felt about her upbringing and her father. With no grandparents or other relatives living close by, there was no way to talk to anybody, Maggie says. "We three girls never talked to each other about it. We never said, 'Isn't that sad?' or, 'Don't you miss Dad?' All three of us were just enormously fearful, sad, and angry. I've likened our family to a family of an alcoholic where nobody says anything, . . . but there's this five-hundred-pound gorilla in the middle of the living room. It's a very isolating thing, a disaster like that.

"I found his letters when I was nine or ten . . . in the back bedroom closet. There was this cedar chest and these letters were at the bottom. I started reading the letters and I couldn't believe it. Is this the guy that they've been telling me about, the one who went to heaven; the one who loved me?

"I developed this fantasy father, based on the man in the letters. That's why I have gone over to see his grave four times. My sister Mary went with me in 1995 for the fiftieth anniversary [of the end of the war], but Kathy and my mom have never been there." Elizabeth Rodney died in 2003.

"He was in an Infantry Regiment of the Thirtieth Division of the Ninth Army, and I went to a Thirtieth Division Reunion. These guys who fought together in the division have been getting together every year ever since the war. The division [originally] was something like four thousand men, but now it's reduced to about eight hundred because they're all dying.

"Luckily, I found this guy who knew my father. He and my dad were the cigarette and alcohol guys for the officers, and Daddy and he got to know each other pretty well. The man, who was nineteen at the time, called my dad, who was thirty-five, 'Papa.'

"'I knew your dad,' he said excitedly when I showed him a photograph. 'This is Papa!' He had lost his father when he was fifteen and was from a Wisconsin farm. 'Your dad really helped me through the war,' he said. 'I was a pretty wild guy, but he would always say, "Don't forget you're *going home*. Don't do something you'll be sorry for when the war's over." So my unit's motto became "We're going home," and I got that from your dad.'" For Maggie, it was great to know that her father had that kind of a strong, caring personality.

"Ever since joining AWON and establishing the true story about my dad, I've been able to say 'Dad' without going boohoo. Before I would say 'my father,' and I'd expect to be told—not literally but [through suggestion]—that I shouldn't talk about him. I attribute learning to like and trust men a lot better to AWON and to researching who my dad really was, like putting flesh on his bones.

"If there's one thing I'm learning in therapy and AWON,

it's that you can't say, 'Oh, it would have been absolutely great if my father had lived.' One has no way of knowing. But I imagine that it would have been very different. My life has turned out to be better and richer than I was ever led to expect it to be. But given the choice, I would always prefer to have known my father. From his letters, I get the idea that all of our lives would have been more stable and happy if he had lived."

WHAT IF YOUR PARENTS DIVORCED?

If your parents divorced (or were never married) when you were a child and your dad became little more than a shadowy figure in your life, the problems surrounding getting to know him are quite different from those faced by women whose fathers have died. Ironically, the most obvious problem is that your father is alive; or, if he is not alive now, he was living when he left; that is, he *chose* to remove himself from your life. This reality can open up a number of emotional issues for everyone involved—your mother, your father, and most of all, of course, for you.

Your Mother's Feelings

If you are the product of divorce, getting to know your father may pose real problems vis-à-vis your mother. Depending on how acrimonious the divorce and who instigated it, your mother may have extremely negative feelings toward your father. She may feel betrayed by your wish to get to know him and may strongly insist that you not contact him.

As one woman said about her mother more than twenty years after her parents' divorce, "She hates my father. Loathes him. These days, she's actually gotten a little more peaceful, but she won't even hear about him. Doesn't want to know anything I tell her."

Most likely, your mother's feelings about your father will have colored yours. Also, you probably have no wish to hurt your mother. However, for your own sake, it is imperative that you find him, or at least find out about him.

WHAT IF YOUR DAD IS "LOST"?

"Lost" fathers come in a number of guises.

He can be lost simply because he chooses to be. One woman I interviewed told me her dad had gone out for a quart of milk in 1952 and never came back. Another woman's father, a respected dentist, was clearly and intentionally remote from his daughter after his divorce from her mother. When she pressed him for more contact and closeness, he refused to see her under any circumstances at all.

A father can be lost because keeping up with his daughter becomes too painful. Often, as a result of acrimonious divorces, fathers slowly withdraw from contact with their children because dealing with the ex-wife is impossible. Also, especially if they remarry, making arrangements to see the children becomes too complicated, and integrating children from divorce into a new family is problematic. Finally, maintaining support for children is expensive.

A father can be lost because circumstances played out in such a way that he is denied access to his child. Particularly among younger couples who have a child and then part, the father is often denied access to the children. In these cases, the father is often required—sometimes legally—to remove himself from his daughter's life.

A father can be lost because he didn't know he was a father. In many adoption cases, the father, for any number of reasons, is not informed that he fathered a child, and even if he does know, he is denied contact with the child.

Finding Lost Dads

Some fathers may not want to be found. In the most painful cases, when the father has disappeared by choice, he may have gone to great lengths to make sure his ex-wife and his children never learn of his whereabouts or the facts of his new life. Joan, whose father literally left to buy a quart of milk and never came home, abandoned his wife and five children to fend for themselves. Twenty-five years later, Joan convinced her mother to search one last time for him. With the help of the Social Security Administration, Joan and her mother tracked him down in California. It turned out he had married again, but he had died by the time Joan located him. His second wife, who had no clue that he had a living wife and several children, was collecting his Social Security. In the end, Joan's mother was also able to collect.

⌁ SUZANNE ⌁

On July 11, 1959, in Santa Monica, California, a baby girl was born to Pat and Richard Peck. Pat was eighteen and Richard was nineteen. The Pecks had married just after their high school graduation, undoubtedly due to the imminent arrival of their child, and to complicate matters, the baby was born prematurely, weighing only two-and-a-half pounds. Still, she survived, and her parents struggled to get their marriage going. During the brief months of their marriage, Pat and Richard lived in a small apartment. The relationship was rocky from the start, and they split when their daughter was only six months old. When the baby was nine months old, Pat met Ed Vega, a student at Santa Monica College who lived in the same apartment complex.

Almost immediately, a serious relationship developed between Pat and her neighbor, and when the baby was two-and-a-half years old, they picked up and moved to Ed's hometown, New York City. They changed her name to Suzanne. She grew up assuming that she was Ed Vega's daughter.

"My stepfather had grown up in East Harlem. We moved to New York, and they had more children. By the time my mother was twenty-four years old, she had four children: me; my sister, Alyson; and my two brothers, Matthew and Timothy."

From the beginning, Suzanne had an awkward relationship with her father, who, of course, was actually her stepfather. But as a child, she spent a great deal of time with his relatives. "His relatives were great with me," Suzanne says. "They really loved me and I loved them. They lived in the South Bronx and also in Puerto Rico. I remember being very close to my grandmother, who taught me how to speak Spanish and how to bathe myself, which I really appreciated, since my mother was so busy.

"Kids in our neighborhood were always making comments

about my skin because I was very pale and they were darker. My sister, who is genuinely half Puerto Rican, still didn't look as though she was Puerto Rican, although her skin is darker than mine and her hair is black. But in our neighborhood, I looked markedly different. I remember feeling self-conscious all the time and not knowing why.

"When I was about nine years old, after we had moved to the Upper West Side of Manhattan, a middle-class neighborhood, we were having one of those talks about feelings that my father had with me all the time, and all of a sudden, he said, 'Well, I really think that you should know. . . . Have you ever wondered why you don't look like me?'

"I didn't remember ever thinking that, or wondering why I didn't look like him. I knew I was very light, but I had always been told that I looked like my mother, so I figured, Well, okay, I look like my mother. At that point, I didn't have a clear idea of what I looked like, anyway. Still, I remember thinking, Well, the 'right' answer is probably yes, so I said yes.

"Then he said, 'Well, I'm not your real father.'

"I just kind of looked at him, and for a crazy moment I remember thinking, Well, who could possibly be my father? If what he is saying is true, then who would be my father? I was thinking about Marvin from next door, who was the only other father figure I had ever known, but that seemed improbable.

"Then my stepfather explained. 'Your father is in California.'

"It all seemed like craziness to me.

"When my mother came into the room, my stepfather said, 'I've told her about Dick.' I looked at my mother to see if she knew what he was talking about. She just said, 'Oh, I guess it's about time.'

"Then, I thought, Wow! The two of them know about this, and there's another man in the world who is my father. It was just so weird.

"On that first day, they told me his full name: Dick Peck. Over the next couple of days, I figured out that my name at birth was completely different. They told me what my real name was, and I thought, Oh, how weird! I had absolutely no connection with this other name.

"But I was also embarrassed. I didn't want to talk about it, and mostly I felt like a freak. Somehow the other kids found out about it (probably from me), and from time to time, would blurt something out. We'd be sitting at the table with a guest and all of a sudden Timothy—he was the youngest—would say, 'Suzy has another father, doesn't she?' Then everyone would tell him to shut up.

"I ended up feeling like I had this shadow, something that was invisible to most people but made me feel stigmatized. I didn't like feeling that I was different, and I didn't want to meet the man who was my father. In fact, I didn't even want to know about him. At first.

"After my stepfather told me that he was not my real father, he began treating me differently. There were a few things that I did that were part of my character that he saw as objectionable, like being reserved. I didn't like talking about my feelings, and he would sort of try to make me come out of myself.

"Still, my stepfather had such a strong personality that I always felt uncomfortable asking anything about my own history. From time to time, my parents would say things about my real father. My mother would say not-so-great things about him, and my stepfather would sometimes say good things. Although my mother always liked my father's hands, which she told me were like my hands. Over the years, I found out things about him—that he was a nice guy, that he was funny, that he was considered good-looking—that he was very good at playing the piano, and that he was talented musically.

"My mother and stepfather separated for a little while when I was eleven, and during this time, my mother took all four of us back to California on a Greyhound bus. While we were there, she asked whether or not I wanted to meet my natural father, and I said, 'No, I don't.' At that point, I had no interest in meeting him.

"Ultimately my parents got back together, we returned to New York, and life continued. I went to New York High School for the Performing Arts, where I studied dance and began writing songs. Later I went to Barnard College, where I studied English literature and theater. After college, I had odd jobs. I also performed often at places like Folk City in Greenwich Village.

"I was influenced by my stepfather in a good way because he was a writer. He also played the guitar and had written a song when I was young in which I appeared. It was actually written for my brother Matthew. But I had my own verse. We would talk about writing, about metaphor and poetry, when I was in my early teens. These talks shaped me in many ways.

"When I was in my twenties, the idea of my real father started to haunt me. I would get drunk, and then it would really hit me—I should find him. I had heard that he was in San Diego, and I happened to be going there. I had a pocketful of dimes, and so I started calling all the Richard Pecks in the phone book and saying, 'Hi. Did you know someone named Patricia Schumacher in high school?' That was fruitless.

"Then when I was in my late twenties, I made a couple of records, and I had enormous success with this song, 'Luka,' which went Top 10 all over the world. It was this astonishing thing that happened in my life, this success that I wasn't really expecting. I thought I was just going to have a more low-keyed kind of poetic career, and instead I had this blatant success. Some of it was overwhelming but also very gratifying; this was something I had always wanted and now it had come to pass. So I started to feel that maybe I could challenge this other part of my life—finding my father—and see if that would make a big difference in my life, too.

"On a long plane trip to Japan, I told my manager my life story regarding my father. He knew the name of a detective, who I met with in August 1987. It turned out that the detective was adopted, too, so he was very interested in helping me out. He found Richard within two weeks.

"The detective called me and said, 'I have this information

for you,' and I said, 'Hold on and I'll get a pen.' I went to get the pen and a piece of paper, and I remember thinking, I feel so calm right now. When I got back to the phone and picked it up, I realized I had hung up!

"Anyway, we finally connected, and he gave me my father's address and telephone number. He also told me that Richard had just separated from his second wife and had another daughter. I kept all the information, but I didn't call him. I just carried the information around for a few months and got used to the idea that he was a real man who lived in the real world, who was my father.

"Also, I had some fears because my mother had not been very encouraging about my interest in my father. I remember telling her once that I might want to see Richard, and her response was, 'Well, maybe he doesn't want to see you.'

"But my mother and stepfather had also told me about a certain incident. Apparently my father had come to visit my mother on Mother's Day, 1960, when I was ten months old, and brought her flowers.

"So I knew that Richard had come with flowers on Mother's Day, and that gesture stayed with me. I believed that if he came on Mother's Day, it meant that he was thinking about me. So I took the chance based on that anecdote that he would be receptive to meeting me. And that's really all I had to go on.

"Finally, six months later I wrote him a letter.

"I had all these fantasies of what he was going to be like—a bookish, intellectual sort of guy—even though my mother had told me that he wasn't like that. And, of course, he wasn't bookish at all. He has a kind of visual-spatial talent and a really good eye for art, and he draws. He's a draftsman; he used to work at McDonnell Douglas as a draftsman.

"Also, he plays the piano by ear. Richard plays fluently; it just pours out of him. He learned how to play by listening, and that talent seems to run through that side of the family—the ability to play music without reading. I can't read the music, but I can remember it and I can play it.

"But I sent him this letter saying who I was, and he called me back on New Year's Eve day of that year, and we had this talk. I was kind of stunned.

"I remember being in a little bit of a daze that day and for the rest of the month. Just listening to the cadence of his voice, which seemed so familiar to me. This struck me as odd because his name wasn't familiar, but his voice was and his way of speaking. When I heard his voice, it contained a soothing kind of a memory.

"I was curious to know whether he would be consistent. We made a date to call each other the next Thursday—the first call had been on a Saturday—and this filled me with relief. It wasn't like, now he's going to call me every day and it's going to be overwhelming. And it wasn't, 'I'll call you in a few months,' and I'd never see him again.

"Then I waited to see if he actually would call or if he'd forget. But he was very consistent, and for a while we would speak a couple of times a week. He sent me pictures of himself and of his family that he had met, and of my half-sister, so everything was very visual, and there was all this visual information.

"It turned out that my father had a very strange family situation. First, my father, my biological father, was himself adopted. Curiously he had found his real family just two years before I found him. He had three biological brothers and sisters. His sisters found him through the Motor Vehicle Bureau because they knew that they had had a younger brother, but they'd never seen him and they were always curious about him.

"It was a very dramatic story actually. My biological grandparents were musicians. My grandfather was a trumpet player and my grandmother was a drummer, and the two of them met on the road, and they were together for a short time. They had four kids in five years. It's so weird the way things repeat.

"She had to put her other children in an institution, give my father up for adoption, and so the kids were kind of in and out of institutions for a lot of their growing-up life. She would visit them on Sundays for a couple of years, and then sometimes her life would be stable and she would have them back.

"I have very glamorous pictures of my biological grandmother behind her drum kit and in this band with other women. It just seemed like she was really courageous, especially for the era, which was the 1930s. She performed all over the Midwest. The press clippings were all from the vaudeville circuit in the Midwest. I don't know how she ended up in Southern California, but the whole family ended up there.

"My stepfather was kind of matter-of-fact about Richard, and he said, 'I really did figure that you would probably do this one day, and I think it's fine.' He didn't seem to feel particularly jealous. He actually seemed to have a fair amount of empathy in that situation, which I really was grateful for.

"My mother was not very happy about it, though, at the time, I think she may have been really annoyed by it. Eventually she got used to it. Now it's not even an issue, but at the time it was a problem.

"The thing about Ed that I have to say I really did appreciate was he could probably read me better than anybody I knew. He was very tuned in. He was not remote and distant. He was very involved.

"I certainly never felt unconditional love from Ed. With him, I always felt a sort of unconditional disapproval unless I did something to earn his respect, and even then it was very tenuous and could disappear at any moment. Whereas when I met my biological father, I could just see he'd kept all the pictures, he kept everything, and he had followed my birthdays every year. He knew exactly how old I was. He didn't know my name, because it had been changed, but he knew how old I was and had been thinking of me those years, and he had come back that Mother's Day. But I didn't have that love between the ages of two and twenty-eight.

"Once I met Richard, I had my issues with struggling with the reality of him as opposed to my fantasy of him. Ed's personality was so huge in so many ways and so extreme, and then I met my father, who's a really nice guy. He's not particularly larger than life as Ed was. He wasn't able to connect with me as a child, but he's been there when I needed him since then. He is a big part of my life and my daughter's life, and we see each other whenever we can. So there is a part of my life that feels settled and put back in place.

"My daughter, Ruby, is now in her teens, and although I am divorced from her dad, she knows her father and talks to him every day. She is a vocal major at the La Guardia High School of Performing Arts and plays many different instruments, so the music has continued down the family line through her."

MAKING PEACE WITH YOUR DAD

I fear I have come to believe that getting to know your father, whether he is alive or dead, whether he agrees to be found or not, ends up being one of those bad news/good news conundrums.

Bad news first: Despite having devoted an entire chapter to getting to know your father, I regret to say that for most fatherless daughters (myself included), truly knowing your father is virtually—and ultimately—impossible. If he has died, it doesn't matter how many of his friends or relatives you interview, you'll only find an echo of him. Rather like reading a brilliant biography of Abraham Lincoln or Thomas Jefferson, you may feel you know him better, but you never believe that you have come to know the real man.

If he left the family and cut off contact with you for years, it is also nearly impossible to ever really know him. Even if you forge some sort of relationship later in life, you and he still have to make up for many lost years and much guilt, anger, and regret.

As I worked on this book, I got to know some of the women I interviewed rather well. One of them, Maggie Malone, had become very involved in the American War Orphans Network (AWON) because her dad had been killed in Europe in March 1945. Maggie and I were having a drink one evening and she asked me about how I was doing on the book. She said hesitatingly, "You know, every time I go to one of those AWON meetings, I think my dad will be there." Then after a moment, almost unable to speak, she said, " . . . But he never is."

I could see that Maggie was close to tears, and I felt much the same way. I had known that feeling of hopelessness myself, but I had never been able to articulate it as clearly as Maggie had. I, too, had gone places and done things, hoping to find my dad. I had driven several times to East Cleveland and looked at the house my dad grew up in. I had made contact with cousins on my dad's side of the family who I had never known before and established a loving relationship with them. I had written this book.

I believe I started out writing this book—even writing this chapter—thinking that I would find my dad, and in a grand stroke of generosity, share that information with other fatherless daughters. But the fact is, as I come close to finishing this book, I have learned that truly *knowing* my dad . . . well, it's just not going to happen.

Now, for the good news: The main reason I wanted to write this book was that I wanted to define what it was that I missed by not having a father. Moreover, I wanted to be able to articulate the meaning of that loss and to share my findings with other fatherless daughters.

I ultimately realized that my quest to know what I had missed was only a part of what I wanted, or, perhaps, just a cover for what I wanted. What I really wanted was to find my father, to make my father come home to me. But what I ultimately came to feel at a much deeper level was, quite simply, that he had died and that he was never coming home. By discovering that fact—by really experiencing that emotion—I have felt liberated. It wasn't a happy, joyful feeling, but more like a sense of peace.

12. HEALING

What I have taken from the cemetery is a sentence that keeps running through my mind like music: Love is stronger than death.

—Mary Gordon, *The Shadow Man*

Recently I saw a film that moved me deeply. It was called *My Architect* and was made by Nathaniel Kahn, the illegitimate son of famed architect Louis Kahn. Nathaniel, like me, longed to know his father, who had died when he was eleven.

Louis Kahn led a messy life. An artist and a workaholic, Kahn died in the men's room at Penn Station in New York City in 1974 at the age of seventy-three, bankrupt not only financially but apparently also professionally and personally. He had been married only once and had one daughter from that union. However, over his lifetime, he also had had two long-term love affairs, and he had a daughter with one of these women, and a son, Nathaniel, with the other.

Over the years of his childhood, Nathaniel had received only sporadic attention from his father, who died before Nathaniel entered his teens. As a result, Nathaniel sought to know his father better, through both his father's architecture and his own art as a filmmaker.

"I'd made other films, but this [film] was something that I had avoided for a long time, because it's scary to go back," Nathaniel said in a quote from the theater's flyer. "You don't know what you're going to find. There's always the risk of embarrassing yourself: here comes what appears to be a middle-aged man asking questions that a child asks. That was difficult."

The fact is Nathaniel Kahn's quest was reassuring to me. Like me, he seemed to believe strongly that it was necessary to actively mourn his father's death and his own personal loss. A significant part of his mourning process involved his search to try to know his father. Through visiting all the buildings his father had designed, through interviewing people who had known his father, and finally, by interpreting his father's art through his own, Nathaniel Kahn was able not only to begin to understand his father but to forgive him.

What moved me most was that by the end of the film, Nathaniel discovered he needed to let go of his father: to forgive him for hurting his mother; forgive him for not providing all the love and assurance he had needed as a child; forgive him for dying too soon.

So, finally, how do we come to terms with the loss of our father? How do we ultimately accept that he was not there for us, for whatever reason? When do we know we have accepted his loss? What does acceptance really mean?

We need to acknowledge our pain and face up to the fact that we must work our way through our grief. Consciously mourning our father's loss, whether he disappeared through death or abandonment, is imperative. An important element in the mourning process is getting to know your father as much as you can and accepting the fact that you can never know him completely. But it is also important to get to know yourself. For this quest, you may need a little help—or maybe even a lot of help—although there are ways you can begin to cope on your own.

HELPING YOURSELF

All sorts of techniques are readily available to help you get to know your father and to help yourself work your way through the mourning process.

Journaling

Journaling is simply the act of keeping a written record of your thoughts, feelings, and activities on a regular basis. You can do this by writing by hand in a notebook or keyboarding your thoughts into a file on your computer.

I have been keeping a journal most of my adult life. I find that writing in my journal is most effective if I write first thing in the morning. I sit down with a cup of coffee and empty my head of whatever occurs to me. At times, I may simply record incredibly banal information, like I'm happy that I've lost five pounds or I'm worried about paying off my MasterCard bill. Usually, though, especially when I'm working through a problem, I just write out my thoughts.

Often I don't know what I am really thinking until I have put it into words. I have even written Freudian slips, or something other than what I was intending, but which often turned out to be closer to the real truth of the matter.

Try not to edit yourself when you write in your journal; just let it out. If you become blocked, write anything that crosses your mind, and don't worry about how it sounds or if your writing is great art. (I have found that spontaneous material often ends up being the most compelling.) Remember, this journal is for your eyes only; no one else should see it, which should free you from self-consciousness.

I don't write in my journal every day; in fact, sometimes I don't write for months on end. But I write frequently when I am going through a troublesome or painful experience, sometimes several times during the day when I'm plagued with self-doubt or working through a problem. It is a great emotional relief to take a problem out of my head and objectify it onto a piece of paper (or, in my case, on my computer screen).

I also find it fascinating and rewarding to go back occasionally and reread past entries. I'm frequently surprised (as well as disconcerted, upset, or even bored) that I'm still struggling with a particular problem after months, or even years. You, too, may quickly see that certain issues crop up over and over again.

With regard to problems of father loss, keeping a journal can serve many purposes. If your father died when you were young, you obviously won't have immediate issues with regard to him. Perhaps, though, you can look at other problems you may be having in your present life—a heartbreaking love affair; guilt over behavior toward your husband; conflict with a boss; health or addiction problems—and consider whether these issues have anything to do with your father or your father's loss. If your father left the family and you are considering making contact with him or have already done so, you can use your journal as a sounding board for the emotions you are experiencing.

In any case, if you are serious about working through your father-loss issues, journaling can be a great help. Also, remember to be especially vigilant about looking for father-related issues when you record your thoughts and feelings in your journal.

Letters—Mailed and Unmailed

Writing letters is another way to articulate your feelings. Instead of talking to yourself as you do in a journal, you are speaking to someone else—specifically, possibly, your father. If he has died, obviously he will never read your missive, yet the act of writing a letter to him directly and articulating long-dormant, unexpressed feelings can be both cathartic and healing.

If your father is alive and you have been out of touch for some time, writing a letter to him expressing your emotions can be equally helpful; however, consider very carefully whether you want to send it to him. My personal rule of thumb: If you are entertaining even a wisp of doubt about sending it—don't. (On a few occasions in my life I have sent letters I have deeply regretted; I should have taken my own advice.) Instead, step back and rethink your potential exchange with him. Perhaps it would be better to meet with him face to face, or, at least, talk to him on the telephone rather than write. Use a briefer letter to explain your wish to meet with him, then follow up with a telephone call to set up a time and place for a meeting, even if it is just a telephone meeting. This will give both of you time to consider what you want to say. Also, if you are seriously considering writing to him to set up a meeting, you might want to work with a therapist as you go through this potentially extremely upsetting process. (See the section on psychotherapy later in this chapter.)

Another way to get at buried feelings through letter writing is to write a letter to yourself: not yourself as you are today, but yourself at another point in your life, such as when your father died or a period in your life when you missed him.

Family Photos

I have found examining old family photos to be not only a pleasure but also a fascinating and informative exercise. Although old photos (as well as old family home movies or videos) may not give you the last word on your father and his relationship with you, your mother, or others in your family, they can tell you a lot.

For example, among my family's albums are several rather formal photographs of my dad fondly cuddling my older brother, Steve, when he was only a few months old. In these pictures, Steve is usually swaddled in lovely hand-knit baby clothes and carefully wrapped in a beautiful blanket. However, as the years passed, fewer photos of my dad holding any of the rest of us in this relaxed and elegant way are evident. Instead, the later shots are all group shots of Dad with kids, invariably with one child crying, one walking out of the frame, and one with his shirttail hanging out, indicating, I suppose, that we were a fairly typical, fairly chaotic family.

Among your family pictures, you may find evidence of your parents' love for each other or of tensions between them. Don't just focus on photos of your dad. Check out pictures of other family members. You may find relatives you didn't know you had; images of an uncle, now ancient, who turns out to have once been breathtakingly handsome; or pictures of your mom, arm-in-arm with a guy you don't recognize, and what does that mean?

Art Therapy

Working through feelings and emotions regarding father loss can be accomplished through many forms of art or craft: short story, novel, memoir, play, poetry writing, painting, sculpture, photography, film, music, dance. You can use whatever art form you choose to express positive feelings about your father, perhaps even create some sort of commemoration or tribute. I once made a collage of old family photos for my mother, and the entire process of searching for the right pictures, deciding what to include and what to leave out, and arranging the material was both fun and informative.

Of course, you can also use art to express negative feelings. Many great artists have used their feelings about their fathers as the basis for a work of art; the plays of Arthur Miller *(Death of a Salesman)* and Sam Shepard *(True West)* come to mind.

Commemoration

Another way to honor your father while getting in touch with your own feelings is through a formal commemoration or celebration. You can celebrate your father's life in many ways. If he has died, you might simply visit his grave; ask that his name be included in prayers at your place of worship on the anniversary of his death, his birthday, or a special holiday; or make a donation in his name to an appropriate charity. You might commemorate him in a poem or story, make a special photo album just about him, or plant a tree in a park in his name. My stepfather was very involved in the establishment of a senior center in the town where he lived. When he died, the directors of the center placed a stone in the garden with his name on it.

If you are working through feelings regarding a father who abandoned the family, a commemorative gesture, including any of the previous suggestions, can be incredibly cleansing for you.

Returning to Your Childhood Home

My ninety-six-year-old mother still lives in the same area where I grew up, as do two of my brothers and their families. Although I now live in New York City, I visit my hometown of Cleveland, Ohio, a couple of times a year, and remain connected to it through my relatives and old friends. Almost every time I go home, I revisit the street where I grew up and drive around my old neighborhood, which, of course, always brings back memories. As I was researching this book, my brother, Herb, who still lives and works in town, gave me a guided tour, pointing out changes, reminding me of people I'd forgotten, and sharing some of his experiences as a kid, which at times were decidedly different from my own, although we lived under the same roof and are only nineteen months apart in age. We had a wonderful day together.

Many fatherless daughters don't have such strong connections to their childhood home. Families often move when the father dies, the parents' marriage dissolves, or, most especially, when the mother remarries. Still, it's important to revisit the home you shared with your father; to walk the streets of your old neighborhood; to visit your school, church or synagogue, parks, or whatever places ground you in that community, especially those that involved your father. The sights and sounds of these places are bound to dredge up memories; you may be surprised at the feelings they evoke.

Visiting Your Father's Grave

Almost every time I visit my mother, I visit my father's grave site, which is also in the town where I grew up. I take fresh flowers, I clean off the stone, and then I quietly stand or sit with my dad. My father is buried next to my grandmother, and, by a rather odd quirk of family real estate, my stepfather. (My mother will also be buried in an adjoining plot.) Other close relatives are buried nearby. My visits to this lovely, serene place allow me time to sort of commune with my dad and other relatives who have passed away. Somehow it is a centering experience, a special way of connecting with my father.

Several women I interviewed were members of the American War Orphans Network, daughters of men who had died during World War II. Visiting their fathers' graves has been one of the most important and compelling aspects of their AWON experience; all of them found the experience unforgettably moving.

Gloria Zuccarella Layne's story is particularly poignant. For years, Gloria's stepfather had encouraged her and her mother to visit her father's grave at Margraten, Netherlands. (Gloria's father, Rocco Zuccarella, died on April 8, 1945, near Werl, Germany, a casualty of the Battle of the Bulge.) Gloria's mother never agreed to go, but finally, in 1985, Gloria decided to stop at Margraten as part of a trip she and her husband were taking to Europe. Although she considered the visit to Margraten to be just a small part of a bigger vacation, as soon as the plane landed in Brussels, Gloria insisted that they travel immediately to the cemetery, although that was not part of their original plan. Gloria's husband, Allen, totally sympathetic, agreed immediately to go. They rented a car and drove for several hours, but by the time they reached the cemetery, it was early evening and the cemetery officials had already gone home for the day.

Here's how Gloria describes what happened next:

"The gates were open, so we went in, but I didn't have any of the papers with me, and I just didn't have it in my mind where the grave was situated or anything. [My husband] Allen said, 'Don't worry about it. We'll be back tomorrow, and they'll bring us to the grave.'

"There are over eight thousand graves [at Margraten]. [Allen] started walking off in one direction, and I can only tell you that there was a pulling. And, Allen as my witness, I was pulled. I was walking this way—I just don't know, but there was something. And I stopped and there was my father's grave. I cannot to this day believe it, but I looked up, and it was his grave. All I remember is screaming, 'Allen. Allen, I found him! I found him!'

"It was truly a feeling that he was waiting for me. I really do believe it. It's not as if he's on the end grave or in the first row. It's K53, like in the middle of everything. How in God's name would you find that? But I did. I really believe it's God's miracle. But I do believe that for all these years now he was waiting for me. There had to be some closure and peace for him. I had to get there. . . . And now I really feel like he's at rest. I think he's more at peace."

PSYCHOTHERAPY

Psychotherapy is a way of treating mental and/or emotional disorders using psychological methods administered by a professional psychiatrist or psychotherapist. Many methods, or models, of psychotherapy are available, from traditional psychoanalysis to a host of contemporary Western and Eastern therapies. Psychotherapy, to my mind, is one of the most effective ways to help you through your mourning process.

Traditional Psychoanalysis

Psychoanalysis, the original form of psychotherapy, evolved about a century ago through the work of Sigmund Freud and his followers (or detractors), including Karl Jung, Karen Horney, Alfred Adler, and many others. Today a psychoanalyst is either a psychiatrist (a medical doctor who has advanced training in psychology) or a psychotherapist (a psychologist who holds a Ph.D. degree in psychology). Both require a state license, and only a psychiatrist (medical doctor) can prescribe drugs, such as antidepressants, antianxiety medication, and the like.

Traditional therapy, sometimes referred to as talk therapy, is when the patient (or client) and the therapist sit opposite each other, and the patient talks about what's on her mind or events that are occurring, or have occurred, in her life, and the therapist responds. The traditional practice of a patient lying on a couch during the session, with the therapist sitting behind her head, taking notes—the theory being that the patient could more easily access and articulate memories (or free associate, to use the therapeutic term) mentally and emotionally in the prone position with the therapist out of sight—is less common these days. Also, traditional analysis involved seeing the therapist four or five times per week, but these days seeing a therapist once a week for several months or a year is more the norm.

Other Methods of Psychotherapy

An enormous number of other therapeutic methods for treating emotional problems have evolved over the past century. These include everything from Jungian therapy, Gestalt therapy, primal therapy, Reichian therapy, and hypnotherapy to Rolfing, transpersonal therapy, drug therapy, and soul retrieval—the list is long.

Many contemporary therapies fall under the umbrella term *behavioral therapy* as opposed to *psychotherapy*. Instead of explaining or working through emotions intellectually, as is done in traditional psychotherapy, work is done to alter overt behavior, with the idea that once the destructive behavior is under control, emotional healing will follow.

Group therapy, as opposed to one-on-one treatment with a therapist, is another approach to coming to terms with emotional problems. Groups can be made up of an eclectic collection of a particular therapist's patients, or of people with a single mutual interest, such as grief, parental loss, or even specifically father loss. Group therapy can be very effective, giving you a chance to air your concerns, as well as hear the similar—or very different—life stories and responses of those who have also experienced father loss.

Why Therapy?

Many people resist entering psychotherapy. Some even take the position that psychotherapy is only for "crazy" people. Others believe that seeking psychotherapy is a sign of weakness and contend that they should be able to solve their emotional problems on their own. Still others consider the need for psychotherapy to be shameful. Finally, many object to the expense—and psychotherapy is expensive—which is only complicated by the fact that most insurance policies do not cover the costs to any significant degree. (Which, in some ways, only underscores the still-prevailing negative beliefs about psychotherapy.)

To make matters worse, not much hard scientific evidence has been found by psychologists to confirm the theory that loss of a parent early in life results in emotional or psychiatric problems in adult children. As Laura Bernay, herself both a psychotherapist and a fatherless daughter, says: "One of the old truisms in psychiatry was that children who lose a parent early in life are more prone to depression later in life. It seems intuitively obvious and makes perfect sense. Well, it turns out when they looked at the numbers, [the numbers] don't come out. . . . There may be a slightly increased incidence of depression in people who have early loss, but by far, there is no one-to-one, cause-and-effect piece of evidence stating that if you have early [parental] loss, then you will have depression later in life. The other old [belief] was increased suicide rate, and I think that one fell by the wayside, too."

Given these findings, why pursue psychotherapy? As Bernay asserts, the issues surrounding father loss are incredibly complex and are difficult, if not impossible, to quantify in a scientific way. As we've seen, how you lose your father (through death, divorce, or abandonment), your age when he died or left, your mother's responses, your place in the family, the presence of other important men in your life, and many other factors affect how you experience the loss of your father. I believe that perhaps the reason psychological researchers have found little hard evidence about the effects of father loss is not because no negative effects exist, but simply because they are too numerous and amorphous to define. This vague-yet-complex quality is precisely why intense psychotherapy of some kind is often necessary for people who have lost fathers early in life.

Psychotherapy, especially one-on-one talk therapy, allows you to articulate your thoughts and feelings about your father's loss and related issues with the support and feedback from an objective professional. This person's job is to help you. Unlike a spouse, a friend, a relative, or even a religious counselor, a therapist has no other agenda but to be of service to you and to your emotional health. He or she has no other relationship with you, except the therapeutic one.

I am a very strong advocate for psychotherapy for people who have lost a parent during childhood. I believe that the emotional problems that almost always result from such a severe childhood trauma and its extenuating circumstances require professional help to define, treat, and work through. Since I am not a trained professional in the field, I can speak only superficially about psychotherapy, but I urge you, if you feel your life has been scarred by father loss, to explore professional psychotherapy as a way of dealing with your father-loss issues.

I participated in traditional, basically Freudian psychotherapy with a psychiatrist for many years. I decided to enter therapy at the time that my marriage was breaking down. Not surprisingly, my disintegrating marriage was only a symptom of much deeper emotional problems that took years for me to work through. During the first year, I went twice a week, and for the next five years or so, I went once a week. For many years thereafter, I would return to therapy for additional weeks or months during periods when I was having problems. I even went back into therapy while I was working on this book. Frankly, I believe that psychotherapy not only shaped my life but may have *saved* my life in certain ways.

In all honesty, my dad's death was not the sole reason for all my troubles; many other factors contributed to the problems I faced. However, the fact that my father died when I was ten was the very first biographical detail that I told my therapist in my first session. I believe that my dad's loss was central in my emotional development and colored the way I experienced the world, particularly my relationships with men.

As Linda, a fatherless daughter and a psychotherapist, says: "I do talk therapy and I think that it's helpful. People [I've treated] have gotten to the point where they can do things they hadn't done before. But I think that there's a unique way that we experience things that even though we can say, 'Oh yeah, I know what it feels like because my father died, too' . . . There's a point where it becomes only your own."

RELIGION

Seeking help from a religious advisor or through prayer is another excellent avenue toward healing the wounds of father loss. Many people turn to their religious leaders for emotional help during times of crisis, but you can go to these same helpers even years after your loss.

Many of the books I consulted on the subject of father loss while researching this book, particularly books on how father loss affects women, are published by religious (particularly Christian) publishers. Some of these books are concerned with the protection of traditional family values and focus on the importance of a strong father at the head of the family and the problems that develop when he is absent. In addition, most of these books are based on the premise that the ultimate father is God, and in His hands, all can be healed, which is a widespread belief.

I believe strongly in the benefits of prayer and religious counseling, but I also think that religious counseling is most helpful and effective in conjunction with psychotherapy in some form. Although religious counselors are almost always compassionate, discreet, and trustworthy, often your priest, minister, or rabbi has some other relationship with you or with other members of your family. You may socialize with your priest or minister at weekly services, weddings, and other church gatherings, possibly making your more intimate talks with him or her problematic. You may feel embarrassed, ashamed, or inhibited about revealing family secrets.

Nevertheless, I believe turning to your religious background, faith, and beliefs is an excellent way to begin the healing process. As I've said, I believe you may well need to combine formal religious guidance with some other therapeutic remedy, but religious support can be an important key to emotional healing.

SPIRITUALISM AND SPIRITUALITY

Spiritualism is the name of a formal religion that is centered on the belief that the dead can communicate with the living. *Spirituality* is a more general term, connoting any sort of dealings with a person's spiritual life, from traditional religions to working in less mainstream areas, such as soul work. In some forms, spirituality might be considered the link between psychotherapy and religion.

Many of the women I interviewed spoke of their belief that their fathers were often with them in spirit, usually as a guide and protector. Margaret believes without question that her father visited her within days of his death, and although he never appeared to her again, she always believed he was there protecting her. Maria felt strongly that her father was guiding her for years after his death. "I'm a Catholic by birth," Maria said. "But . . . I believe in spirits. For the longest time, I felt my father's presence. Actually, on my wedding day, I felt that there had been a departure and that my husband was almost taking over the protection of me. But I felt like I had been guided. When my father passed away, I felt like he was there protecting me."

Other women I talked to experienced strong, vivid dreams about their fathers. Ellen described what she called an "odd little story." She had dreams about Frank Sinatra, but she actually believed the man in the dreams was her father, because her dad had strongly resembled Sinatra. "But in my dreams he's always leaving," she says. "I see him and [then] he's gone. I can't catch up with him. He's on a train, I run after him, he's gone, always. I never get around to asking him the questions I want to ask."

I am not a skeptic. I utterly accept the reality of a spiritual dimension in our lives, and under certain circumstances (usually extreme emotional trauma), I do believe we can be visited by those who have died. However, I also believe that more than psychotherapy and traditional religion, the world of spiritualism and spirituality is peopled with so-called experts who are not properly trained and may even have questionable motives. Studying about spiritual cures and attending lectures and forums can be instructive and incredibly liberating. Perhaps, as I said regarding traditional religion, the best advice is to combine explorations of spirituality with formal therapy.

WHEN ARE YOU HEALED?

How will you know when you are healed?

Many years ago, a therapist said to me something that at first glance might seem very depressing, but somehow it didn't upset me. He said that losing my father at a young age was rather like going blind or deaf or being crippled from polio. It was something that was never going to heal; it was an event that could not be fixed.

Somehow that bold statement was a relief. I accepted his statement—how could I not?—and believe this was the beginning of my accepting my father's death.

Accceptance is, of course, the end result of the mourning process. However, I have also learned that we must cross one more bridge before acceptance is complete and we can let go and find peace. That bridge is built on the act of forgiveness.

13. STARTING FRESH

People, in general, would rather die than forgive. It's that hard. If God said in plain language, "I'm giving you a choice, forgive or die, a lot of people would go ahead and order their coffin."

—Sue Monk Kidd, *The Secret Life of Bees*

I began this book with the idea that I wanted to go on a journey—a pilgrimage, if you like—to find out what I had missed having grown up without the presence of my father. I knew the journey involved a considerable amount of work: interviewing, researching, writing, thinking, and possibly experiencing emotions I had not expected. I was even aware that chances were good that I would come face-to-face with certain truths that might not thrill me.

Originally I thought this book would take me about eighteen months to write, but for reasons I couldn't at first define, it ultimately took me eight years. Although, admittedly, I'm not a particularly speedy writer, I had already written several books, and the longest it had ever taken me to prepare a manuscript was one year, not three or five, and certainly not eight. Clearly, something else was at work here.

In fact, I sailed through the interview and research phases of the book. I loved meeting other fatherless daughters and hearing their stories, and managed to conduct, rather efficiently, more than a hundred interviews. I also read and took notes on scores of articles and books. However, every time I sat down to write about my findings, I was faced with an enormous choir of demons. For starters, I often felt overcome by the amount of information I'd uncovered. I also wondered if I had the right to my opinions on this subject; after all, I wasn't a professional sociologist or a trained psychologist. Paradoxically, I eventually felt paralyzed by my own tardiness!

But most of all, I was often absolutely floored by the depth of my emotions. I would outline a chapter, pull together my research, begin to write (which often uncovered even more fresh ideas), and then suddenly I would be presented with some notion that would utterly overwhelm me. I would be awash in a wave of feelings that included loss, regret, fear, sadness, and very often, anger. Sometimes I would be so saddened that I would have to take a nap. (A note to other writers: this was different from the "writer's nap," a mode of procrastination that sometimes, but not always, means that the creative juices are flowing but need time to collect and gel.)

These overwhelming emotions should not have come as a surprise, and, in fact, in many ways, they did not. For example, I'd been dealing with my anger for years in one form or another, usually as depression. I was most in touch with this feeling as it pertained to my mother (as opposed to my father and his death), and I'd worked over this ground ad nauseam in therapy. I'd also experienced anger repeatedly in my relationships with men. I was well aware that my anger resulted from fears of abandonment and sometimes real rejection. As I did my interviews for this book, I became aware that anger was a common emotion among fatherless daughters. Still, these emotions seemed to paralyze me in terms of finishing my book, and I didn't know what to do about them.

But I persevered and gradually completed chapter after chapter. I thought through my ideas and expressed them the best way I could. I came up with suggestions for coping with loss, like getting to know your dad, and various methods for healing. And yet these difficult emotions persisted. In the midst of this ongoing dilemma, I had an experience that had nothing to do with father loss but ended up leading me to a final revelation and to closure.

I took a job writing publications for the Brooklyn Public Library. (Like many writers, I have to do other work to earn my living.) I loved the work, I loved the library, believed that I was doing a good job, and, indeed, received lots of feedback to that effect. However, one person was not pleased with me or my performance, and unfortunately, that person was my boss. I worked at the library for about nine months, and she and I butted heads continually. I simply could not please her. In the end, she fired me.

I was devastated and for several months was deeply depressed, upset, and, not surprisingly, *really pissed off.* Here was that old bugaboo *anger* again. Although I was experiencing this emotion in an entirely different context from father loss, I saw that this situation was clearly linked to feelings of rejection, abandonment, and helplessness, emotions that I had defined as hallmarks of father loss. The circumstances also had everything to do with my fears regarding my ability to support myself financially, another issue frequently linked to father loss.

The anger was paralyzing me. I wasn't moving forward; instead, I was wallowing in my own despair. Finally, after meditating, praying, reading lots of self-help literature—and, yes, more wallowing—I realized that in order to move on from this setback, I had to *let it go.* And in order to let it go, I had to *forgive* this young woman who had been, to my mind, so cruel and unfair to me.

I can't say that my rage and depression shifted overnight as a result of this realization; it didn't. But I worked at it, and finally the anger began to evaporate and my depression and paralysis lifted. I came to see that the key to dissolving the anger was *forgiveness.*

Yet I still had questions. What exactly does forgiveness mean? With regard to father loss, who was I supposed to forgive? My father? My mother? God? And was I capable of it? To answer these questions, I began reading everything I could find on the subject; thinking; meditating.

WHAT IS FORGIVENESS?

At its most fundamental level, forgiveness means pardoning or excusing an offense, a debt, or a fault. At a deeper level, forgiveness means that we must renounce any bad feelings associated with an offense. We must try to see the absolute truth of a troubling situation, then make a conscious, committed decision to give up all condemnation, resentment, and anger surrounding it.

To invoke the old cliché, forgiving is easier said than done. Forgiveness is difficult in any anger-provoking situation, but particularly unique with reference to father loss, a situation over which we had no control, and because we were children, we were and are in no way at fault.

What Forgiveness Is Not

Perhaps the best way to understand the concept of forgiveness is to look at what it is *not*. For many of us, the notion of forgiveness has a number of associations that run deep, but to my mind they are not necessarily either true or helpful, especially as we work our way toward resolution with regard to father loss. In order to have truly forgiven, we often mistakenly believe we must:

- Pretend the injury doesn't matter
- Forget the offense
- No longer feel pain when remembering the offense
- Expect that our relationship will return to what it once was

Hey, No Problem

Many of us believe that in order to forgive, we must pretend that an injury doesn't really matter. Even when someone apologizes for hurting us in some way, we feel compelled to say, "Oh, that's all right. It really didn't bother me." That is not forgiveness; it is lying. Instead, we need to acknowledge that a particular offense did hurt us; that it mattered.

This attitude of feigned forgiveness came up frequently among the fatherless women I interviewed, particularly women whose fathers had purposefully abandoned the family. As Judith Wallerstein stated in her book *Second Chances,* "Girls have a powerful need to create a protective, loving father, one who would never intentionally let them down. . . . Without any sense of contradiction, they are able to maintain a benign image of the loving father side by side with a history of repeated rejections and failures."

This attitude of "Hey, no problem" often masks deep rage. If your father left the family, you may think that the quickest route to forgiveness—and possibly his attention—is to pretend your parents' divorce and your father's desertion wasn't a big deal. This may be especially true if your dad remained accessible to some extent. In recent years, divorce has become breathtakingly commonplace—ergo, supposedly, not hurtful. This, of course, is not true. Your parents' divorce and your father's loss has been central to your life, and you need to acknowledge it before you can truly forgive.

If your father has died, you may feel that forgiveness isn't relevant and isn't a problem, because, after all, how could you be angry at someone who didn't choose to leave you? As irrational as it may seem, anger toward someone who has died is not uncommon. Unfortunately, such feelings tend to arouse guilt, so they are often quickly denied. Your mother or other family members may also have hurt you as a result of, or in relation to, your father's death. All of these emotions need to be acknowledged and dealt with before true forgiveness can take place.

Forgive and Forget

When it comes to forgiveness, many of us dredge up the old adage "Forgive and forget." We think that in order to excuse a personal offense, we must decide to forget it ever happened. Of course, we don't forget, especially when it involves an issue as serious as the loss or abandonment of our father. The attempt to forget what cannot be forgotten only puts you in an emotional bind and confuses the meaning of forgiveness. We need to not only remember the pain of our father's loss but make a concerted effort to deal with those feelings. When the negative feelings of grief have been worked through, then we may not cease to experience pain, but we can begin to cope with sad memories or painful feelings.

Pain, No Gain

Some of us believe that we have not truly forgiven if we continue to experience pain over our father's loss. I have heard it said that one way to test if we have forgiven a transgression is to note how it feels if we hear something positive about the person who has hurt us. If we feel no pain, we've forgiven the person; if we feel anger or hurt, we haven't.

Frankly, I don't completely believe this notion, especially with regard to pain as intense as father loss. Recently I heard that the woman who had fired me from the Brooklyn Public Library had taken a very good job at another nonprofit organization. I thought I had completely forgiven her and moved on, but when I heard this news, I felt a rush of resentment. The moment I felt this, I tried something I'd also read about in my research on forgiveness: I sent her a blessing. I caught myself feeling resentful; I stopped it; and I simply said to myself: "God, bless her." I must confess, I said it with a twinge of sarcasm. Yet it worked; my pain eased and I let it go.

With regard to father loss or abandonment, remembered pain is going to be far more powerful than an insult from a former boss; it will probably last forever. This is particularly true for women whose fathers have consciously abandoned them. When you learn that your father has happily remarried, has had another child (or is indulging stepchildren from his new wife), is living a more affluent life than yours (or you think he is), or is just plain happier to be gone, you are going to feel resentment. Even women whose fathers have died may experience anger at certain moments for any number of reasons. Our father may not have been there to protect us from an abusive or neglectful mother; to help pay for our college education; to walk us down the aisle on our wedding day; to cuddle our firstborn.

These sorts of negative feelings are going to present themselves over and over again, probably for the rest of our lives. However, that doesn't mean we can't forgive our fathers. I think that it is important to acknowledge and explore these feelings. When this exploratory work is completed, the feelings can be put aside. When they bubble up again (and they almost certainly will), they can be dealt with in a kind but firm manner.

It Never Happened

Many of us assume that true forgiveness means that the relationship between us and the transgressor must return to what it was before the offense. Whether it's a spat over a forgotten appointment, an explosion over a spouse's love affair, or the construction of an adult relationship with a father who left when we were very young, the relationship will never be the same as it was originally. In many situations, the relationship may ultimately be better, but it can never go back to what it was before the transgression.

With regard to father loss, the change in our relationship with our dad is obvious. Our fathers died or left the family when we were children, and we are now adults. Obviously, we'll never be Daddy's little girl again—if we ever were! For women whose fathers are still alive, an opportunity to create a new relationship is possibly open. (Whether a new relationship can or should be forged is something that needs to be considered and acted upon, or not.) For a woman whose father has died, the fact that he can never be truly known must be acknowledged and accepted. In either case, we must face the fact that the loss has colored and changed our lives, often in a negative way. This needs to be examined, forgiven, and let go.

WHO MUST WE FORGIVE?

So, who must we forgive? Obviously, for starters, we must pardon our fathers. Some women, especially women whose dads have died, do not consciously experience rage at their fathers in any way. As a result, forgiveness may seem like a non sequitur. However, I believe this rosy view of an abandoning father—even if the abandonment is due to death— is usually a defense against feeling real pain. Daughters of fathers who have died are often as angry as daughters of fathers who literally walked out, but their anger is usually masked in some way, often as depression.

This truth came as a complete surprise to me and was one of the pivotal personal discoveries I made as a result of researching and writing this book. I have always thought and said that I adored my father. But underneath that veneer of adoration, I was carrying around a tremendous amount of anger. Consciously, I knew, of course, that my father didn't want to die, but subconsciously I experienced his death as abandonment, as sharply as if he had chosen to leave. Moreover, I was furious that he had left behind such a financial and emotional mess in our home.

Many of the women I interviewed whose fathers had literally abandoned their families were very clear that they were angry with their fathers, and most of these women were in no frame of mind to forgive them. As one young woman said, in language that clearly mirrored her rage: "I'm very unforgiving. If my dad got his shit together and came to me and said, 'I fucked up and let's just start [again],' I don't know how I would act. I would try to be open-minded. [But] I don't think I would ever be totally forgiving."

Forgiving Mom

A major part of the resentment of fatherless daughters has to do with the fact that they were left with neglectful, abusive, or overwhelmed mothers without the protection of their fathers. Many women who are widowed or divorced harbor their own deep rage toward their lost husbands. Their anger is often accompanied by loneliness and fear, which in turn frequently evolves into a plethora of problems. (As I noted earlier, one of the most frequent trends I encountered in my interviews was alcoholism among the mothers of fatherless daughters.) Their children, perhaps particularly their daughters, often incur the brunt of their mothers' emotional turmoil.

Not only must we forgive our fathers, many of us must also forgive our mothers for not being there for us, and sometimes for very real neglect and abuse. Forgiving our mothers can be as hard as forgiving our fathers; it may be even harder. Often our anger toward our mothers is more obvious, more concrete, more real. We're able to be in touch with that anger simply because she is, or was, present.

Forgiving Others

Most of the time, other family members are as affected by our father's death or abandonment as we are, although probably not in the same way. This includes sisters and brothers, grandparents, aunts and uncles, and even close family friends. We may have been saddled with responsibility for younger siblings, endured sexual abuse from a brother or uncle, or felt neglected by an older sister or aunt who should have been more responsive to our needs. One woman I interviewed recalled that her uncle bragged that he had promised her father, as her father went off to fight in Europe during

World War II, that he would take care of his wife and children if anything happened to him. After her father was killed, this uncle's ultimate contribution was that he showed up at their house once a month to clean out the refrigerator and to berate her mother for being a lousy housekeeper. The woman who related this anecdote told it with great humor, but vestiges of her resentment, even after sixty years, were still evident.

Regardless of whether it's a major violation or a minor (even amusing) transgression, if we are still harboring any anger or negative feelings, we need to look at them carefully, come to terms with them however we can (and humor helps!), forgive the transgressors, and move on.

Forgiving Ourselves

Fatherless daughters experience guilt for any number of reasons. For the most part, until I began working on this book, I was not in touch with any anger I had toward my dad. Still, I experienced feelings of guilt every time I came up against a flickering thought that I might be furious with him for, in effect, abandoning me and my brothers. I finally had to allow myself to fully experience those feelings; and, in addition to forgiving him, I had to forgive myself for feeling them.

As women who have grown up without the guidance of a loving father, we all suffer from various problems, especially involving our relationships with men. Almost every woman I interviewed expressed some sense of regret or shame over a relationship (or relationships) with a man (or men). I, of course, include myself as one who made many mistakes and who has many regrets in this regard. We have all behaved uncaringly, impulsively, shamefully at times, with regard to men, very possibly because we are fatherless daughters. (As I write this, I suspect that many women who grew up with a strong father, even a loving one, have just as many regrets.) In any case, we must forgive ourselves.

WHY MUST WE FORGIVE?

Many studies have been conducted on the subject of forgiveness as it relates to physical health. Not only does forgiveness cut stress, improve the quality of sleep, and elevate mood, it can ease chronic back pain, reduce the chances for heart attack, help avoid addiction relapse, and even aid in treating cancer.

Forgiveness also goes a long way toward raising self-esteem. Wayne Dyer, the well-known psychologist and author, writes extensively about the benefits of forgiveness in order to achieve a sense of value. In his book *Manifest Your Destiny,* Dyer writes:

> The inclination to bond to our wounds rather than move past them traps us in a constant state of feeling unworthy. A person who has experienced traumatic events in life, such as sexual abuse, the death of loved ones, traumatic illnesses, accidents, family disruptions, drug addictions and the like, can become bonded with the past painful events and replay them for attention or pity. . . .
>
> When you go backward and continuously relive your pain, including labeling yourself (incest survivor, alcoholic, orphan, abandoned), you do not do so for strength. You do it because of your inner experience of bitterness. This bitterness shows itself in hatred and anger as you discuss these events. This bitterness infects the body and prevents healing . . . [and] . . . keeps you from feeling worthy. . . .
>
> The way out of bonding to your wounds is through forgiveness. Forgiveness is the most powerful thing that you can do for your physiology and your spirituality. . . . Forgiveness means that you fill yourself with love and you radiate that love outward and refuse to hang onto the venom or hatred that was engendered by the behaviors that caused the wounds. Forgiveness is a spiritual act of love for yourself, and it sends a message to everyone, including yourself, that you are an object of love.

HOW DO WE FORGIVE?

Forgiveness is a complex, difficult, long-term, painful process. I love Sue Monk Kidd's comment about forgiveness in her novel *The Secret*

Life of Bees: "People, in general, would rather die than forgive. It's that hard. If God said in plain language, 'I'm giving you a choice, forgive or die,' a lot of people would go ahead and order their coffin."

Still, it is imperative that we forgive all transgressions, mostly for selfish reasons. Only when we have truly forgiven will we be free to move on. This is particularly true when forgiving the people most involved with our experience of father loss.

12 Steps to Forgiveness

Here are my thoughts on steps toward reaching forgiveness as it relates to our fathers or anyone else involved in the pain we experienced as a result of father loss.

1. Clarify the facts about the transgression(s) and the pain these transgressions caused you. This may appear obvious, but many fatherless daughters are reluctant or unable to acknowledge the pain of father loss and to direct the blame in the appropriate direction.

For example, some women excused their fathers repeatedly, sometimes over a lifetime, for disappointments. Both Marsha and Jane, now in their mid-sixties, had permitted their father, who had abandoned the family when the girls were very young, to repeatedly blow in and out of their lives, leaving them devastated after every encounter. Marsha, the elder sister, had clearly been the father's favorite (if you could call it that), and she seemed quite pleased that her father always exclaimed about how beautiful she was. Nevertheless, one of Marsha's earliest memories was literally waiting by the garden gate for her father to take her out on her fourth birthday, as he had promised. He never showed up. Still she expressed a loving and forgiving attitude toward him. Jane, however, who had essentially been ignored by her father, was clearly angry at him, although she, too, had remained in touch with him throughout her life.

Just a few years ago, their father, now well into his eighties, died. At his wake, the sisters stood talking to a man who had introduced himself as their father's best friend. After chatting with this man for several minutes, the man, with a rather puzzled expression on his face, finally said, "You know, I didn't know Dick had any kids."

Both sisters told me the same story. Jane registered substantial anger and pain, but Marsha, although she remembered the comment, reported it with a small laugh. She seemed to know intellectually that her father had never been interested in her, but emotionally, she remained unmoved. I suspect the hurt was simply too deep.

2. Be willing to forgive. One of the fundamental steps toward forgiveness is simply deciding that you are going to forgive. This means letting go of blame and self-pity, especially self-pity. Try to accept the fact that it wasn't your fault and there is nothing you can do, or could have done, to change the situation. The past is past. This means facing difficult feelings with courage and making tough decisions about important people in your life.

3. Work with a sympathetic listener or advisor. You must articulate your feelings, and sharing them with a sympathetic listener is a good idea. As a writer, I obviously respect the power of putting feelings into words. As soon as a feeling is verbalized, it has been taken outside of us and objectified; we can look at it more clearly. You can do this alone by writing in a journal or speaking into a tape recorder.

In addition to simply talking about your feelings about your father, you can express them to a responsive and sympathetic listener, such as your spouse, a good friend, a religious advisor, or, most especially, a psychotherapist. Talking to a sibling may also be useful. (One of my brothers was a rock for me during the writing of this book, serving as a reality check and a constant source of information.) However, even though you grew up in the same household, as siblings you may have experienced situations and personalities differently. You may also have your own relationship issues with a sibling. As a result, siblings may not be the most objective listeners.

4. Clearly articulate who the transgressor is. You probably have more than one person to forgive, including your father, your mother, and anyone else directly associated with the effects of the loss of your father. You need to define the transgressions that are causing the pain and who is responsible for them. Transgressions (and transgressors) will vary and may be numerous. Each situation needs to be worked out separately.

5. Focus on the facts. Highlight clearly the offenses that were done to you; not how you felt about them but simply the offenses themselves. As odd as it may sound, try not to take these offenses personally.

6. Try to understand and empathize with the transgressor. Focus on the humanity of the transgressor. Do you know of problems he or she faced growing up? What was life like for this person at the time of the offense? As soon as you begin thinking along these lines, you will feel a certain softening toward the person you are forgiving.

7. Understand that you don't have to condone transgressions. Although you have decided to forgive and you may well be feeling softer or warmer toward the transgressor(s), understand that you need not—and indeed *should not*—condone serious transgressions, such as abandonment, sexual or emotional abuse, or alcoholism. Remember that you are trying to forgive a transgressor; you are not acknowledging that the transgression was right.

8. Understand that you don't have to continue a relationship with the person you are forgiving. To forgive another does not necessarily mean that you have to like him, want to associate with him, or indeed should associate with him. For example, if an abandoning father was also an abusive, hurtful man, he can be forgiven, but you are not obligated to associate with him or be responsible for or toward him in any way. You can wish health, happiness, peace, joy, and all the blessings in life for him, but you need not offer anything more. Indeed, you don't even have to tell him you have forgiven him. Your forgiveness is for your own spiritual well-being, not for his or for anyone else's.

9. Realize that you are *not* responsible for the transgressions. Usually when you are involved in the act of forgiveness, you must hold yourself responsible in some way. If you are asking for forgiveness, you are obviously taking responsibility for something you have done wrong and are hoping the one you hurt can forgive you. If you are trying to forgive a transgression, you often need to take into account your own offensive behavior that may have contributed to the problem.

However, when it comes to the loss of your father, you are not responsible for what happened. You certainly are not responsible for your father's death. Nor are you responsible if he left the family or if you were abused in any way. You were a child, and children are not accountable for their parents' behavior.

10. Accept that you *are* responsible for your own life today. Although you are not responsible for what happened when you were a child, you are responsible for finding your own peace of mind today. View this process of forgiveness as an opportunity for your own emotional, psychological, and spiritual growth.

11. Understand that forgiveness cannot be forced. If there have been some serious transgressions in your life, forgiveness may take time. However, even if your initial gesture of forgiveness is halfhearted, it will still give you a sense of release and lightness. Lifelong pain, like that associated with father loss, cannot be erased in a moment; you must keep working on it.

12. Start fresh. Forgiveness involves taking out all those bad feelings you've been hiding, examining them, coming to terms with them, and then letting them go. This isn't easy, because you've probably spent much of your life lugging these nasty feelings around with you, but once you've managed to confront them, they lose their power. You can kiss them good-bye and let them go. Then your work will be finished. You can forgive and forget, and start fresh. The pain will be gone, the anger will evaporate, and you'll be free to be who you really want to be.

14. FINAL IMAGES

"I have to tell you something: I think about him every day. I miss him still."

—Mary, age 94, whose father died when she was 5

This book began as a pilgrimage for me, a journey to find out how the loss of my father when I was only ten years old had affected my life. I also hoped to share this information with other women who had lost their dads, either through death or through abandonment. Issues surrounding father loss are thick and complicated. Now as I approach the end of this book, I want to try to present a sharp, clear picture of all that I have learned. Toward that end, here's a brief summation:

WHAT I HAVE LEARNED ABOUT FATHER LOSS

1. The depth of a woman's attachment to her father is profound. Whether the relationship was good or bad, long or short, happy or sad, it has had an enormous impact on her life, and it will never end.

2. Fear of abandonment is the hallmark of the fatherless daughter. Directly linked to fear of abandonment are many other emotional problems, including issues with regard to intimacy, sex, commitment, and most of all, anger.

3. Death of a father, because of its finality, is commonly thought to offer closure to a fatherless daughter. This is not necessarily true.

4. Abandonment by a father following divorce is commonly thought to offer hope to a fatherless daughter, if the father is still alive. This is not necessarily true.

5. If your mother showed strength, intelligence, and empathy toward you after your father's death or abandonment, the chances are good that you were spared many of the problems faced by fatherless daughters.

6. Stepfathers can be a godsend or a tragedy.

7. Alcoholism is a very frequent problem among the mothers, fathers, and stepfathers of fatherless daughters.

8. If you have put together a happy relationship with a husband or partner, you are well on your way to resolving your father-loss issues.

9. Your life would not necessarily have been better if your father had been present in the family; different, certainly, but not necessarily better.

10. You are not responsible for hurts you endured as a child, but you are responsible for your life today. You must rely on yourself.

11. It's never too late to find your dad and to come to terms with his loss.

12. Coming to terms with the loss of your dad, and forgiving all those who let you down, is liberating, freeing you to experience life, love, peace, and happiness.

ANOTHER PICTURE OF MY DAD

I began this book by describing a photograph of my father kneeling on the lawn with a little girl on his lap, whom he apparently adored, a little girl who was *not* me. I had vivid memories of this photograph and believed firmly that I had seen it often among our family albums.

As I got deeper and deeper into the writing of this book, I decided to ask my mother to send me a copy of that photograph. Her initial response to that request was: "I don't remember that picture." Still, she agreed to look for it, but a short time later she called and told me that she could not find the picture and reconfirmed that she had no memory of it. After also asking my brother and my aunt if they had any memory of such a photo (they did not), I could only conclude that it did not exist and most likely had never existed, except in my mind.

I then set out to find some other photo of my father and me. I wanted one of those shots like I'd seen of Caroline Kennedy, cuddling with her handsome dad, and him looking at her adoringly. I assumed there had to be one, right? After all, I was his only daughter! Well, no such luck; I couldn't find a single one.

I did uncover a few photos of my dad with me, always together with one or more of my brothers. Like my other memories of him, the photos are always of some special event, a boat ride on Lake Erie, a picnic, a day at the beach. In one, I'm about fifteen months old, decked out in a pair of not very attractive rubber pants, standing on a bench at a beach. My dad and I are making eye contact, and he seems to be saying something possibly rather harshly to me. My brother Steve is between us, oblivious to our exchange, a skinny five-year-old in his bathing suit, holding a jar for collecting lightning bugs. I asked my mom about this and she laughed. "He was probably telling you to get down," she said. "You were a very active child, always off doing something. I remember that vacation. We were constantly chasing after you, worried that you'd go in the water or climb up someplace."

So the truth has nothing to do with my fantasies. The good news is that there was no other little girl—a beautiful child he cuddled and adored. The bad news is there is no gauzy shot of me cuddling with my handsome dad and him looking on adoringly. Instead, there are a few pictures reflecting the rather ordinary reality of our lives.

My brother has told me repeatedly that during the last years of his life, my father worked long, grueling twelve-hour days. He would be gone at 6:00 A.M. before we got up and wouldn't return until 8:00 or 9:00 P.M. after we had been put to bed. This is probably the reason I have so few memories and certainly the reason we have so few photographs.

Still, I know some things to be true. Throughout all my interviewing for this book, although I discovered some new information about my dad, I didn't learn anything that ran counter to what I always thought I had known about him. He was a kind, hardworking, funny, fun-loving man. I know he loved his wife, and I know he loved his children. I just didn't have enough of him.

It is the Fourth of July as I write this. And as I am writing, an old memory of another Fourth of July when I was about four or five years old has bubbled up. My brother Steve and some of his friends were playing in our backyard, setting off cherry bombs and firecrackers. Steve decided to stuff one in a plastic toy gun and set it off to see what would happen. As usual, I was hanging around. He told me to get back, but I didn't get back far enough. When the gun exploded, a small piece of plastic flew into my eye.

I got hysterical, more out of fear than pain. My dad swooped down from someplace, carried me into the house, washed out my eye, and then sat with me on our front porch swing, cuddling me until I settled down. My uncle and another man were there, and Daddy was engrossed in talking to them. And yet I remember sitting there, curled up in the crook of his arm, feeling safe and loved. I don't have a photo of this moment. But I know that it's true.

ACKNOWLEDGMENTS

When I began to work on *Fatherless Daughters,* I thought it would take me eighteen months to complete the manuscript, but in the end, it took me almost nine years. As I say in the Introduction, I wanted this book to be a sort of pilgrimage for me, a journey to discover the meaning of my father's death when I was so young. However, when I began, I had no idea the trip would be so long! In fact, this book turned out to be far more difficult than I had ever imagined, both with regard to dealing with the creative elements (the interviewing, the researching, the writing), but also coping with the emotional issues that bubbled to the surface as I delved deeper and deeper into the subject of "lost dads." I could never have written this book without the commitment and support of a vast number of people.

Six of these people were "absolute necessities" for me. I feel blessed to have had them in my life and am enormously grateful to them.

My mother, Roberta Bosworth Mathews, has supported me emotionally, intellectually, and occasionally financially throughout the writing of *Fatherless Daughters.* Needless to say, my mom's private history is an enormous and profound element in my own "fatherless daughter" story, and I'm so thankful that she trusted me to tell this story, which was as much hers as mine. I can't begin to thank her for her love, generosity of spirit, and insights, and send her great love and gratitude in return.

My brother, Steve Thomas, was an endless source of information regarding our dad, reflections on life in general and our lives in particular, reality checks, and humor. He was my rock throughout the writing of this book. I am so thankful that he is my brother.

My editor, Sydny Weinberg Miner, took a chance on me by acquiring this book, and throughout this long process has provided me with infinite patience and support, down-to-earth and intelligent guidance, and welcome friendship. I thank her profusely.

My friend Betsy Harris served as an indefatigable "fatherless daughter agent" and researcher (in addition to being a fatherless daughter herself), finding many of the women I interviewed for this book as well as feeding me vast amounts of useful information. I am so grateful to Betsy for all her help.

My friend of over forty years, Mimi Morton, served as my "literary guide" throughout the long journey of this book. She read most of the working chapters, frequently in two or three incarnations, and always returned with honest, intelligent, useful advice. I would have been at a loss without her wit, humor, and friendship.

My friend (and long-ago boss!) Betty Kelly Sargent, came to my rescue in the last weeks of work on the manuscript for *Fatherless Daughters*. She generously and tirelessly jumped into the process, offering editorial advice and service, professional guidance, and emotional and moral support. I am so grateful for her help and for her friendship.

Several other family members contributed time, memories, insights, and support in countless ways, and I am enormously grateful to them. They are: Ruth Bosworth Andrews, Sally Andrews Baldwin, Joyce White Cima, Ralph Evans, Frances Evans Land, Alice Andrews Hickethier, Gregory Mathews, Robert H. Mathews, Meg Negilski McCartney, Gail Mathews Negilski, Matthew Negilski, Clifford Quinn, Joanna Quinn Ravasio, Andrea Thomas Semmens, Brianna Semmens, Amanda Thomas, Bradley Thomas, Bronwyn Thomas, Christopher Thomas, Erin Thomas, Herbert R. Thomas, Jessica Thomas, Katherine Ryan Thomas, Michael J. Thomas, Robert J. Thomas, Seth Thomas, Shirley Simon Thomas, Stephan M. Thomas, Stephanie Thomas, Geraldine Quinn Town, Marjorie Evans Tucker, Andrew Weis, and Holly Thomas Weis.

Many other friends and acquaintances helped me in ways too numerous to mention, and I offer enormous thank-yous to: Anna Lee Phillips Andrews, Maggie Anson, Carl Apollonio, Deborah Bacon, Lucinda Baker, Alan Barnett, M.D., Eleanor Berman, Linda Cole Brennan, Gayle Mikula Cajka, Ariane Cañas, Narcisse Chamberlain, Connie Clark, Tom Crawford, Nina DeMartini Day, Jonathan Day, Carol Dix Eady, Josephine Fagan, Patricia Ellisor Gaines, Rachel Ginsburg, Tom Hatch, Venable Herndon, Marty Jezer, Lauranne Jones, Mary Judge,

Naomi Kleinberg, Barbara Machtiger, Bruce Macomber, Jeanette Mall, Sonia Mankowitz, Barbara Elliott Michael, Barbara Morgan, Susanne Ocasic, Stephanie Chalmers O'Rourke, Cynthia Edwards Page, Adam Park, Jennifer Perry, Susan H. Peters, Parker Phillips, Carol Devoe Riese, Susan Seibel, Julee B. Shapiro, Elizabeth Sheldon, Cinda Siler, Chip Simpson, Patricia R. Simpson, Frank Sorensen, M.D., Andrea Sperling, Robert Stein, Barry Tyo, Rachel Weiss, Laine Whitcomb, Geraldine Youcha, and Ezekiel Youcha, M.D.

A number of people helped me tremendously with the nuts-and-bolts of taking this book from the half-formed idea in my head to its final publication. First, I thank my agent Jane Dystel for her infinite patience, honesty, and support. I also am very grateful to everyone at Simon & Schuster for their special contributions, especially Gypsy da Silva, Mary Dorian, Paul Dippolito, Amber Husbands, Victoria Meyer, Michelle Rorke, and Dina Siljkovic, Jackie Seow, and Design-works.

Of course, central to this book are the more than 100 fatherless daughters who so generously shared their memories and insights with me, frequently stimulating ancient and difficult emotions of their own in the process. Although I could not begin to include all their stories, the thoughts and feelings from each and every one of these women informed this book's content, and I am exceedingly grateful to them. They are: Katherine Abbe, Daphne Abeel, Lois Akner, Linda Atkinson, Elizabeth Baker, Roni Baronowitz, Sharon Baxter, Ann Landers Beatus, Sally Ann Berk, Laura Bernay, Ellen Jones Blackburn, Sally Blackett, Kathleen Bliss, Leslie Bridgeman, Judy Garvin Brock, Millie McConnell Cavanaugh, Patricia Silo Chalmers, Joyce Cima, Anne Coleman, Rita Sawa Conallen, Jo Dolcimascolo Connor, Elyse Coster, Karen Cunningham, Jane Wilmot Crane, Dana Devoe, Joan Coventry Dickason, Rachel Doob, Daline Dudley, Alice Eady, Yasmin Eady, Amy Eason, Susan Edwards Eidson, Shawn Blass Feuerstein, Carol Fishberg, Paula Fodor, Anita Corona Fox, Patty Garbe, Estella Gayossa-Mendoza, Frances McLaughlin Gill, Lauren Goldberg, Danielle Hayes, Eulalah Henricks, Betsey Stein Horovitz, Marilyn Kamile, M.J. Karmi, Pamela Kiernan, Amy King, Aki Kirimoto, Terry Berman Klewan, Nancy Wilson Kline, Andrea Kott, Karen

Landers, Sue Landers, Gloria Layne, Sandra Chichella MacDuffee, Medrie MacPhee, Maggie Malone, Elizabeth Ledbetter Marino, Joan Marlow, Katey Mears, Victoria Mears, Susan Meyer, Pam McWethy, Ann Bennett Mix, Nancy Jo Morrell, Rhonda Moore Ortiz, Marjorie Palmer, Linda Cook Pelaccio, Lynne Eicher Peterson, Lys Rogers, Sky Rogers, Cynthia Roney, Betty Kelly Sargent, Alisa Schulman, Kathleen Shafer, Nancy Shuker, Mary Simpson, Maxine Sylvester Stanley, Marsha Stober, Jay Stouppe, Peggy Tagliarino, Jill Dove Teetor, Ellen Macomber Thomas, Gretchen Goebel Thomas, Pamela B. Thomas, Kathy Titakis, Marjorie Traverso, Gail Trechsel, Mary Giesen Tucker, Diane Vasil, Suzanne Vega, Barbara Vitanza, Ellen Wertheim, Holly Witte, Eileen Wolkstein, and Yolande Zahler.

NOTES

INTRODUCTION

Page

ix *"My mother died when I was nineteen":* Anna Quindlen, "Mothers," *Living Out Loud* (New York: Ivy Books, 1988), 210.

xi *According to Whitehead:* "Dan Quayle Was Right," by Barbara Dafoe Whitehead, *The Atlantic Monthly*, April 1993.

1. SNAPSHOTS OF MY FATHER

Page

3 *Losing a father in childhood:* Victoria Secunda, *Women and Their Fathers: The Sexual and Romantic Impact of the First Man in Your Life* (New York: Delta Books, 1992), 195.

2. SO, WHAT'S A FATHER?

Page

18 *It is a father's task:* David Popenoe, *Life Without Father* (New York: The Free Press, 1996), 139.

21 *the concept of fathering:* Luigi Zoja, *The Father: Historical, Psychological and Cultural Perspectives* (East Sussex, England: Brunner-Routledge, 2001).

22 *"Hector is both patriot and father":* Ibid., 83.

23 *The simultaneous emergence of industrialization:* Robert L. Griswold, *Fatherhood in America: A History* (New York: Basic Books, 1993), 16–17.

24 *"In the formal, patriarchal [Italian] home":* Ibid., 69–70.

26 *"forged their screen identities as fathers":* Ibid., 191.

27 *"striking how clearly the men saw breadwinning":* Ibid.

27 *"Quite clearly fatherly responsibilities":* Ibid., 194.

27 *"Fathers emphasized":* Ruth Jacobson Tasch, "The Role of the Father in the Family," *Journal of Experimental Education,* June 1952.

30 *"As you recall":* Dan Quayle's comment to CNN's Wolf Blitzer.

34 *Father's play tends to be:* Popenoe, *Life Without Father,* 139.

3. DEATH, DIVORCE, OR SIMPLY FADING AWAY

Page

39 *Today the principal cause of fatherlessness:* David Blankenhorn, *Fatherless America: Confronting Our Most Urgent Social Problem* (New York: Basic Books, 1995), 22.

43 *When a father dies:* Ibid., 24.

47 *love is stronger than death:* Mary Gordon, *The Shadow Man* (New York: Random House, 1996), 274.

58 *"Divorce is the closest thing to the death":* Secunda, *Women and Their Fathers,* 196.

59 *"Many of the issues highlighted":* Beverley Raphael, *The Anatomy of Bereavement* (Northvale, N.J.: Jason Aronson, 1994), 122.

59 *"have a powerful need":* Judith S. Wallerstein and Sandra Blakeslee, *Second Chances: Men, Women and Children a Decade After Divorce* (Boston: Houghton Mifflin Company, 1996), 243.

4. THE TIME IN A GIRL'S LIFE

Page

72 *"The death of a loved one":* William C. Kroen, Ph.D., LMHC, *Helping Children Cope with the Loss of a Loved One* (Minneapolis, Minn.: Free Spirit Publishing, 1996), 46.

73 *"Most researchers agree that divorce":* Secunda, *Women and Their Fathers,* 196.

5. THE MOM FACTOR AND OTHER FAMILY MATTERS

Page

91 *Me, I never knew the love of a father:* Karen V. Kukil, ed., *The Unabridged Journals of Sylvia Plath* (New York: Anchor Books, 2000), 431.

116 *"Biological fathers are more likely":* Popenoe, *Life Without Father,* 198.

6. THE EMOTIONAL LEGACY OF FATHER LOSS

Page

125 *"In Sylvia Plath's work"*: Elizabeth Hardwick, *Seduction & Betrayal* (New York: Vintage Books, 1975), 104.

126 *"Always, behind every mood"*: Ibid., 115.

143 *"In most instances, persons who have suffered"*: W. Hugh Missildine, M.D., *Your Inner Child of the Past* (New York: Simon & Schuster, 1963), 259.

7. OUR BODIES, OUR DADS

Page

151 *"It's really so interesting"*: "When Fergie Met Rosie," *Rosie*, August 2001.

8. LOVE AND SEX, SEX AND LOVE

Page

156 *"A woman's capacity for a mutually loving"*: Secunda, *Women and Their Fathers*, xvi.

157 *"The father-daughter relationship"*: Ibid.

158 *"girls without fathers often became"*: Wassil-Grimm, *Where's Daddy?*, 159.

165 *"I felt for the first time"*: Donald Spoto, *Marilyn Monroe: The Biography* (New York: HarperCollins Publishers, 1993), 265.

168 *"I was her lover, husband, and father"*: Gloria Steinem and George Barris, *Marilyn* (New York: MJF Books, 1986), 103.

169 *"By exciting and arousing"*: Ibid., 118.

169 *"offered sex in return"*: Ibid., 69.

171 *"the attitude of a father"*: Ibid., 117.

171 *"What Marilyn wanted"*: Ibid., 103.

172 *"How often, in the dawn of life, are we presented"*: Maggie Scarf, *Intimate Partners: Patterns in Love and Marriage* (New York: Ballantine Books, 1987), 92.

186 *Care, responsibility, respect, and knowledge*: Erich Fromm, *The Art of Loving* (New York: Harper Perennial Classics, 1956), 30.

191 *"rise to prominence as young women"*: Judith S. Wallerstein and Sandra Blakeslee, *Second Chances: Men, Women and Children a Decade After Divorce* (Boston: Houghton Mifflin Company, 1989), 62.

9. THE DILEMMAS OF WORK

Page

193 *One of my failings:* Martin Gottfried, *Balancing Act* (New York: Pinnacle Books, 1999), 420.

199 *"Fatherless women are a hardworking group":* Elyce Wakerman, *Father Loss* (New York: Doubleday, 1984), 254.

205 *The childhood of persons:* Missildine, *Your Inner Child of the Past,* 240.

206 *"She had idealized Olivier":* Arthur Miller, *Timebends: A Life* (New York: Grove Press, 1987), 422.

206 *"What gradually began to dawn on me":* Ibid., 419.

208 *"One of my failings":* Gottfried, *Balancing Act,* 420.

208 *"Having that rock":* Ibid., 416.

10. MOURNING

Page

213 *Forever [is] a difficult concept:* William C. Kroen, Ph.D., LMHC, *Helping Children Cope with the Loss of a Loved One: A Guide for Grownups* (Minneapolis, Minn.: Free Spirit Publishing, 1996), 6.

214 *"We only call it the 'stages of dying'":* Elisabeth Kübler-Ross, *On Life After Death* (Berkeley, CA: Celestial Arts, 1991), 26.

224 *"In contrast to the stage of denial":* Elisabeth Kübler-Ross, *On Death and Dying* (New York: Macmillan, 1969), 50.

225 *"Anger is prominent":* Raphael, *The Anatomy of Bereavement,* 123.

225 *buy time:* Kübler-Ross, *On Death and Dying,* 83.

225 *good behavior:* Ibid., 84.

228 *reactive depression and preparatory depression:* Ibid., 87.

229 *"should not be encouraged":* Ibid., 87.

230 *"In the preparatory grief":* Ibid.

230 *"I am convinced":* Ibid., 142.

231 *"Acceptance should not be mistaken":* Ibid., 113.

231 *"If a patient has had enough time":* Ibid., 112.

231 *"a natural process":* Ibid., 116.

11. GETTING TO KNOW YOUR DAD

Page

237 *Even if Dad never sets eyes:* Wassil-Grimm, *Where's Daddy?*, 158.

240 *"Even if Dad":* Ibid.

240 *"Children need to have an unbiased well-rounded picture":* Ibid., 159.

12. HEALING

Page

261 *What I have taken from the cemetery:* Gordon, *The Shadow Man*, 274.

268 *"The gates were open":* Susan Johnson Hadler and Ann Bennett Mix, edited by Calvin L. Christman, *Lost in the Victory: Reflections of American War Orphans of World War II* (Denton, Tex.: University of North Texas Press, 1998), 202–204.

13. STARTING FRESH

Page

275 *People, in general, would rather die:* Sue Monk Kidd, *The Secret Life of Bees* (New York: Penguin Books, 2002), 277.

278 *Girls have a powerful need:* Judith S. Wallerstein and Sandra Blakeslee, *Second Chances: Men, Women and Children a Decade After Divorce* (Boston: Houghton Mifflin, 1996), 243.

BIBLIOGRAPHY

Akner, Lois F., with Catherine Whitney. *How to Survive the Loss of a Parent: A Guide for Adults.* New York: Quill, 1993.

Alderman, Linda. *Why Did Daddy Die? Helping Children Cope with the Loss of a Parent.* New York: Pocket Books, 1989.

Appleton, William S. *Fathers & Daughters: For Every Woman—the Startling Truth About You and the First Man in Your Life.* New York: Berkley Books, 1981.

Bair, Dierdre. *Anaïs Nin: A Biography.* New York: Penguin Books, 1995.

Ball, Lucille. *Love, Lucy.* New York: A Berkley Boulevard Book, The Berkley Publishing Group, 1996.

Barras, Jonetta Rose. *Whatever Happened to Daddy's Little Girl? The Impact of Fatherlessness on Black Women.* New York: The Ballantine Publishing Group, 2000.

Becker, Ernest. *The Denial of Death.* New York: The Free Press, 1973.

Bettelheim, Bruno. *A Good Enough Parent: A Book on Child-Rearing.* New York: Vintage Books, 1963.

Blankenhorn, David. *Fatherless America: Confronting Our Most Urgent Social Problem.* New York: Basic Books, 1995.

Bogart, Stephen Humphrey, with Gary Provost. *Bogart: In Search of My Father.* New York: A Plume Book, 1995.

Boose, Lynda E., and Betty S. Flowers, eds. *Daughters & Fathers.* Baltimore and London: The Johns Hopkins University Press, 1989.

Brokaw, Tom. *The Greatest Generation.* New York: Dell Publishing, 1998.

Carlson, Randy L. *Father Memories: How to Discover the Unique, Powerful, and Lasting Impact Your Father Has on Your Adult Life and Relationships.* Chicago: Moody Press, 1992.

Chodorow, Nancy. *The Reproduction of Mothering: Psychoanalysis and the Sociology of Gender.* Berkeley: University of California Press, 1978.

Conway, Jill Ker. *The Road from Coorain.* New York: Vintage Books, 1989.

Cook, Blanche Weisen. *Eleanor Roosevelt: Volume 1, 1884–1933.* New York: Viking Press, 1992.

Corneau, Guy. *Absent Fathers, Lost Sons: The Search for Masculine Identity.* Boston: Shambhala, 1991.

DeWitt, Henry, and James Alan McPherson, eds. *Fathering Daughters: Reflections by Men.* Boston: Beacon Press, 1998.

Didion, Joan. *The Year of Magical Thinking.* New York: Alfred A. Knopf, 2006.

Dodson, Fitzhugh. *How to Father.* New York: New American Library, 1974.

Dyer, Wayne W. *Manifest Your Destiny.* New York: HarperPerennial, A Division of HarperCollinsPublishers, 1998.

———. *The Power of Intention: Learning to Co-Create Your World Your Way.* New York: Hay House, 2005.

Edelman, Hope. *Motherless Daughters.* New York: Addison-Wesley, 1994.

Elium, Jeanne, and Don Elium. *Raising a Daughter: Parents and the Awakening of a Healthy Woman.* Berkeley, California: Celestial Arts, 1994.

Erickson, Beth M. *Longing for Dad: Father Loss and Its Impact.* Deerfield Beach, Fla: Health Communications, 1998.

Ferraro, Geraldine A. *Framing a Life: A Family Memoir.* New York: A Lisa Drew Book/Scribner, 1998.

Fitzgerald, Helen. *The Grieving Child: A Parent's Guide.* New York: Simon & Schuster, 1992.

Freud, Sigmund. *Three Essays on the Theory of Sexuality.* New York: Basic Books, 2000.

Friedan, Betty. *The Feminine Mystique.* New York: W. W. Norton, 2001.

Fromm, Erich. *The Art of Loving.* New York: Perennial/Imprint of Harper-Collins Publishers, 2000.

Goetz, Masa Aiba. *My Father, My Self: Understanding Dad's Influence on Your Life.* Boston: Element Books, 1998.

Gordon, Mary. *Circling My Mother: A Memoir.* New York: Pantheon Books, 2007.

———. *The Shadow Man: A Daughter's Search for Her Father.* New York: Random House, 1996.

Gottfried, Martin. *Balancing Act: The Authorized Biography of Angela Lansbury.* New York: Pinnacle Books, 1999.

Goulter, Barbara, and Joan Minninger. *The Father-Daughter Dance.* New York: G. P. Putnam's Sons, 1993.

Greene, Bob. *Good Morning, Merry Sunshine: A Father's Journal of His Child's First Year.* New York: Penguin Books, 1985.

Greer, Germaine. *Daddy, We Hardly Knew You.* New York: Alfred A. Knopf, 1990.

————. *The Female Eunuch.* New York: McGraw-Hill, 1970.

————. *The Whole Woman.* New York: Anchor Books, 1999.

Griffin, Donna. *Fatherless Women: What Every Daughter Needs from a Father.* Los Angeles: Milligan Books, 1998.

Griswold, Robert L. *Fatherhood in America: A History.* New York: Basic Books, 1993.

Guiles, Fred Lawrence. *Legend: The Life and Death of Marilyn Monroe.* New York: Scarborough House, 1991.

Hadler, Susan Johnson, and Ann Bennett Mix, Calvin L. Christman, ed., *Lost in the Victory: Reflections of American War Orphans of World War II.* Denton: University of North Texas Press, 1998.

Hardwick, Elizabeth. *Seduction & Betrayal: Women and Literature.* New York: Vintage Books, 1975.

Harris, Maxine. *The Loss That Is Forever: The Lifelong Impact of the Early Death of a Mother or Father.* New York: A Plume Book, The Penguin Group, 1995.

Harrison, Kathryn. *The Kiss, A Memoir.* New York: Avon Books/Bard, 1997.

Heilbrun, Carolyn G. *The Education of a Woman: The Life of Gloria Steinem.* New York: Ballantine Books, 1995.

Hollis, Judi. *Fat Is a Family Affair: A Hope-Filled Guide for Those Who Suffer from Eating Disorders and Those Who Love Them.* New York: Harper & Row, 1985.

Ingerman, Sandra. *Soul Retrieval: Mending the Fragmented Self.* San Francisco: HarperSanFrancisco, 1991.

Kidd, Sue Monk. *The Secret Life of Bees.* New York: Penguin Group, 2003.

Kopp, Heather Harpham. *Daddy, Where Were You?: Healing for the Father-Deprived Daughter.* Ann Arbor: Servant Publications, 1998.

Kroen, William C. *Helping Children Cope with the Loss of a Loved One: A Guide for Grownups.* Minneapolis: Free Spirit Publishing, 1996.

Kübler-Ross, Elisabeth. *On Death and Dying.* New York: Macmillan, 1969.

————. *On Life After Death.* Berkeley: Celestial Arts, 1991.

Kukil, Karen V. *The Unabridged Journals of Sylvia Plath.* New York: Anchor Books, 2000.

LaRossa, Ralph. *The Modernization of Fatherhood: A Social and Political History.* Chicago: The University of Chicago Press, 1997.

Lash, Joseph P. *Eleanor and Franklin.* New York: W. W. Norton, 1971.

Leonard, Linda Schierse. *On the Way to the Wedding: Transforming the Love Relationship.* Boston: Shambhala, 1987.

————. *The Wounded Woman: Healing the Father-Daughter Relationship.* Boston: Shambhala, 1982.

Lerner, Harriet Goldhor. *The Dance of Intimacy: A Woman's Guide to Courageous Acts of Change in Key Relationships.* New York: Harper & Row, 1989.

Levinson, Daniel J. *The Seasons of a Woman's Life.* New York: Alfred A. Knopf, 1996.

Levinson, Daniel J., with Charlotte N. Darrow, Edward B. Klein, Maria H. Levinson, and McKee Braxton. *The Seasons of a Man's Life.* New York: Alfred A. Knopf, 1978.

Lewis, C. S. *A Grief Observed.* New York and San Francisco: HarperSanFrancisco, 1996.

Lifton, Betty Jean. *Lost & Found: The Adoption Experience.* New York: Harper & Row, Perennial Library, 1993.

Lifton, Betty Jean. *Journey of the Adopted Self: A Quest for Wholeness.* New York: Basic Books, 1994.

Louv, Richard. *Father Love.* New York: Pocket Books, 1993.

Mailer, Norman. *The Prisoner of Sex.* New York: Penguin (Donald I. Fine), 1971.

Maine, Margo, Ph.D. *Father Hunger: Fathers, Daughters, and Food.* Carlsbad, Calif.: Gürze Books, 1991.

Marone, Nicky. *How to Father a Successful Daughter.* New York: Fawcett Crest, 1988.

Meeker, Meg. *Strong Fathers, Strong Daughters: 10 Secrets Every Father Should Know.* Washington, DC: Regnery, 2006.

Milford, Nancy. *Savage Beauty: The Life of Edna St. Vincent Millay.* New York: Random House, 2001.

Miller, Arthur. *Timebends: A Life.* New York: Grove Press, 1984.

Missildine, W. Hugh. *Your Inner Child of the Past.* New York: Simon & Schuster, 1963.

Mitscherilick, Alexander. *Society Without the Father: A Contribution to Social Psychology.* New York: Harper Perennial, 1993.

Mowday, Lois. *Daughters Without Dads.* Nashville: Thomas Nelson, 1990.

Murdock, Maureen. *The Hero's Daughter: Through Myth, Story, and Jungian Psychology, An Exploration of the Shadow Side of Father Love.* New York: Fawcett Columbine, 1994.

Murphy, Joseph, revised by Ian McMahan. *The Power of Your Subconscious Mind.* New York: Bantam Books, 2001.

Nin, Anais. *The Diary of Anais Nin, Volume II, 1934–1939.* New York and London: Harcourt Brace Jovanovich, 1967.

O'Keefe, Claudia, ed. *Father: Famous Writers Celebrate the Bond Between Father and Child.* New York: Pocket Books, 2000.

Phillips, Adam. *On Flirtation: Psychoanalytic Essays on the Uncommitted Life.* Cambridge, Mass.: Harvard University Press, 1994.

Pittman, Frank. *Man Enough: Fathers, Sons, and the Search for Masculinity.* New York: G. P. Putnam's Sons, 1993.

Plath, Aurelia Schober. *Letters Home by Sylvia Plath: Correspondence 1950–1963.* New York: Harper & Row, 1975.

Popenoe, David. *Life Without Father: Compelling New Evidence That Fatherhood and Marriage Are Indispensable for the Good of Children and Society.* New York: The Free Press, 1996.

Pruett, Kyle D. *Fatherneed: Why Father Care Is as Essential as Mother Care for Your Child.* New York: The Free Press, 2000.

Quindlen, Anna. *Living Out Loud.* New York: Ivy Books, 1988.

Rank, Maureen. *Dealing with the Dad of Your Past.* Minneapolis, Minn.: Bethany House, 1990.

Raphael, Beverley. *The Anatomy of Bereavement.* Northvale, NJ: Jason Aronson, 1983.

Rimm, Sylvia. *See Jane Win: The Rimm Report on How 1,000 Girls Became Successful Women.* New York: Crown Publishers, 1999.

Rivers, Caryl, Rosalind Barnett, and Grace Baruch. *Beyond Sugar and Spice: How Women Grow, Learn & Thrive.* New York: Ballantine Books, 1979.

Rodriguez, Kathy. *Healing the Father Wound.* Enumclaw, Wash.: Pleasant Word (division of WinePress Publishing), 2008.

Rosin, Mark Bruce. *Stepfathering: Stepfathers' Advice on Creating a New Family.* New York: Ballantine Books, 1987.

Rubin, Lillian B. *Intimate Strangers: Men and Women Together.* New York: Harper & Row, 1983.

Russert, Tim. *Wisdom of Our Fathers.* New York: Random House Trade Paperbacks, 2006.

Sagan, Eli. *Freud, Women, and Morality: The Psychology of Good and Evil.* New York: Basic Books, 1988.

Samuels, Andrew, ed. *The Father: Contemporary Jungian Perspectives.* New York: New York University Press, 1985.

Sanford, Linda Tschirhart, and Mary Ellen Donovan. *Women & Self-Esteem: Understanding and Improving the Way We Think and Feel About Ourselves.* New York: Penguin Books, 1984.

Scarf, Maggie. *Intimate Partners: Patterns in Love and Marriage.* New York: Ballantine Books, 1987.

Secunda, Victoria. *Women and Their Fathers: The Sexual and Romantic Impact of the First Man in Your Life*. New York: Delta Books, 1992.

Shapiro, Jerrold Lee. *The Measure of a Man: Becoming the Father You Wish Your Father Had Been*. New York: A Perigee Book, 1993.

Simon, Clea. *Fatherless Women: How We Change After We Lose Our Dads*. New York: John Wiley & Sons, 2001.

Smiley, Jane. *A Thousand Acres*. New York: Fawcett Columbine, 1991.

Smith, Harold Ivan. *On Grieving the Death of a Father*. Minneapolis: Augsburg, 1994.

Staal, Stephanie. *The Love They Lose: Living with the Legacy of Our Parents' Divorce*. New York: Delacorte Press, 2000.

Steinem, Gloria. *Outrageous Acts and Everyday Rebellions*. New York: An Owl Book, Henry Holt and Company, 1983.

———. *Revolution from Within: A Book of Self-Esteem*. Boston: Little, Brown, 1993.

Steinem, Gloria, and George Barris. *Marilyn*. New York: Henry Holt, 1986.

Stevenson, Anne. *Bitter Fame: A Life of Sylvia Plath*. Boston: Houghton Mifflin, 1989.

Streiker, Lowell D. *Fathering: Old Game, New Rules*. Nashville: Abingdon Press, 1989.

Tasch, Ruth Jacobson. "The Role of the Father in the Family," *Journal of Experimental Education*, June 1952.

Wakerman, Elyce. *Father Loss: Daughters Discuss the Man That Got Away*. New York: Doubleday, 1984.

Wallerstein, Judith S., and Sandra Blakeslee. *Second Chances: Men, Women and Children a Decade After Divorce*. Boston: Houghton Mifflin, 1996.

Wallerstein, Judith S., and Joan B. Kelly. *Surviving the Breakup*. New York: Basic Books, 1979.

Wallerstein, Judith S., Julia M. Lewis, and Sandra Blakeslee. *The Unexpected Legacy of Divorce*. New York: Hyperion, 2000.

Wassil-Grimm, Claudette. *Where's Daddy? How Divorced, Single and Widowed Mothers Can Provide What's Missing When Dad's Missing*. Woodstock, NY: The Overlook Press, 1994.

Whitehead, Barbara Dafoe. "Dan Quayle Was Right," *The Atlantic Monthly*, April 1993.

———. *The Divorce Culture*. New York: Alfred A. Knopf, 1996.

Whitfield, Charles L. *Healing the Child Within: Discovery and Recovery for Adult Children of Dysfunctional Families*. Deerfield Beach, Fla: Health Communications, 1987.

Williams, Jett, with Pamela Thomas. *Ain't Nothin' as Sweet as My Baby: The Story of Hank Williams' Lost Daughter.* New York: Harcourt Brace Jovanovich, 1990.

Winokur, Jon, ed. *Fathers.* New York: A Dutton Book, 1993.

Woititz, Janet G. *Healing Your Sexual Self.* Deerfield Beach, Fla: Health Communications, 1989.

Yablonsky, Lewis. *Fathers & Sons: The Most Challenging of All Family Relationships.* New York: Gardner Press Trade Book Company, 1990.

Zoja, Luigi. *The Father: Historical, Psychological and Cultural Perspectives.* Philadelphia: Taylor & Francis, 2001.

FICTION AND POETRY

Bernstein, Jane. *Departures.* New York: Holt, Rinehart & Winston, 1979.

Eicher, Terry, and Jesse D. Geller, eds. *Fathers and Daughters: Portraits in Fiction.* New York: NAL Books, 1990.

French, Marilyn. *Our Father.* New York: Ballantine Books, 1994.

Gordon, Mary. *Final Payments.* New York: Random House, 1978.

Millay, Edna St. Vincent. *Collected Poems.* New York: Harper & Row, 1956.

Plath, Sylvia. *Ariel: Poems by Sylvia Plath.* New York: Harper & Row, 1966.

Simpson, Mona. *The Lost Father.* New York: Alfred A. Knopf, 1992.

INDEX

Printed in the United States
By Bookmasters